O Taste & Sing

*Time-tested recipes with a Southern flair
from the homes of Richmond, Virginia*

St. Stephen's Choir
St. Stephen's Episcopal Church
6004 Three Chopt Road
Richmond, Virginia 23226

ISBN 0-9647438-0-9

| First Printing | 5,000 copies | July, 1995 |
| Second Printing | 10,000 copies | October, 1996 |

Printed in the USA by

WIMMER

The Wimmer Companies, Inc.

Memphis

About the artists

Emma Lou Martin

Artist Emma Lou Martin provided the cover watercolors, pen-and-ink divider pages, and interior food illustrations. A life-long Episcopalian, she resides in Richmond, VA, where she is a communicant at St. Stephen's. She founded the Uptown Gallery, a Richmond area artists' cooperative and served as its first director. A prize-winning professional artist, she has directed Art Camp at Shrine Mont, the Diocesan Conference Center, and teaches occasional classes. Her paintings hang in many private homes and corporate collections.

Mark Burnett

Cover designer Mark Burnett is the owner and creative director of Burnett Advertising, Inc., Richmond, VA. With a 30-year background in graphic design and advertising, Mark provides creative services individually tailored to a wide variety of clients. He is a communicant and vestry member of St. Stephen's.

Table of Contents

Acknowledgments

Editorial Committee

Nancy Hodder, Editor
Barbara Fleming, Assistant Editor
Ruth Prevette, Assistant Editor
William Fleming, Finance
E. Gordon Johns, Marketing
Frank Warren, Accounting

Choir Cookbook Committee

Susan Albert	Sheila Freeman
Walter Amacker	Betty Graham
Bobbie Arnall	Bob Hodder
Eugenia Borum	Ann Hyer
Neal Campbell	Molly Hyer
Douglas Carleton	Emily McLeod
Liz Cone	Mary Ann Sartin
Leslie Douthat	Marianne Watkinson
Phyllis DuVal	Rob Watkinson

Acknowledgments

The Choir Cookbook Committee of St. Stephen's Episcopal Church would like to express its appreciation to the following for their invaluable support:

Endowment Fund Trustees, St. Stephen's Church, for providing the financial backing and encouragement to carry out this project.

Virginia Historical Society, Richmond, VA: Mrs. Frances Pollard, Senior Librarian, for her assistance in locating the historical recipes and background material in *The Compleat Housewife* (1742, 1747); *The Prudent Housewife* (1750); *Lady's Assistant* (1750, 1773); *Cooking of the Old Dominion Prior to 1838* (©1938, Miss Aileen Brown and Miss Gertrude Drinker); *Colonial Recipes* (©1907, Miss Maude Bomberger); Occasional Bulletin Nos. 31-45, Virginia Historical Society. The historical recipes in the Faith and Food inserts are exact copies of the originals which were found in the previously mentioned sources.

Heritage Books, Bowie, Maryland, for their kind permission to reprint the etchings of the colonial churches that accompany the historical recipes. These etchings originally appeared in their book *Old Churches, Ministers, and Families of Virginia*, Vols. I and II, ©1992.

 *O Taste & Sing* celebrates two time-honored community traditions—the church supper and choral singing. This collection of more than 500 favorite recipes evokes memories of dinner-time fellowship experiences inspired by the suppers that accompany weekly choir rehearsals at St. Stephen's Episcopal Church in Richmond, Virginia. Contributed by a host of choristers, parishioners, and friends, these recipes capture the essence of Southern hospitality—Richmond-style.

History records that the first permanent English settlers arrived in the New World in 1607 at Jamestown, Virginia, a town some 60 miles due east of Richmond. They and their descendants sustained themselves on two indispensable ingredients: food and faith. A special feature of this book is the inclusion of historical commentaries on eight colonial Episcopal Churches whose roots spring from the earliest days of the colony. Accompanying each church profile is a recipe typical of the period to demonstrate that traditions passed down to us by our forbearers still live today in community gatherings such as the church supper.

The phrase "O Taste and Sing" connotes both eating and singing as expressed in Psalm 34:8 that begins with these words, "O taste and see how gracious the Lord is. . ." Frequently, church liturgy provides the settings for many types of musical accompaniments, both instrumental and vocal. English composer Ralph Vaughan Williams set these familiar words to music in his motet of the same name, a work often sung in churches like St. Stephen's.

The members of St. Stephen's Choir sing for a wide variety of services throughout the church year and have long shared a camaraderie born of worship experiences and social fellowship. Weekly rehearsals often evolve into group gatherings that inevitably center on food.

Choir members cook and serve Thursday evening suppers for members, spouses, and friends. These meals, usually prepared by teams of individuals or married couples, have enhanced the sense of community. The dinner group doubled its size several years ago with the addition of the youth choir and their families, who also assume responsibility for meal preparation.

Since Colonial times, Episcopalians have maintained strong ties with the mother church, the Church of England, in worship and musical traditions. For many years, the choir has wanted to travel as a group to England to tour and possibly to sing in some churches and cathedrals. This and other projects, such as musical scholarships and professional recordings, mandate a significant fund-raising effort. What could be a more natural solution than a cookbook inspired by the weekly suppers?

More about St. Stephen's. . .

Parables and stories featuring food figure prominently in the New Testament scriptures. Jesus's feeding of the 5,000 and celebration of the Last Supper with his disciples are but two reminders that Christians are "very members incorporate in the mystical body of thy Son." Since the agape suppers of the early church, communal meals have satisfied not only man's physical but also his spiritual needs.

Choir suppers are just one facet of food production and Christian hospitality in this busy parish of 2,300 communicants. The parish kitchen pulses as a nerve center for this church community. Each year the kitchen serves more than 8,000 persons attending services, conferences, and concerts. Church and community groups also use the kitchen to prepare over 3,800 meals annually for the homeless. The Women of St. Stephen's oversee the operation of the May Fair House, a nonprofit gift shop that sells food specialties prepared in the church's kitchen.

Worship services form the backbone for all church activities, many of which take place on Sunday mornings. The organist and choirmaster is responsible for the four choirs who support the clergy in leading the worship services of the church. St. Stephen's Choir, a group of 30-40 mixed voices, sings at the 11:15 a.m. Sunday service as well as for other special services such as the All Saints' Evensong, Thanksgiving Festival Service, Christmas Eve Holy Eucharist, and the Maundy Thursday Eucharist.

The choir's eclectic repertoire includes a variety of literature ranging from Gregorian Chant to Bernstein's *Chichester Psalms*. In addition to standard favorites like *Messiah* and *Elijah*, the choir has sung such lesser known works as *The Star of Bethlehem* by Rheinberger, *The Seven Last Words of Christ* by Franck, and a recently discovered Mass by Brahms.

The choir has sung for the Protestant Hour radio broadcast series and has recorded a professional album of hymns, carols, and anthems. The choir has also sung for services at the National Cathedral and at Christ Church in Alexandria, Virginia.

Three choirs of students sing for the 9:15 a.m. Sunday services. St. Stephen's Singers (elementary students) and the Sine nomine Cantores (secondary students) sing for the family service in the church; the Palmer Hall Choir (second and third graders) sings for the children's service in Palmer Hall,  a small chapel built in 1911 that was the first St. Stephen's Church.

St. Stephen's jointly sponsors a summer recital series featuring well-known regional, national, and international artists. One such acclaimed musician was Francis Jackson, retired organist of England's York Minster. In 1987 he played at St. Stephen's for the United States première of his *Concerto for Organ, Strings, Timpani and Celesta* with members of the Richmond Symphony, conducted by organist and choirmaster Neal Campbell.

St. Stephen's Church, located at the corner of Grove Avenue and Three Chopt Road, Richmond, was designed by Frank E. Watson of

Philadelphia and was initially completed in 1928. The Gothic revival style structure was built with rubble stone walls pierced by tall arched windows, this Gothic Revival style building is an adaptation of an early English parish-style church. Under the direction of Philip H. Frohman, architect of the National Cathedral, the church was lengthened and received a new facade in 1950. Among its appointments are stained-glass windows by the Willet, D'Ascenzo and J. & R. Lamb studios and a polychromed triptych reredos executed by the woodcarvers of Oberammergau, Germany.

Designed by G. Donald Harrison and built by the Aeolian-Skinner Organ Company of Boston in 1951, the organ at St. Stephen's is an outstanding example of the American Classic Organ. The main portion of the organ is located behind the facade on the Gospel side of the chancel. In 1968 Aeolian-Skinner supervised the additions of several ranks in the main organ, a four-manual console, the Antiphonal Organ flanking the Patriot's Window on the west wall, and the Positiv Organ on the Epistle side of the chancel.

ST. STEPHEN'S EPISCOPAL CHURCH   RICHMOND, VIRGINIA
EDWARD H. WINKS ARCHITECTURE, P.C.   RICHMOND, VIRGINIA

Illustrations

St. Stephen's Church with additions to be completed November, 1996, *page 8* (above)
St. Stephen's Church, West Facade, *page 5*
Palmer Hall, *page 7*

Crowd-Pleasers

Contents

The CROWD-PLEASERS section includes many exciting menus which have been prepared for St. Stephen's Choir suppers. Each recipe can be easily multiplied several times to feed large groups. All of the menus work well in casual settings, but several could also be used for more formal dining, such as the **Festival Chicken Dinner** or **Casual Elegance.**

Two menus that are especially popular with children are the **We Aim to Please**, with a delicious *White Chili*, and **A Reason to Celebrate**, which includes two guaranteed hits, *Turkey Tetrazzini* and *Punch Bowl Cake*. The **Souper Supper** and **Favorite Fall Dinner** make great cool weather meals; each entrée features a spicy Mexican flavor. When the weather changes from cool to warm, the Southern **Summer Picnic** menu of barbecue, baked beans, and coleslaw always scores high marks.

Following the supper suggestions are menus for three parties, hosted by choir members, that have become annual traditions. Typically, the Christmas holiday season demands many choir commitments and these celebrations are part of the pay-off for singers and their families. The last two recipes in the section were contributed by the May Fair House. Great for serving very large groups, both *Currituck Casserole* and *Hunter's Spaghetti* are sold in this nonprofit gift shop operated by the Women of St. Stephen's.

Good 'n Easy Supper

Easy Baked Pork Chops
Baked White Rice
Good 'n Easy Lettuce Salad
Commercial Italian Bread
Really Good Buttermilk Pound Cake

❧

Easy Baked Pork Chops

8	butterflied pork chops
2	(1-ounce) packages dehydrated onion soup mix
4-6	tablespoons water

Trim fat from chops and place them in 2 lightly greased 13" x 9" x 2" baking dishes. Shake soup in package and sprinkle over chops. Add water. Cover tightly with aluminum foil and bake at 325° for at least 2 hours. After 1½ hours of baking time, check chops and rearrange if necessary to insure even baking. Serve, with drippings, over rice.
Yield: 8-16 servings

Baked White Rice

4   cups rice
6⅔   cups water

Combine rice and water in greased large casserole dish. Cover tightly with aluminum foil. Bake at 350° for one hour. **Variation:** Substitute broth for part of the water; may add dried herbs of choice. **Yield: 15 servings**

Good 'n Easy Lettuce Salad

½   cup olive oil
1   tablespoon minced garlic
½   teaspoon salt
2   tablespoons lemon juice
¼   teaspoon dillweed
5-6   cups torn lettuce or salad greens
1   cup grated Parmesan cheese
1   (2-ounce) can sliced black olives, drained
1   (2-ounce) jar chopped pimiento (optional)

Combine oil, garlic, salt, lemon juice, and dill; set aside. Just before serving, put greens in a large bowl. Sprinkle cheese over top; add olives and pimiento. Pour dressing over salad; toss to mix. **Yield: 6 servings**

Really Good Buttermilk Pound Cake

2½   cups granulated sugar
½   cup shortening
½   cup butter or margarine
4   eggs
1   teaspoon vanilla
½   teaspoon lemon extract
3   cups all-purpose flour
½   teaspoon baking soda
1   cup buttermilk

Cream together sugar, shortening, and butter until light and fluffy. Add eggs, one at a time, beating well after each addition. Stir in vanilla and lemon extract. Combine flour and soda and add to creamed mixture alternately with buttermilk, beginning and ending with dry ingredients. Pour into a greased and floured 10" tube pan. Bake at 325° for 1¼ hours. Check for doneness. Cool in pan for 10 minutes. Remove from pan and cool on rack. **Yield: 16 servings**

We Aim to Please

White Chili
Jessie's "Fresh" and Fancy Fruit Salad
Ultimate Double Chocolate Brownies

℘

White Chili

2½	cups water
1	teaspoon lemon pepper
2	teaspoons cumin, divided
4	chicken breast halves, skinned
1	cup chopped onion
1	(16-ounce) bag frozen shoepeg corn
1	(4-ounce) can chopped green chilies, drained
2-3	tablespoons lime juice
2	(15-ounce) cans great northern beans

Grated Monterey Jack cheese
Commercial salsa verde
Corn chips

In a large saucepan, mix together water, lemon pepper, 1 teaspoon cumin, and chicken. Bring to a boil. Reduce heat, cover, and simmer until chicken is done, about 20 minutes. Remove chicken and reserve stock. Chop chicken into bite-sized pieces and return to saucepan. Microwave (or sauté) onion until transparent and add to chicken mixture. Stir in corn, chilies, 1 teaspoon cumin, and lime juice. Bring to a boil ; add beans; heat through. Top with grated cheese and salsa verde and serve with corn chips.
Yield: 8 servings

Jessie's "Fresh" and Fancy Fruit Salad

1	(28-ounce) can pear halves, drained
1	(29-ounce) can sliced peaches, drained
1	(16-ounce) can pineapple tidbits, drained
1	(10-ounce) package frozen strawberries, thawed and drained
1	(21-ounce) can peach pie filling
2	bananas, sliced

Drain pears, peaches, pineapple, and strawberries on paper towels. Cut into bite-sized pieces. Combine with pie filling in large bowl. Cover and refrigerate. Just before serving, fold in banana slices. **Yield: 12 servings**

Ultimate Double Chocolate Brownies

¾	cup cocoa
½	teaspoon baking soda
⅔	cup melted butter or margarine, divided
½	cup boiling water
2	cups granulated sugar
2	eggs
1⅓	cups all-purpose flour
1	teaspoon vanilla
¼	teaspoon salt
½	cup chopped pecans
2	cups semi-sweet chocolate chips

In a large bowl, combine cocoa and baking soda; blend in ⅓ cup melted butter. Add boiling water; stir until well blended. Stir in sugar, eggs, and remaining butter. Add flour, vanilla, and salt. Stir in pecans and chocolate chips. Pour into a lightly greased 13" x 9" x 2" pan. Bake at 350° for 35-40 minutes. Cool in pan before cutting. **Yield: 3 dozen**

Favorite Fall Dinner

Taco-Beef Casserole
Pretty Pear Salad
Commercial French Bread
Goldies

❧

Taco-Beef Casserole

1	pound ground beef
½	cup chopped onion
1	(15-ounce) can tomato sauce
½	cup water
1	(1¼-ounce) envelope taco seasoning
2	(5-ounce) packages medium egg noodles
2	cups small-curd cottage cheese
¼	cup sour cream
1	tablespoon all-purpose flour
2	teaspoons beef bouillon granules
¼	cup chopped green onion
1	cup shredded mozzarella cheese

(Recipe continues on next page)

(Taco-Beef Casserole continued from previous page)

Brown ground beef and onion; drain excess grease. Add tomato sauce, water, and taco seasoning; bring to a boil. Reduce heat and simmer for 10 minutes. Cook noodles according to manufacturer's instructions; drain well. Combine noodles, cottage cheese, sour cream, flour, bouillon granules, and green onion; mix well. Spoon noodle mixture into a greased 2½-quart casserole. Top with meat mixture. Bake at 350° for 25 minutes; sprinkle with cheese and bake 5 minutes more or until cheese melts. Let stand 10 minutes before serving. **Yield: 8 servings**

Pretty Pear Salad

1	(3-ounce) package cream cheese
1	(6-ounce) jar stemmed maraschino cherries, juice reserved
8	lettuce leaves
2	(28-ounce) cans pear halves, drained

In a small bowl, stir cream cheese until softened. Add a small amount of juice from cherries and blend until smooth. Add enough juice to achieve a rosy pink color. Line salad plates with lettuce leaves. Place 2 pear halves on each. Top each half with a tablespoon of cream cheese mixture. Garnish each with a cherry. **Yield: 8 servings**

Goldies

1	(18¼-ounce) package yellow cake mix
½	cup butter or margarine, softened
3	eggs, divided
1	(8-ounce) package cream cheese, softened
2½	cups confectioner's sugar

Combine cake mix, butter, and 1 egg. Press into the bottom of a lightly greased 13" x 9" x 2" pan. In another bowl, beat cream cheese, sugar, and remaining eggs until smooth. Pour over cake mixture; bake at 325° for 45 minutes. Cool in pan; cut into squares. **Yield: 2 dozen**

Souper Supper

Spicy Chicken Soup
Marinated Broccoli and Cauliflower
Commercial French Bread
Buttermilk-Chocolate Cake

ᏽᏽ

Spicy Chicken Soup

2	(14½-ounce) cans chicken broth
½	cup water
½	cup commercial picante sauce
¼	cup long-grain rice, uncooked
1	teaspoon ground cumin
½	teaspoon chili powder
1	cup diced, cooked chicken or turkey
1	small zucchini, cut into match-sticks
½	cup diced red bell pepper
1	ripe avocado, peeled, seeded, and chopped
¼	cup sliced green onions with tops

Chopped fresh cilantro or parsley

Combine broth, water, picante sauce, rice, cumin, and chili powder in large saucepan. Bring to a boil. Reduce heat and simmer, uncovered, for 15 minutes. Add chicken, zucchini, and bell pepper; simmer 5-6 minutes more. Just before serving, stir in avocado. Green onion and cilantro or parsley may be added with avocado or sprinkled on top in tureen or individual serving bowls. **Yield: 4 servings**

Marinated Broccoli and Cauliflower

1	bunch broccoli, cut into bite-sized pieces
1	head cauliflower, cut into bite-sized pieces
½	cup minced onion
1	cup grated sharp Cheddar cheese
1	cup mayonnaise
2	tablespoons cider vinegar
½	teaspoon sugar
½	teaspoon salt
¼	teaspoon pepper

Mix broccoli, cauliflower, onion, and cheese together in large bowl. Shake mayonnaise, vinegar, sugar, salt, and pepper together in a jar; pour over vegetables and refrigerate overnight before serving. **Yield: 12 servings**

Buttermilk Chocolate Cake

2	cups granulated sugar
1	cup vegetable oil
2	eggs, beaten
2	cups all-purpose flour
½	teaspoon salt
1	teaspoon baking soda
¼	cup cocoa
½	cup buttermilk
1	cup water
1	teaspoon vanilla

Combine sugar, oil, and eggs; beat well. Combine flour, salt, baking soda, and cocoa; gradually add to sugar mixture, beating well after each addition. Blend in buttermilk, water, and vanilla. Batter will be thin. Pour into lightly greased 13" x 9" x 2" pan. Bake at 350° for 25 minutes. Spread Buttermilk Chocolate Frosting (recipe below) over hot cake; cool in pan. Cut in squares to serve. **Yield: 12 servings**

Buttermilk Chocolate Frosting:

1	pound confectioner's sugar
¼	cup cocoa
¼	cup butter or margarine, melted
1	teaspoon vanilla
⅓	cup buttermilk

Blend sugar and cocoa together. Stir in butter, vanilla, and buttermilk and mix well. Spread over hot cake.

Tips for Pleasing Crowds

For large crowds, use 2 buffet lines--let guests serve themselves. Desserts and drinks can be served from separate tables.

Be sure to determine time needed to brew large pots of coffee.

Concentrated iced tea can be made ahead of time; dilute with water.

Casual Elegance

Chicken Curry
Steamed Rice and Condiments
Green Beans Elegante
Chewy Toffee Cookies

℃

Chicken Curry

4-5	tablespoons minced onion
5	tablespoons vegetable oil
5	tablespoons all-purpose flour
4	cups chicken stock
1	cup seedless raisins
2	tablespoons lemon juice

Strips of lemon zest

1	cup heavy cream
3-4	teaspoons curry powder
2	cups diced, cooked chicken

Salt to taste
Hot fluffy rice
Condiments: chutney, grated coconut, chopped nuts, crumbled bacon, green onion slices, grated hard-cooked egg yolks and whites

In a large skillet, sauté onion in hot vegetable oil. Stir in flour. Add chicken stock; cook and stir until slightly thickened. Add raisins, lemon juice and zest. Simmer for 5 minutes. Stir in cream. Mix curry powder with a little water and add to skillet. When well blended, add chicken and salt. Simmer over low heat until sauce is reduced to desired consistency. Serve over rice with condiments. **Yield: 6 servings**

❡ *Remember that many casseroles can be prepared ahead of time and refrigerated. Allow extra cooking time so they will be hot in the center.*

❡ *For easy serving, any gelatin-based salad can be individually molded in muffin tins using paper liners.*

Green Beans Elegante

2   (16-ounce) cans whole Blue Lake green beans, drained
½   cup chopped onion
1   cup chopped celery
½   cup cider vinegar
½   cup olive oil
¾   cup granulated sugar
½   teaspoon salt
Lettuce leaves

In large bowl, combine green beans, onion, and celery. In a jar, combine vinegar, oil, sugar, and salt; shake well to combine. Pour over bean mixture; cover; refrigerate overnight. Drain and serve on lettuce leaves. **Yield: 8-10 servings**

Chewy Toffee Cookies

2½   cups all-purpose flour
1   teaspoon baking soda
½   teaspoon salt
½   cup butter or margarine, softened
¾   cup granulated sugar
¾   cup light brown sugar
1   teaspoon vanilla
2   eggs
1   (10-ounce) package English toffee bits

Sift together flour, soda, and salt; set aside. Cream together butter, sugar, brown sugar, and vanilla; add eggs. Gradually add dry ingredients; beat well. Stir in toffee bits. Drop by rounded teaspoonfuls onto lightly greased cookie sheets. Bake at 350° for 9-11 minutes. Cool slightly on cookie sheet before removing to wire racks. **Yield: 4 dozen**

A Toast

**Chicken when you're hungry,
Champagne when you're dry,
Loved ones when you're lonely,
And heaven when you die.**

Summer Picnic

Beef Barbecue on Buns
Baked Beans
Coleslaw
Bob's Chocolate Delight

❧

Beef Barbecue

1½	cups vegetable oil
1	cup chopped onion
2	cups ketchup
2	cups water
½	cup lemon juice
½	cup cider vinegar
½	cup granulated sugar
½	cup Worcestershire sauce
6	tablespoons prepared mustard
5	teaspoons salt
1½	teaspoons pepper
1	teaspoon hot pepper sauce
4-5	pounds boneless or bone-in chuck roast

In large saucepan, combine oil, onion, ketchup, water, lemon juice, vinegar, sugar, Worcestershire sauce, mustard, salt, pepper, and hot pepper sauce. Bring to a boil, reduce heat, and simmer for 15 minutes or until slightly thickened. Place meat in crock pot; cover with half the sauce. Cook on high for 2 hours and then reduce heat to low and cook for 4 hours more. After cooking, remove meat and discard accumulated liquid. Shred meat by pulling apart with two forks. Discard gristle, fat, and bone. Mix half of reserved sauce into meat. Reheat before serving on buns. Use remaining sauce on the side. *This is better made a day ahead. Refrigerate and reheat before serving.* **Yield: 20-25 servings**

Baked Beans

1	pound mild bulk sausage
1	pound hot bulk sausage
1	cup minced onion
¾	cup chopped green pepper
3	(32-ounce) cans pork and beans
¾	cup ketchup
½	cup brown sugar
¼	cup prepared mustard

Salt, pepper to taste

Brown sausage, onion, and green pepper, breaking up meat with fork; drain thoroughly. Combine with beans, ketchup, brown sugar, mustard, salt and pepper. Spoon into 2 lightly greased 3-quart casseroles. Bake at 325° for 90 minutes. **Yield: 20 servings**

Coleslaw

2	large heads cabbage, shredded
4	carrots, peeled and shredded
1	cup cider vinegar
1	cup granulated sugar
2	teaspoons salt
2	teaspoons dry mustard
2	teaspoons celery seed
1	cup vegetable oil

Combine cabbage and carrots in large bowl. In medium saucepan, mix together vinegar, sugar, salt, mustard and celery seed; bring to a boil. Remove from heat and whisk in oil; immediately pour over cabbage. Refrigerate until thoroughly chilled. **Yield: 20 servings**

Bob's Chocolate Delight

1	(15-ounce) package cream-filled chocolate sandwich cookies
1	(half-gallon) carton vanilla ice cream, softened
1	(12-ounce) carton frozen whipped topping, thawed

Put cookies into plastic bag; break into small pieces with rolling pin. Stir into ice cream; fold in whipped topping. Spread in a 13" x 9" x 2" pan and freeze. Cut into squares to serve. **Yield: 15-20 servings**

BILLS OF FARE.

Cod's Head and
Shoulders grilled,
remove for
a Pheafant, or Woodcocks.

Broccoli.	Mock Turtle Soup.	Stewed Cardoons.
Mince Pyes.	Brandy Fruit and Sweetmeats.	Veal Olives.
Beuf Tremblant.	Floating Ifland of Chocolate.	Stewed Turkey.
Sweetbreads roafted.	Brandy Fruit and Sweetmeats.	Pompadour Cream.
Artichoke Bottoms fricafeed.	Mock Turtle Soup.	Savoys forced.

Chine of Houfe
Lamb.

[Sauce on the Side Board.]

[A Defert.]

FAMILY

Old Smithfield Church
(LATER NAMED ST. LUKE'S CHURCH)
SMITHFIELD, VIRGINIA
CIRCA 1632 - 1680

OLD SMITHFIELD CHURCH is thought to be the oldest standing original church in Virginia. It was built around 1632 within a few miles of the main Smithfield-Suffolk road. The thick walls, buttresses, and sturdy tower reflect English castle heritage and gothic style. Using English workmanship, the church was built of the best available brick, stone, and earthen materials which accounts for its present excellent condition. The woodcut above, which reproduces an illustration drawn by Henry Howe in 1845, is the earliest surviving pictorial representation of the church. No longer a parish church, St. Luke's has now been designated a shrine by the Diocese of Southern Virginia.

A Reason to Celebrate

Turkey Tetrazzini
Tasty Green Salad
Refrigerator Biscuits
Punch Bowl Cake

৬৯

Turkey Tetrazzini

1	(8-ounce) package spaghetti
1	cup minced celery
½	cup minced onion
½	cup minced green pepper
¼	cup butter or margarine
1	(8-ounce) can sliced mushrooms, drained
3 or more cups chopped, cooked turkey (or chicken)	
2	cups water or turkey broth
2	(10¾-ounce) cans cream of mushroom soup
½	cup grated sharp Cheddar cheese

Cook spaghetti according to manufacturer's instructions; drain well. Sauté celery, onion, and green pepper in melted butter. Remove from heat; drain juices, and add mushrooms and turkey. Place half the spaghetti in a greased 4-quart casserole dish. Spoon half the turkey-vegetable mixture over spaghetti. Add broth or water. Spread 1 can soup over turkey. Repeat all layers. Sprinkle top with cheese. Bake at 350° for 45-60 minutes. **Yield: 8-10 servings**

Tasty Green Salad

1	head iceberg lettuce, washed, drained, and torn
1	(7-ounce) can tiny green peas, drained
¼	cup minced onion
1	cup salad dressing
⅓	cup grated Romano cheese
4	slices bacon, cooked, drained, and crumbled

In a large salad bowl, layer (in this order) lettuce, peas, and onion. Spread salad dressing over vegetables. Sprinkle with cheese and bacon. Cover tightly and refrigerate at least 10 hours before tossing gently to serve. **Yield: 8-10 servings**

Refrigerator Biscuits

1	package active dry yeast
2	tablespoons warm water
2	cups buttermilk
3	tablespoons granulated sugar
1	teaspoon salt
5	cups all-purpose flour, sifted
1	tablespoon baking powder
1	teaspoon baking soda
¾	cup shortening

Dissolve yeast in water. Combine with buttermilk, sugar, and salt; set aside. Mix together flour, baking powder, and soda. Cut in shortening. Stir in liquid mixture. Mix lightly; do not knead. Turn into greased bowl; cover; and refrigerate overnight. Roll dough ½″ thick; cut into 2″ rounds; place on ungreased cookie sheets. Bake at 450° for 10 minutes.
Yield: 2 dozen

Punch Bowl Cake

1	(18¼-ounce) package yellow cake mix
3	eggs
1⅓	cups water
⅓	cup vegetable oil
1	(6-ounce) package instant vanilla pudding mix
3	cups milk
1	(20-ounce) can crushed pineapple, drained
2	(10-ounce) packages thawed frozen strawberries, undrained
2	bananas, sliced
1	(16-ounce) carton frozen whipped topping, thawed

Combine cake mix, eggs, water, and oil, and prepare according to package directions. Bake in 2 greased and floured 9″ cake pans. Remove from oven; cool on wire racks. Meanwhile, combine pudding mix and milk and beat for 2 minutes; refrigerate.

Cut one cake layer into chunks and put in the bottom of a large bowl. Stir pudding and pour half over cake chunks. Spread half the pineapple over pudding; continue with half the strawberries, half the bananas, and half the whipped topping. Repeat entire process, beginning with cake layer. Cover tightly and refrigerate until ready to serve. **Yield: 12-15 servings**

Fancy Buffet

Super Creamed Chicken
Buttermilk Waffles
Mrs. Anderson's Tomato Aspic
Japanese Fruit Pie

ళు

Super Creamed Chicken

½	cup chopped onion
½	cup chopped celery
2	tablespoons butter or margarine
2	tablespoons all-purpose flour
1⅓	cups undiluted evaporated milk
1	(10-ounce) can cream of chicken soup
⅔	cup water
2	tablespoons green olives, sliced
⅛	teaspoon poultry seasoning
¼	teaspoon salt
1	cup cooked zucchini, cubed
3	cups cooked chicken, cubed

Sauté onion and celery in butter; stir in flour. Add evaporated milk; cook, stirring constantly, over medium heat until mixture thickens. Add soup, water, green olives, poultry seasoning, salt, zucchini and chicken one at a time, stirring after each addition. Simmer, covered, for 15 minutes, stirring occasionally. Serve over waffles or in 4" pastry shells. *This freezes well.* Yield: 10-12 servings

Buttermilk Waffles

2	cups all-purpose flour
1	tablespoon baking powder
1	teaspoon baking soda
1	teaspoon salt
2	cups buttermilk
4	eggs, separated
1	cup melted butter or margarine or vegetable oil

Sift together flour, baking powder, baking soda, and salt. Combine buttermilk and egg yolks; add to dry ingredients; mix until moistened. Fold in melted butter. Beat egg whites stiff; fold into batter. Pour batter onto griddle; close lid. Bake until steaming stops. **Yield: 8 servings**

Mrs. Anderson's Tomato Aspic

1	envelope unflavored gelatin
1¾	cups tomato juice, divided
3	tablespoons lemon juice
1½	teaspoons cider vinegar
½	teaspoon salt
2	tablespoons granulated sugar

Pepper to taste
Lots of celery salt
Lots of onion salt or powder

Dissolve gelatin in ½ cup tomato juice; set aside. Add 1 cup hot tomato juice to gelatin mixture, stirring well to completely dissolve gelatin. In a small bowl, mix lemon juice, vinegar, salt, sugar, pepper, celery salt, and onion salt with remaining ¼ cup tomato juice. Add to gelatin mixture. Pour into 4-cup mold and refrigerate. **Yield: 4 servings**

Japanese Fruit Pie

½	cup butter or margarine, melted
1	cup granulated sugar
3	eggs
½	cup flaked coconut
½	cup raisins
½	cup chopped pecans or walnuts
1	teaspoon vanilla
1	9" unbaked pastry shell

Combine butter, sugar, eggs, coconut, raisins, nuts, and vanilla; pour into prepared pastry shell. Bake at 350° for 45 minutes. **Yield: 6-8 servings**

Festival Chicken Dinner

Chicken Spaghetti
Milwaukee Spinach Salad
Herbed French Bread
Rum Cake

ⲟⲋ

Chicken Spaghetti

1	(3½-4-pound) broiler-fryer, cut up
1½	teaspoons salt, divided
1	(28-ounce) can whole tomatoes, undrained
¼	cup plus 3 tablespoons butter or margarine, divided
3	tablespoons all-purpose flour
½	cup heavy cream
⅛	teaspoon nutmeg
⅛	teaspoon pepper
¼	pound ground beef
¼	pound bulk pork sausage
½	pound fresh mushrooms, sliced
2	cups finely chopped onion
1½	cups finely chopped celery
1½	cups chopped green pepper
2	cloves garlic, minced
1	bay leaf
½	teaspoon dried red pepper flakes
1	(16-ounce) package spaghetti
2	cups grated sharp Cheddar cheese

Grated Parmesan cheese

Place chicken, 1 teaspoon salt, and water to cover in a Dutch oven. Bring to a boil; cover and simmer 45 minutes. Remove chicken from broth; cool, reserving 2½ cups broth. Bone chicken, and cut meat into bite-sized pieces; set aside. Place tomatoes in a heavy saucepan. Bring to a boil; reduce heat, and simmer 15 minutes; set aside.

Melt 3 tablespoons butter in a heavy saucepan over low heat; add flour, stirring until smooth. Cook 1 minute. Gradually stir in cream and 1 cup reserved broth; cook over medium heat, stirring, until thickened and bubbly. Stir in nutmeg, pepper, and remaining salt; set aside. Brown beef and sausage in skillet; drain and set aside.

(Continued on next page)

(Chicken Spaghetti continued from previous page)

Sauté mushrooms, onion, celery, green pepper, and garlic in remaining butter in a Dutch oven 5 minutes. Add tomatoes, white sauce, meat, bay leaf, and red pepper flakes to Dutch oven; stir well. Simmer over low heat 15 minutes. Discard bay leaf. Cook spaghetti according to package directions; drain and set aside. Spoon one third of meat sauce into a lightly greased 5-quart casserole. Top with half of spaghetti, half of chicken, one third of meat sauce, and half of Cheddar cheese. Repeat layers, beginning with spaghetti and ending with Cheddar cheese. Pour remaining reserved broth over layers. Bake, covered, at 350° for 15 minutes. Uncover and bake an additional 15 minutes. Serve with Parmesan cheese.
Yield: 12 servings

Milwaukee Spinach Salad

1	pound fresh spinach, washed and torn
2	heads Bibb lettuce, washed and torn
2	avocados, peeled and sliced in wedges
2	(11-ounce) cans mandarin oranges, drained
1	cup thinly sliced sweet onion
1	cup vegetable oil
½	cup granulated sugar
½	cup cider vinegar
1	tablespoon dry mustard
1	tablespoon celery seed
2	green onions, thinly sliced
1	teaspoon salt

In a large salad bowl toss together spinach, lettuce, avocado, oranges, and sweet onion. Whisk together oil, sugar, vinegar, mustard, celery seed, salt, and green onion; refrigerate 3-4 hours before tossing with salad greens.
Yield: 10 servings

Herbed French Bread

1	tablespoon chives
1	tablespoon parsley
½	teaspoon tarragon
½	teaspoon chervil
½	cup butter or margarine, melted
2	loaves French bread, sliced

Combine chives, parsley, tarragon, chervil, and butter; brush on bread. Re-assemble loaves; wrap in foil. Bake at 350° for 20 minutes.
Yield: 12 servings

Rum Cake

½   cup finely chopped pecans
1   (18¼-ounce) package yellow cake mix
1   (3.4-ounce) package instant vanilla pudding mix
¾   cup cold water
4   eggs
⅓   cup vegetable oil
¼   cup light rum

Syrup:

1   cup granulated sugar
½   cup butter or margarine
6   tablespoons water
2   tablespoons light rum

Generously grease a 12-cup Bundt pan; sprinkle pecans in bottom. Combine cake mix, pudding mix, water, eggs, oil, and rum in large bowl Beat at medium speed of mixer for 2 minutes. Spoon batter into prepared pan. Bake at 325° for 1 hour. During the last five minutes of baking, combine sugar, butter, and water in small saucepan and bring to a boil. Remove from heat; add rum. Pour over hot cake immediately after baking. Cool cake in pan. **Yield: 16 servings**

Party Time

Meal and party times vary according to local custom, but within standard schedules.

Morning Coffee: Between 10:00 a.m. and noon

Brunch: Between 10:30 a.m. and 1:00 p.m.

Luncheon: Begins at 12:30 or 1:00 p.m.

Tea: From 4:00 to 5:00 or 5:30 p.m.

Cocktails: Begin around 5:00 and last until about 7:00 p.m.

Dinner: Depends entirely upon local custom, but may begin as early as 6:30 p.m. In metropolitan areas, the usual time is 8:00 p.m.

Choir Christmas Party

*A choir tradition hosted by Barbara and Bill Fleming
following the annual Carol Concert*

Eggnog Extraordinaire
Spiced Cider
Sliced Eye of the Round
Horsie Sauce
Sweet 'n Sour Meatballs
Liver Paté
Hot Artichoke Dip
Spinach Surprise Dip

᪐

Egg Nog Extraordinaire

*This is an adaptation of a wonderful recipe found in a
Jeffersonian cookbook from Monticello.*

18	large eggs, separated
3½	cups confectioner's sugar, divided
2	cups brandy
2	cups light rum
1	quart half-and-half
2	quarts heavy cream, divided
1½	tablespoons vanilla

Freshly grated nutmeg

With an electric mixer, whisk the egg yolks until light and fluffy. Gradually add confectioner's sugar. Whip egg whites to soft peaks; fold into yolk mixture. Pour in the brandy and rum, mixing thoroughly; refrigerate overnight. Next day, add the half-and-half and 1 quart cream. Cover; refrigerate 3 days. At serving time, whip remaining cream; flavor with vanilla and remaining confectioner's sugar. Pour into punch bowl; fold a proportionate amount of whipped cream into top surface. Sprinkle generously with freshly grated nutmeg. **Yield: 20-30 servings**

Spiced Cider

2	gallons apple cider
12	cinnamon sticks
2	tablespoons whole cloves
1	tablespoon whole allspice
1	orange, sliced thinly
1	lemon, sliced thinly

Pour cider into large kettle. Tie cinnamon sticks, cloves, and allspice in square of clean white cotton; drop into cider. Bring to a boil; reduce heat; simmer 30 minutes. Pour into punch bowl; float orange and lemon slices on top. **Yield: 50 servings**

Eye of the Round

1	(5-pound) eye of round roast
3-4	tablespoons all-purpose flour

Salt, pepper to taste

Rub fat side of roast with flour; sprinkle surface liberally with salt and pepper. Place in roasting pan, fat side up. Bake in preheated 500° oven for 30 minutes. Turn off oven. Leave oven door closed and allow roast to cool for 1 hour. Refrigerate overnight before slicing. Serve on rye or pumpernickel party bread with Horsie Sauce (recipe below).

Horsie Sauce:

2	cups sour cream
1	cup mayonnaise
1	(5-ounce) jar prepared horseradish

Combine sour cream, mayonnaise, and horseradish; refrigerate. Serve as accompaniment to beef. **Yield: 3 cups**

Sweet 'n Sour Meatballs

15	ounces commercial chili sauce
½	cup brown sugar
1	(1-pound) can jellied cranberry sauce
1	(5-pound) package frozen cooked meatballs, thawed

Combine chili sauce, brown sugar, and cranberry sauce in saucepan; cook over medium heat; stir until blended and bubbly. Pour over thawed meatballs. Keep warm over low heat until serving time.
Yield: 5-6 dozen

Liver Paté

½ pound chicken livers
1 medium onion, minced
4 tablespoons butter or margarine, melted
2 eggs, hard-boiled
¼ cup half-and-half
½ teaspoon salt
¼ teaspoon pepper
⅛ teaspoon nutmeg
1 teaspoon Worcestershire sauce

Cook chicken livers and onion in butter until tender. Place liver mixture in food processor with eggs, half-and-half, salt, pepper, nutmeg, and Worcestershire sauce; process to a paste-like consistency. Pack into a mold, or form by hand. Store in plastic wrap in the refrigerator until ready to serve. *Tastes best on shredded or flat wheat crackers.* **Yield: 2 cups**

Hot Artichoke Dip

1 (14-ounce) can drained artichoke hearts
½ cup mayonnaise (more if desired)
1 cup Parmesan cheese
8 ounces grated mozzarella cheese
Garlic powder, paprika to taste

Chop artichokes; mix together with mayonnaise, cheeses, and garlic powder to taste. Place in 13" x 9" x 2" glass oven proof baking dish. Bake at 350° for 30 minutes. Sprinkle with paprika after removing from oven. Serve immediately with plain, stoned wheat or shredded wheat crackers.

Spinach Surprise Dip

1 (10-ounce) package frozen, chopped spinach, cooked and drained
1 cup sour cream
1 cup mayonnaise
1 (1.5-ounce) package dehydrated onion soup mix
Hot pepper sauce to taste
1 teaspoon lemon juice
½ teaspoon seasoned salt
¼ teaspoon seasoned pepper

Mix spinach, sour cream, mayonnaise, soup mix, hot pepper sauce, lemon juice, salt and pepper; chill. Serve with raw vegetables. **Yield: 3 cups**

Soul Food for New Year's Day

The Flemings invite family and friends for brunch.

Garlic Grits
His Stewed Tomatoes
Her Stewed Tomatoes
Curried Baked Fruit
Black-eyed Peas with Smithfield Ham
Cornbread

ᘒ

Garlic Grits

4	cups salted water
1	cup hominy grits
½	cup butter or margarine
1	cup milk
4	eggs, slightly beaten
1½	cups shredded sharp Cheddar cheese
2	cloves garlic, pressed and minced

Bring salted water to boil; stir in grits slowly. Bring water back to brisk boil; cover; reduce to medium-low heat. Cook until water is absorbed, stirring often to make sure grits do not stick. Remove from heat; stir in butter and milk. Cool to lukewarm; add eggs, cheese, and garlic. Pour into greased 2-quart baking dish. Bake at 350° for 60 minutes.
Yield: 6-8 servings

His Stewed Tomatoes

The more traditional style in the South--a sweet variety that many feel complements the black eyed peas perfectly!

1	cup butter or margarine
4	(15-ounce) cans whole tomatoes
2-3	cups granulated sugar
10-12	slices stale bread, toasted, torn into 2" pieces

Salt and pepper to taste

Melt butter in large skillet; add tomatoes. Stir and cook until tender. Add sugar; stir until dissolved. Then add bread, salt, and pepper. Cover; cook over low heat about 30 minutes. **Yield: 25 servings**

Her Stewed Tomatoes

Each year Barbara and Bill vie for honors!

1   cup butter or margarine
8   stalks celery, cut diagonally into 1" pieces
4   (15-ounce) cans whole tomatoes
Salt and pepper to taste

In large saucepan or electric fry-pan, melt butter and add celery; sauté until transparent. Pour in tomatoes and cook slowly until all is bubbly and well blended. Salt and pepper as necessary. **Yield: 25 servings**

Curried Baked Fruit

1   (16-ounce) can peach halves, drained
1   (16-ounce) can pear halves, drained
1   (16-ounce) can sliced pineapple, drained
1   (16-ounce) can apricot halves, drained
12   maraschino cherries, drained
¾   cup light brown sugar
1   tablespoon curry powder
⅓   cup butter or margarine, melted
1   cup pecan halves or slivered almonds

Arrange fruit in 11" x 17" x 2" glass baking dish. Mix together brown sugar, butter, and curry, pour over fruit. Sprinkle nuts over top. Bake at 325° for 1 hour. Refrigerate overnight. Reheat at 350° before serving. **Yield: 10-12 servings**

Cornbread

An old family recipe--very Southern, very Virginian

1½   cups white cornmeal (no substitutes)
1   teaspoon salt
2   teaspoons baking powder
2   eggs, beaten
1⅔   cups milk
4   tablespoons shortening

Preheat oven to 400°. Sift cornmeal, salt, and baking powder; set aside. Combine eggs and milk; add to dry ingredients. Blend thoroughly. Put shortening into a 9" x 9" x 2" square pan; put pan in oven to melt shortening. Pour melted, hot shortening into batter; mix well. Pour batter into hot greased pan; bake for 30 minutes or until browned. *Can be baked in muffin tins or iron corn stick pans.* **Yield: 9-12 servings**

Prospect Hill Leftovers Party

For years, Molly and Walter Hyer have entertained choir
families and friends at this brunch held after church
one Sunday early in the new year.

Toe's Bloody Marys
Screwdrivers
Mushroom Paté
Leftover Turkey Brunswick Stew
Lentil Soup
Pork Barbecue with Rolls
Macy's Cookies
Margaret's Fruit Bars

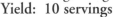

Toe's Bloody Marys

1	(46-ounce) can tomato juice
2	cups vodka
¾	cup lemon juice
½	cup Worcestershire sauce
¾	teaspoon salt
¼	teaspoon pepper
1	tablespoon horseradish
¼	teaspoon hot pepper sauce

In large container, combine juice, vodka, lemon juice, Worcestershire sauce,
salt, pepper, horseradish, and hot pepper sauce. Prepare several hours before serving; refrigerate. Shake or stir well before serving.
Yield: 10 servings

Mushroom Paté

¾ pound chopped mushrooms with stems
2 tablespoons butter or margarine
1 (8-ounce) package cream cheese, softened
½ teaspoon curry powder
1 teaspoon Worcestershire sauce
1 tablespoon dry white wine
½ cup finely chopped pecans
Watercress or parsley for garnish

Sauté mushrooms in butter until dark, about 5 minutes. Drain. In blender, combine mushrooms, cream cheese, curry powder, Worcestershire sauce, and white wine; process until puréed. Fold in pecans. Refrigerate. Garnish with watercress. Serve with crackers.

Leftover Turkey Brunswick Stew

1 turkey carcass
Water to cover
4 cups chopped potatoes
1 (16-ounce) bag frozen tiny lima beans
2 cups chopped celery
2 cups chopped onion
2 (16-ounce) cans whole tomatoes, chopped
2 (16-ounce) cans white shoepeg corn, drained
1 tablespoon Worcestershire sauce
Salt, pepper to taste
1 teaspoon granulated sugar
2-4 cups chopped, cooked turkey
Leftover stuffing, gravy (optional)

Place turkey carcass in heavy kettle; cover with water. Cover; bring to a boil. Reduce heat; simmer 2 hours. Cool broth; strain. Pour broth back into kettle; bring to a boil. Add potatoes and lima beans. Simmer 10 minutes; add celery, onions, tomatoes, corn, Worcestershire sauce, salt, pepper, sugar, and turkey. If desired, add stuffing and gravy. Simmer 30-45 minutes. Adjust seasoning. *Better cooked a day ahead, refrigerated, and then re-heated.* If soup is too thin, add more vegetables; if too thick, add more tomatoes, broth, or water. **Yield: 10-12 servings**

Lentil Soup

1	pound lentils, rinsed and drained
1-2	cups chopped onion
1-2	cups chopped celery
1-2	cups grated or chopped carrots
1	clove garlic, minced
1	teaspoon oregano
½	teaspoon thyme
¼	teaspoon ground cloves
Water	
1	pound Polish sausage, cut into bite-sized pieces
Salt to taste	
2	tablespoons cider vinegar

Combine lentils, onion, celery, carrots, garlic, oregano, thyme, and cloves in Dutch oven. Cover with water; add 2 additional cups water. Bring to a boil; reduce heat. Cover; simmer for 1 hour. After 30 minutes, add more water if necessary. When lentils are soft, add sausage; heat through. Taste for seasoning; add salt as desired. Before serving; add vinegar. *May substitute ham bone and chopped ham for sausage.* **Yield: 8 servings**

Pork Barbecue

2	(4-5 pound) pork shoulder roasts
1	cup water

Place pork in large roaster; add water; cover. Bake at 300° until meat falls apart. This may take 4-6 hours. Cool in pan; reserve cooking liquid. Remove all fat and bone from roasts; chop meat coarsely. Skim grease from reserved pan drippings; bring liquid to a boil; simmer until reduced by half. Pour over chopped meat. Refrigerate or freeze until ready to serve. Before serving, combine meat and sauce. Warm in crock pot or place in covered roaster and   bake at 300° until heated through. Stir occasionally.

Barbecue sauce:

½	cup butter or margarine, melted
1½	cups cider vinegar
1	teaspoon granulated sugar
1	teaspoon salt
1	cup Worcestershire sauce
¼	teaspoon hot pepper sauce

Combine butter, vinegar, sugar, salt, Worcestershire sauce, and hot pepper sauce; simmer 15-30 minutes. Cool; refrigerate. **Yield: 3 cups**

Macy's Cookies

My Aunt Macy made these years ago; I make them
every Christmas to serve at this party.

7   cups all-purpose flour
1   teaspoon baking soda
2   cups butter or margarine, softened
2⅔   cups light brown sugar
2   eggs
1   teaspoon vanilla
2   cups chopped pecans

Combine flour and soda; set aside. In large bowl, cream butter and brown sugar until light and fluffy. Beat in eggs and vanilla. Gradually add reserved dry ingredients, beating after each addition. If necessary, use hands to incorporate all flour. Add chopped pecans. Divide dough into fourths; shape each into a roll; wrap in plastic wrap. Refrigerate 3-4 hours or freeze until firm. Slice into rounds; place on lightly greased cookie sheets. Bake at 350° for 8-12 minutes. **Yield: 8 dozen**

Margaret's Fruit Bars

A former neighbor used to make these.

1½   cups all-purpose flour, sifted
½   teaspoon salt
½   cup shortening
2   cups granulated sugar
3   eggs
1   cup chopped pecans
2   tablespoons lemon juice
1   teaspoon vanilla
½   cup chopped candied orange peel
½   cup chopped candied citron

Combine flour and salt; set aside. In large bowl, cream shortening and sugar until light and fluffy. Add eggs one at a time, beating well. Add reserved dry ingredients. Stir in pecans, lemon juice, and vanilla. Spoon batter into lightly greased 13" x 9" x 2" pan. Sprinkle fruit over batter. Bake at 350° for 35-40 minutes; do not overbake. Cool in pan; cut into squares or bars. **Yield: 3 dozen**

May Fair House Specialties

Hunter's Spaghetti
Currituck Casserole

℘

Hunter's Spaghetti

10	pounds ground beef
10	onions, sliced
6	green peppers, chopped
2½	No. 10 cans tomato sauce
6	cups Burgundy
2	tablespoons salt
3	tablespoons garlic salt
1	teaspoon pepper
1½	cups granulated sugar
5	pounds spaghetti (break into 2" lengths)
10	cups grated cheese, divided

Brown beef, onions, and green peppers; drain. In a large pot, combine tomato sauce, Burgundy, salt, garlic salt, pepper, and sugar; add beef mixture and simmer for 20 minutes. Cook spaghetti in boiling salted water, then drain and mix with 6 cups of the grated cheese. Combine spaghetti and cheese with beef mixture. Pour into large casseroles and top with remaining cheese. Bake at 350° until hot and bubbly. **Yield: 40 Servings**

Currituck Casserole

15	pounds ground beef
2½	cups chopped onion
1	cup meat drippings
2	No. 10 cans lima beans (drain, save 2½ cups)
3⅓	cups vinegar
½	cup prepared mustard
⅓	cup Worcestershire sauce
1	tablespoon salt
5	teaspoons oregano
2	(48-ounce) cans tomato soup

Brown beef and save drippings. Sauté onion in meat drippings. Combine lima beans, vinegar, mustard, Worcestershire, salt, oregano and tomato soup in a large kettle. Add meat and onions to soup mixture. Pour into large baking pans. Bake at 350° until hot and bubbly. **Yield: 40 servings**

Hors D'Oeuvres

Contents

Bourbon Slush

2   tea bags
1   cup boiling water
1   cup granulated sugar
3½   cups water
3   ounces frozen lemonade concentrate, thawed
6   ounces frozen orange juice concentrate, thawed
½   cup bourbon

Steep tea bags in boiling water. Add sugar. Stir in water, lemonade, orange juice and bourbon. Freeze until ready to serve. **Yield: 10-12 servings**

Frozen Daiquiris

1   (12-ounce) can frozen limeade concentrate
2   cups light rum
4½   cups water

Combine limeade, rum, and water in a plastic pitcher. Freeze. This drink freezes to a mushy consistency. Serve and enjoy! **Yield: 12 servings**

Damson Liqueur

10-11   cups damsons, unpeeled
2   cups granulated sugar
½   gallon vodka

Wash damsons; split each on 1 side. Fill 1 half-gallon jar about ⅔ full of damsons. Add sugar. Fill jar with vodka. Turn jar every day until sugar dissolves. This may take as long as 10 days. Allow to sit for 10 weeks. Strain liqueur; pour into bottles. Keeps forever. **Yield: 2 quarts**

Mulled Cider

½   gallon apple cider
½   teaspoon ground mace
½   teaspoon whole allspice
3   sticks cinnamon
½   cup brown sugar
½   cup rum (optional)
½   cup brandy (optional)

Mix cider, mace, allspice, cinnamon, and brown sugar in a large saucepan; boil for 5 minutes. Add rum and/or brandy and simmer. Serve with lemon slices. **Yield: 16 servings**

Burgundy Apple Punch

2   fifths Burgundy or Rosé wine, chilled
1   quart apple juice or cider, chilled
2   tablespoons lemon juice
1   cup granulated sugar
1   quart ginger ale

Combine Burgundy, apple, and lemon juices with sugar; stir to dissolve sugar. Pour into punch bowl; add ginger ale. Add a block of ice. **Variation:** Combine as listed above in a Dutch oven and warm gently over low heat. **Yield: 15 servings**

Champagne Punch

1   fifth Chablis, chilled
½   fifth Triple Sec, chilled
1½ (6-ounce) cans frozen lemonade concentrate
1   quart club soda, chilled
2   fifths champagne, chilled

Mix Chablis, Triple Sec, and lemonade. Pour over block of ice placed in punch bowl. Add club soda and champagne, stirring gently. **Yield: 40 (8-ounce) servings**

Coffee Punch

1	gallon strong coffee
1	stick cinnamon
1	quart heavy cream
5	tablespoons granulated sugar
5	teaspoons vanilla
½	gallon French Vanilla ice cream

Brew coffee with cinnamon stick in water. Cool. Whip cream; add sugar and vanilla gradually. Put ice cream and whipped cream in punch bowl. Add coffee. Mix well. **Variation:** Rum, brandy, or coffee liqueur may be added to taste. **Yield: 50-60 servings**

Prospect Hill Punch

1	(12-ounce) can frozen orange juice concentrate, thawed
1	(6-ounce) can frozen lemonade concentrate, thawed
3	cups brewed tea, chilled
3¾	cups vodka
1½	cups club soda, chilled

Place orange juice concentrate, lemonade concentrate, tea, and vodka in punch bowl. Stir until well mixed. Just before serving, pour in club soda and stir well. Serve over cracked ice. **Variation:** If you omit vodka, use a total of 5 cups club soda for punch. **Yield: 20 (4-ounce) servings**

Russian Tea Mix

Makes a nice Christmas gift.

2	cups orange breakfast drink powder
1	cup granulated sugar
½	cup instant tea with lemon
1	teaspoon cinnamon
½	teaspoon ground cloves

Place all ingredients in food processor. Blend to a fine powder. Store in jars; use as needed. Reconstitute using 2 teaspoons mix per 6 ounces boiling water. May be served hot or cold. **Yield: 96 servings**

Cracker Snackers

1	(.6-ounce) package Italian dressing mix
¼	teaspoon dill weed
⅛	teaspoon garlic powder
¼	teaspoon lemon pepper seasoning
2	(11-ounce) packages oyster crackers
½	cup vegetable oil

Combine dressing mix, dill, garlic powder and lemon pepper, then stir in oyster crackers. Drizzle oil over mixture, mixing well again. Place in large paper bag, fold to close and let stand for two hours. Shake bag and store in airtight container. Enjoy!

Oriental Cashew Crunch

1	(16-ounce) package oat squares cereal
1	(3-ounce) can chow mein noodles
1	cup cashew nuts
⅓	cup vegetable oil
3	tablespoons soy sauce

Combine cereal, noodles, and nuts and place in a 13" x 9" x 2" pan. Combine oil and soy sauce and pour over cereal mixture; stir to coat evenly. Bake at 250° for 1 hour, stirring every 20 minutes. **Yield: 10 cups**

❡ *Natural almonds are almonds that have not been blanched but still have their brown skins.*

Great Poppy Almonds

2	tablespoons butter or margarine
½	teaspoon salt
1½	teaspoons chili powder
1	teaspoon celery salt
⅛	teaspoon cayenne
1	teaspoon Worcestershire sauce
1½	cups whole almonds

Melt butter. Stir in salt, chili powder, celery salt, cayenne, and Worcestershire sauce. Add almonds and coat thoroughly with seasoning mix. Place on a cookie sheet and bake at 300° until crispy, stirring twice. Or place in a glass baking dish; microwave on high for 7 minutes, stirring twice. *Great with drinks. Makes a nice Christmas gift for a man.*
Yield: 1½ cups

Texas Barbecued Pecans

We always serve these at our annual Christmas party.

2   tablespoons butter or margarine, melted
¼   cup Worcestershire sauce
1   tablespoon ketchup
⅛   teaspoon hot pepper sauce
4   cups pecan halves
Salt to taste

Combine butter, Worcestershire sauce, ketchup, and hot pepper sauce. Pour over pecans, stirring gently to coat. Spread pecans on cookie sheet coated with non-stick vegetable spray. Bake at 300° for 30 minutes, stirring often to prevent burning. Immediately after baking, spread pecans on paper towels; sprinkle generously with salt. Cool. Store in airtight container. **Yield: 4 cups**

Tortilla Pie

2   (8-ounce) packages cream cheese, softened
1   (4-ounce) can chopped green chilies
1   (4-ounce) can chopped black olives
1   (20-ounce) package 10" flour tortillas
1   (11½-ounce) jar mild salsa, drained

Combine cream cheese, chilies and olives, mixing until smooth. Spread between layers of tortillas. Refrigerate until chilled. With a sharp knife, slice into pie-shaped wedges and transfer to serving plate. At the last minute, pour drained salsa on top. **Yield: 15-20 servings**

South Carolina Cheese-Its

2½   cups all-purpose flour
½   teaspoon salt
Several shakes cayenne pepper
1   cup butter or margarine, softened
4   cups shredded sharp Cheddar cheese

Combine flour, salt, and cayenne. Add butter; mix in cheese until well blended. Fill cookie press with dough; press out into star shapes. Bake at 375° for 10 minutes. **Yield: 4 dozen**

Tea Time Cheese Puffs

from the Mainstay Inn, Cape May, NJ

2	cups sharp Cheddar cheese, shredded, at room temperature
½	cup shortening, at room temperature
½	cup butter or margarine, at room temperature
½	teaspoon cayenne
1	teaspoon salt
1	tablespoon water
⅓	cup grated Parmesan cheese
2	rounded cups all-purpose flour, sifted
⅓	teaspoon baking soda

Combine cheese, shortening, butter, cayenne, salt, water, and Parmesan; beat until well blended. Sift together the flour and soda; spoon into cheese mixture. Pack into cookie press with star tip; press 1″ star shapes on ungreased cookie sheet. Bake at 350° for 10-15 minutes. **Variation:** Add bacon bits or cooked sausage bits to the dough. Also, experiment with Cayenne pepper - some like it hot! **Yield: 5-6 dozen**

Cheese Blinkers

2	cups grated extra sharp Cheddar cheese
½	cup butter or margarine, softened
¼	cup minced onion
Salt to taste	
1	(1-pound) loaf thinly sliced white or wheat bread, crusted

Combine cheese, butter, onion, and salt to make a spreadable mixture. Spread on bread; roll up, jelly-roll fashion. Cut into thirds. Bake at 350° for about 3 minutes; then broil briefly to toast. Serve warm. *Can be frozen beforehand and baked just prior to serving.* **Yield: 4-5 dozen**

Texas Hot Eggs

This is a tasty appetizer that men usually like.

6	eggs, hard-boiled and shelled
Jalapeño juice	
Crackers	

Place eggs in quart jar; add Jalapeño juice to cover. Seal and marinate in refrigerator for at least 2 weeks. Remove eggs, slice, and serve with crackers. **Yield: 30 servings**

Marinated Chicken Wings

1	cup soy sauce
1	tablespoon granulated sugar
¼	cup white wine
¼	cup corn oil
⅛	teaspoon monosodium glutamate
1	teaspoon ground ginger
2-3	pounds chicken wings, tips discarded

Combine soy sauce, sugar, wine, corn oil, monosodium glutamate, and ginger. Pour over prepared chicken wings, cover, and marinate 16-20 hours. Remove wings from marinade; arrange in single layer in a large, shallow baking pan lined with heavy-duty aluminum foil. Moisten with reserved marinade. Bake at 325° for 1½-2 hours. **Yield: 1 dozen**

Burgundy Eye of Round

1	(3-4 pound) eye of round roast
¼	teaspoon seasoned salt
⅛	teaspoon garlic powder
⅛	teaspoon freshly ground pepper
1	medium-sized oven cooking bag
¾	cup Burgundy wine

Sprinkle roast with salt, garlic powder, and pepper. Place roast in oven cooking bag; add Burgundy. Tie bag securely; place in shallow dish; refrigerate overnight. At cooking time, cut 6 (½") slits in top of bag. Place on roasting pan. Bake at 325° for 50-60 minutes, or until thermometer registers 140°. Cool and slice. Serve with biscuits. **Yield: 25 servings**

Hot Sausage Ryes

1	pound bulk pork sausage (hot)
1	pound pasteurized process cheese spread, cubed
1	loaf party rye bread
Oregano	

Brown sausage in large skillet; drain well. Stir cheese cubes into sausage; cook, stirring, until cheese melts. Spread on rye slices. Sprinkle tops with oregano. Freeze on cookie sheets; package later in bags. Bake at 400° for 10 minutes. Serve hot. *These are good for lunch, cocktail fare, or snacks.* **Yield: about 40**

Shrimp Toast

½   pound uncooked shrimp
¼   cup minced water chestnuts
1   egg, slightly beaten
½   teaspoon salt
½   teaspoon sugar
1   tablespoon cornstarch
¼   cup onion, chopped
½   teaspoon seasoned salt flavor enhancer
6   slices stale white bread, crusted
2   cups peanut or corn oil

Shell and de-vein shrimp, wash, drain, and mince. Combine shrimp, water chestnuts, beaten egg, salt, sugar, cornstarch, onion, and seasoned salt; set aside. Cut each bread slice into 4 triangles; spread 1 teaspoon shrimp mixture over each triangle. In a saucepan, heat 2 cups oil to 375°. Lower bread into hot oil with shrimp side down. After 1 minute, turn; fry on other side until golden brown. Drain on paper towels; serve immediately. *Use stale bread because it absorbs less oil than fresh bread. Shrimp toast should be crisp. It is best when served immediately, but can be made ahead and reheated. Can be frozen and reheated without thawing.* **Yield: 24**

❡ *To make homemade celery salt, thoroughly dry celery leaves, crush them to a powder, or rub them through a sieve; then mix with salt.*

Marinated Asparagus

20 small, thin asparagus
¾   cup olive oil
¼   cup white wine vinegar seasoned with hot peppers
¼   teaspoon granulated sugar (optional)
Garlic powder to taste
½   tablespoon basil
½   tablespoon dill
Other herbs as desired

Blanch asparagus for 2 minutes; drain, but do not cool. Mix thoroughly oil, vinegar, sugar, garlic powder, basil, and dill; pour over warm asparagus. Cover and allow to cool to room temperature. Drain dressing; chill asparagus before serving on bed of lettuce as salad or appetizers. **Yield: 4-5 servings**

Marinated Mushrooms

2   cups red wine vinegar, divided
2   cups vegetable oil, divided
1   large onion, quartered
1   tablespoon salt
2   tablespoons parsley
2   tablespoons prepared mustard
⅓   cup brown sugar
2   pounds fresh mushroom caps, rinsed

Combine ¼ cup *each* vinegar and oil in blender. Add onion; process until onion is finely chopped. Pour into Dutch oven; add remaining vinegar, oil, salt, parsley, mustard, and brown sugar. Bring to a boil, reduce heat, cover; simmer 15 minutes. Add mushrooms in batches; simmer each batch for 5-6 minutes. With slotted spoon, remove cooked mushrooms; put in plastic container. When all mushrooms have been cooked, pour marinade in; refrigerate several hours or overnight. Drain before serving with toothpicks. **Yield: 20 servings**

Hot Spinach Balls

4   (10-ounce) packages chopped frozen spinach
4   cups herb-flavored stuffing mix
2   large onions, diced
8   eggs
1   cup grated Parmesan cheese
1½   cups butter or margarine, melted
1   tablespoon thyme
2   cloves garlic, minced
Salt and pepper to taste

Thaw spinach; squeeze out all liquid. Mix with stuffing, onions, eggs, Parmesan cheese, butter, thyme, garlic, salt, and pepper. Refrigerate at least 2 hours. Roll into balls the size of walnuts. Freeze or refrigerate until ready to use. Defrost before baking. Bake at 300° for 30 minutes. **Yield: 11-12 dozen**

Vegetable Sandwiches

2	stalks celery, strung and chopped finely
½	green pepper, seeded and chopped finely
1	medium onion, chopped finely
1	cucumber, seeded and chopped finely
2	carrots, peeled and grated
1	envelope unflavored gelatin
2	tablespoons water
2	cups mayonnaise
2	teaspoons salt
2	dashes hot pepper sauce
1	(1½-pound) loaf commercial wheat bread, crusted

Combine celery, green pepper, onion, cucumber, and carrots in large bowl. Dissolve gelatin in water in double boiler over simmering water. Combine gelatin, mayonnaise, salt, and hot sauce; mix with vegetables. Refrigerate until ready to use. Spread on half of crusted bread slices; top each with another slice. Cut into thin strips or triangles. **Yield: 4 dozen**

Veggie Pizza

2	(8-ounce) cans refrigerated crescent rolls
2	(8-ounce) packages cream cheese
¾	cup mayonnaise
1	(1-ounce) package ranch dressing mix
1	cup finely chopped raw vegetables: carrots, green and red pepper, broccoli, cauliflower, green onion
2	cups grated Cheddar cheese

On a greased cookie sheet, spread crescent rolls without separating them so that they cover the pan. Push edges together; bake at 350° for 7 to 8 minutes. Mix cream cheese, mayonnaise, and dressing mix; spread on cooked and cooled crescent dough. Sprinkle mixed vegetables over top and press down lightly. Sprinkle grated cheese over all. Cut into small (1½"-2") squares and refrigerate until serving time.

Avocado Dip

1   cup sour cream
½   (.7-ounce) package Italian salad dressing mix
2   tomatoes, peeled and diced
Dash hot pepper sauce
¼   cup mayonnaise
2   avocados, peeled and diced
1½   tablespoons lemon juice

Mix together sour cream, dressing mix, tomatoes, hot pepper sauce, mayonnaise, avocados and lemon juice. Increase recipe by adding more sour cream or avocado. Serve with corn chips. **Yield: 2 cups**

Black Bean Dip

1   (15-ounce) can black beans, rinsed and drained
⅓   cup sour cream
½   cup chopped onion
1¼   cups grated Cheddar cheese, divided
2   tablespoons chopped jalapeño peppers
2   tablespoons salsa
Corn chips

Combine beans, sour cream, chopped onion, 1 cup cheese, peppers and salsa. Sprinkle remaining cheese on top. Spoon into a greased 11" x 7" x 2" ovenproof serving dish. Bake at 350° for 20-25 minutes. Serve with corn chips. May be reheated in microwave. *This is great served with Pico de Gallo (recipe below).*

Pico de Gallo (Rooster's Beak)

4   ripe avocados, peeled, pitted and chopped
2   medium tomatoes, chopped
1   medium onion, chopped
2   cloves garlic, minced
1-2   green chilies, seeded and chopped
3   tablespoons fresh lemon juice
1   tablespoon olive oil
Salt and pepper to taste
Corn Chips

Mix avocados, tomatoes, onion, garlic, chilies, lemon juice, olive oil, salt and pepper. Place in serving dish, cover and refrigerate 1 to 2 hours before serving. Serve with corn chips. **Yield: 3 cups**

Seven Layer Mexican Dip

2   ripe avocados, mashed
Lemon juice, to taste
1   clove garlic, minced
1   cup sour cream
1   (1½-ounce) package taco seasoning
1   (16-ounce) can refried beans
2   tomatoes, seeded and chopped
1   (6-ounce) can black olives, chopped
1-2   cups shredded Cheddar cheese
½   cup chopped green onion
1   (4-ounce) can chopped green chilies

Combine avocado, lemon juice, and garlic to make guacamole; set aside. Mix sour cream with taco seasoning; set aside. In a serving dish, layer the following ingredients in this order: beans, guacamole, sour cream mixture, tomatoes, olives, cheese, onion, and chilies. Serve with Tortilla Chips.

Chili Con Queso

½   pound ground beef
½   pound bulk sausage
1   medium onion, chopped
1   tablespoon butter or margarine, melted
1   pound pasteurized, processed cheese, cubed
1   (14½-ounce) can Italian-style stewed tomatoes, chopped

Brown ground beef and sausage; drain and set aside. In a saucepan, sauté onion in butter until transparent. Add cheese, meat and tomatoes. Stir over low heat until cheese is melted. Serve hot with tortilla chips. **Variation:** For a spicier taste, try hot sausage and/or hot Mexican cheese.

Hummus

1   (14-16-ounce) can chickpeas (garbanzo beans), drained
2-3   cloves garlic, crushed
1   tablespoon tahini
1½   tablespoons lemon juice
3-4   tablespoons olive oil

Combine chickpeas and garlic in food processor; process to a consistency resembling grits. Add tahini and lemon juice. With motor running, add olive oil in a thin stream and process until fluffy. Refrigerate. *Serve with tortilla chips or crackers.* **Yield: 2 cups**

Peppy Pimiento Dip

8 sun-dried tomato halves
2 (7-ounce) jars pimiento, drained well
1 tablespoon lemon juice
2 tablespoons fresh parsley
4 ounces cream cheese
½ cup sour cream
½ teaspoon salt
Bagel chips

Soak tomatoes in hot water to cover for 5 minutes; drain and pat dry. In food processor, purée tomatoes, pimiento, lemon juice, and parsley. Add cream cheese, sour cream, and salt; process until well mixed. Refrigerate. *Also goes well with raw veggies and toasted pita triangles.* Yield: 1½ cups

Susan's Chili Dip

1 (8-ounce) package cream cheese
1 small onion, chopped
1 (4-ounce) can green chilies
1 (15-ounce) can chili with beans
1 cup grated Cheddar cheese
1 cup grated Monterey Jack cheese

Layer ingredients in order given in 13"x 9" x 2" glass baking dish. Cover with plastic wrap. Microwave on high for 4 minutes or until cheese melts. Serve with tortilla chips.

Hot Crab on Ham

1 cup butter or margarine
2 pounds backfin crabmeat
¼ cup white wine
¼ cup cream of mushroom soup, undiluted
Several dashes Worcestershire sauce
Dash garlic powder

Combine butter, crabmeat, white wine, soup, Worcestershire sauce, and garlic powder in a frying pan. Warm slowly; transfer to chafing dish. Serve with melba rounds. **Variation:** Serve on thin slices of country ham as an entrée.

Crabmeat Hors D'oeuvre

½   cup butter or margarine
¼   cup all-purpose flour
2   cups half-and-half
Salt and onion salt to taste
Dash hot pepper sauce
1   pound backfin crabmeat, picked over
⅓   cup dry Sherry

Make a white sauce from butter, flour, and half-and-half. Add salt, onion salt, and hot pepper sauce. Add crabmeat and Sherry; heat, stirring often. Pour into chafing dish and serve with melba toast rounds or small pastry shells. *Can be prepared a day ahead and reheated in a double boiler.* Yield: 25 servings

Shrimp Dip

1   (8-ounce) package cream cheese
¼   cup mayonnaise
1½   tablespoons lemon juice
2-3   tablespoons ketchup
⅛   teaspoon salt
2-3   tablespoons finely minced onion
8-10   medium shrimp, cooked and chopped

Blend cream cheese, mayonnaise, and lemon juice. Add ketchup until desired color is achieved; add salt and onion. Add shrimp; pack into mold or form into a ball. Refrigerate; serve with crackers. **Yield: 1½ cups**

Ginger Dip

1   cup chilled mayonnaise
1   cup chilled sour cream
¼   cup minced onion
¼   cup finely chopped parsley
¼   cup finely chopped water chestnuts
2   tablespoons grated ginger root
2   cloves garlic, minced
1   tablespoon soy sauce
Dash salt

Combine mayonnaise and sour cream; add onion, parsley, water chestnuts, ginger, garlic, soy sauce, and salt. Mix well; refrigerate. *Serve with wheat crackers, or fresh vegetables.* Yield: 2½ cups

Crunchy Ginger Nut Dip

1	(8-ounce) package cream cheese, softened
¼	cup Dr. Pepper carbonated drink
1	tablespoon minced crystallized ginger
1	tablespoon grated orange zest
2	tablespoons coarsely chopped salted peanuts

Beat cream cheese and Dr. Pepper until light and fluffy. Fold in ginger, orange zest, and peanuts. *Serve with grapes, bananas, pineapple chunks, mandarin orange sections or strawberries.* **Yield: 1½ cups**

Horseradish Dip

1	(1-pound) package pasteurized, process cheese spread
1	cup mayonnaise
1	(5-ounce) jar prepared horseradish

Melt cheese in top of double boiler over simmering water. Add mayonnaise and horseradish; mix well and refrigerate. *Serve with cut fresh veggies or ginger snaps.* **Yield: 5 cups**

Beer Cheese

This is an original from Cooking Capers.

1	pound sharp Cheddar cheese
1	pound mild Cheddar cheese
2-3	cloves garlic
3	tablespoons Worcestershire sauce
1	teaspoon salt
1	teaspoon dry mustard

Dash of hot pepper sauce or cayenne pepper

| 1 | cup beer |

Using food processor, chop or grind cheeses with garlic. Add Worcestershire sauce, salt, mustard, and hot pepper sauce. Slowly add enough beer to make a paste smooth enough to spread. Store in refrigerator in covered containers. **Variation:** Can be eaten with crackers, used for sautéed sandwiches, or melted over hot water for Welsh rarebit. **Yield: 8 cups**

Poor knights of Windſor.

TAKE a French roll and cut it into thin ſlices, ſoak them in ſack, then dip them in yolks of eggs, and fry them, ſerve them up with butter, ſack, and ſugar.

Syllabubs.

TAKE three fine lemons, and pare the rind of one, ſqueeze the juice of the three, then ſtrain the juice thro' a fine ſieve, and put it into a large pan with the rind, then take a quarter of a pound of double re-fin'd ſugar beat very fine, a pint of ſack and a quart of cream, then whiſk them as long as they will bear froth, and fill your glaſſes.

St. John's Church
HAMPTON, VIRGINIA
CIRCA 1660

SETTLED IN 1610, Hampton became a jumping-off point for settlers heading west to Jamestown and Williamsburg. In keeping with the English law of that period, each plantation had its own church. Surviving court records indicate that St. John's Church, the first church established in Hampton, was built in 1644 on the Kichton Plantation which encompassed most of the Hampton area at the time. St. John's is believed to be the oldest active parish of the Anglican communion in America.

Boursin Cheese

This is a snap to make for 3 generous gifts accompanied by crackers.

1	(8-ounce) carton whipped butter
2	(8-ounce) packages cream cheese
1	(4-ounce) carton whipped cream cheese
½	teaspoon garlic salt
½	tablespoon garlic powder
¼	teaspoon marjoram, crushed
¼	teaspoon basil, crushed
½	teaspoon dill, crushed
¼	teaspoon oregano, crushed
¼	teaspoon celery salt
¼	teaspoon seasoning salt

Combine whipped butter, cream cheese, whipped cream cheese, garlic salt, garlic powder, marjoram, basil, dill, oregano, celery salt, and seasoning; beat with mixer until fluffy. **Yield: 2½ cups**

Brie in Pastry

1	sheet frozen puff pastry from (17½-ounce) package
1	pound Brie cheese
¼	cup sliced, toasted almonds
¼	cup chopped fresh parsley
1	egg beaten with 1 teaspoon water

Thaw pastry for about 20 minutes before rolling out into a 15" circle. Slice Brie in half horizontally; layer almonds and parsley on the bottom half. Reassemble with top of cheese; place in the center of pastry. Brush the edges with the egg wash; pull up the sides to enclose Brie. Place seam side down on ungreased baking sheet. Decorate the top with pastry scraps. Brush all over with egg wash. May wrap in plastic wrap and refrigerate overnight before baking. Bake at 400° for 20 minutes. *Let stand 10 minutes before serving with crackers.* **Yield: 12 servings**

Christmas Brie

1	pound Brie cheese
1	(6-ounce) jar pesto sauce
1	large clove garlic, crushed, then finely chopped
⅓	cup sundried tomatoes in olive oil, finely chopped

Allow Brie to ripen. Cut top crust from Brie. Cover with pesto sauce. Add garlic to sundried tomatoes in olive oil. Gently spread garlic-tomato mixture over pesto layer. *Serve with a plain crackers, such as melba toast (recipe below).*

Homemade Melba Toasts

1	loaf thinly sliced white bread

Trim bread crusts; cut each slice into 4 small squares. Spread in shallow pan. Bake at 200° for 2 hours. *This is much better than commercial Melba toast, and keeps almost indefinitely in an airtight container.* **Yield: 7-8 dozen**

Herbed Cheese

1	(8-ounce) package nonfat cream cheese
2	cloves garlic, pressed
1	tablespoon fines herbes

Chopped parsley for garnish

Using food processor or blender, mix together cream cheese, garlic and fines herbs. Shape into ball; roll in chopped parsley. Refrigerate. Serve with crackers. **Yield: 1 cup**

Onion and Cheese Spread

1	pound Swiss cheese, grated
1	cup mayonnaise
1	large onion, finely chopped

Melt cheese with mayonnaise in microwave. Stir in onion. Spoon mixture into shallow oven-proof dish. Bake at 350° for 30 minutes, or until browned. Serve hot with party rye or crackers. *May prepare ahead of time and then reheated in oven or microwave.* **Yield: 20 servings**

Cheese Spread

2	cups grated sharp New York Cheddar cheese
2	cups grated extra sharp Cheddar cheese
¼	cup grated onion
1¼	cups mayonnaise
3-4	dashes hot pepper sauce
1-2	shakes ground red pepper

Mix cheeses, onion, mayonnaise, hot pepper sauce, and red pepper together thoroughly. Store in crocks. Refrigerate overnight. **Yield: 3 cups**

Lulu Paste

1	pound American cheese, grated
½	teaspoon salt
1	small onion, grated
Chopped parsley to taste	
¼	teaspoon red pepper
1	teaspoon dry mustard
1	teaspoon hot pepper sauce
⅓	cup butter or margarine, melted
½	cup ketchup
¼	cup Worcestershire sauce
2	tablespoons Sherry

In large bowl, blend grated cheese, salt, and onion together to creamy consistency. Add parsley, red pepper, dry mustard, hot pepper sauce, butter, ketchup, Worcestershire sauce, and Sherry; mix thoroughly. Store in refrigerator, but serve at room temperature. Spread on crackers of your choice. **Yield: 4 cups**

Pimiento Cheese Spread

1	pound pasteurized processed cheese
2-3	drops milk
¼	cup cider vinegar
3	tablespoons granulated sugar
1	egg, beaten
1	(4-ounce) jar pimiento
1	cup mayonnaise

Melt cheese in top of double boiler over simmering water. Add 2-3 drops of milk as it melts. Stir in vinegar, sugar, egg, and pimiento. Cook for 30 minutes, then cool. Add mayonnaise. Refrigerate. *This is a great spread for crackers or sandwiches.* **Yield: 2 cups**

Ranch Cheese Ball

2	(3-ounce) packages cream cheese (not light cheese)
2	cups shredded Cheddar cheese
1	(1-ounce) package ranch salad dressing mix
½	cup mayonnaise
½	cup milk
5	ounces sliced almonds, toasted

Let Cheddar cheese and cream cheese stand at room temperature for 1 hour. Mix salad dressing mix, mayonnaise, and milk. Add cream cheese; beat well. Add Cheddar. Cover; freeze for 30 minutes. Shape cheese mixture into a ball. Roll cheese ball in toasted almonds.

Curry Paté

2	(3-ounce) packages cream cheese, softened
1	cup grated sharp Cheddar cheese
2	tablespoons dry Sherry
½	teaspoon curry powder
¼	teaspoon salt
1	(8-ounce) jar mango chutney, finely chopped
½	cup minced green onion

Combine cream cheese, Cheddar cheese, Sherry, curry powder, and salt. Carefully spread on serving platter, shaping into a ½" thick layer. Refrigerate until firm. At serving time, spread with chutney and sprinkle with green onion. *Serve with unsalted crackers.* **Yield: 8 servings**

Smoked Salmon Horseradish Mousse

¾	teaspoon unflavored gelatin
1	tablespoon water
¾	cup sour cream, divided
⅓	cup chopped smoked salmon
1	tablespoon grated horseradish
2	teaspoons minced fresh dill

Salt and pepper to taste

In a small saucepan, sprinkle gelatin over water to soften. Heat mixture over low heat, stirring, until gelatin dissolves. Add ¼ cup sour cream. Cook the mixture, whisking, until smooth. In a food processor, puree chopped salmon. In small bowl, whisk together gelatin mixture, remaining sour cream, pureed salmon, horseradish, dill, salt, and pepper. Spoon into 2-cup mold coated with non-stick vegetable spray. Refrigerate, covered, for 1 hour, or until firm. *May be prepared up to 2 days in advance.*

Smoky Salmon Spread

12	ounces cream cheese, at room temperature, and cut into pieces
¼	teaspoon dill weed
1	(7¾-ounce) can red salmon, drained
1	teaspoon liquid smoke
2	teaspoons lemon juice
7-9	drops hot pepper sauce

Process cream cheese in food processor; add dill weed. Add salmon, liquid smoke, lemon juice, and hot pepper sauce. Refrigerate. Serve with melba toast (see recipe on page 61). **Yield: 2 cups**

Shrimp Spread

1	(8-ounce) package cream cheese
1	tablespoon horseradish
1	teaspoon lemon juice
Salt to taste	
½	pound shrimp, cleaned, de-veined, cooked, and chopped

Combine cream cheese, horseradish, lemon juice, and salt. Fold in shrimp. Taste. If desired, add additional horseradish, lemon juice and salt, but do not overwhelm the shrimp taste. **Variation:** This is a good basic recipe. Add a little Worcestershire sauce, or a little ketchup, again, taking care not to lose the flavor of the shrimp.

Soups & Stews

Contents

Our Thanks

L ORD, MAKE US thankful for these and all our many blessings. *Amen.*

B LESS, O LORD, this food to our use and us to thy service, and make us ever mindful of the needs of others. Through Jesus Christ, our Lord. . .*Amen.*

Colonial Chowder

2	tablespoons butter or margarine
3	ounces finely diced Canadian bacon
1	pound chicken breast, boned and skinned, cubed
¾	cup EACH diced celery, onion, carrot
1½	cups diced red potatoes
1	teaspoon EACH: basil, oregano, thyme
½	teaspoon EACH: parsley, sage
3-4	bay leaves
¼	cup all-purpose flour
4	cups chicken broth
1½	cups corn kernels (fresh or frozen)
1	(16½-ounce) can cream-style corn
1	cup milk
½	teaspoon salt
⅛	teaspoon white pepper

In a large skillet over medium heat, melt butter. Add bacon; cook until slightly browned. Add chicken; cook until it is no longer pink. Add the celery, onion, and carrot; cook until onion is soft. Add the potatoes, basil, oregano, thyme, parsley, sage, and bay leaves. Add flour; continue to cook and stir for 3 more minutes. Slowly stir in chicken broth and corn. Bring to a boil; then lower heat. Simmer, stirring frequently, until vegetables are tender, about 5 minutes. Add milk; cook until slightly thickened, stirring frequently, about 30 minutes. Season with salt and pepper. Remove bay leaves before serving. **Yield: 8 servings**

Cream of Turkey Soup

Here's a great way to maximize holiday turkey leftovers!

1	quart turkey broth
⅔	cup finely chopped celery
½	cup chopped onion
¼	cup butter or margarine
¼	cup all-purpose flour
1	cup finely chopped cooked turkey
¾	cup cooked rice
1	cup half-and-half

Salt, pepper, and curry powder to taste

Simmer broth, celery, and onion together in large saucepan. In large skillet, melt butter; add flour. Slowly stir in broth mixture. Simmer 15 minutes. Return to saucepan. Add turkey, rice, and half-and-half. Season to taste with salt, pepper, and curry. **Yield: 6 servings**

Mary's Timothy's White Chili

1	pound large white beans
6	cups chicken broth
2	cloves garlic, minced
1	cup chopped onion, divided
1	tablespoon vegetable oil
2	(4-ounce) cans chopped mild green chilies
2	teaspoons oregano
¼	teaspoon ground cloves
¼	teaspoon cayenne pepper
4	cups diced cooked chicken breast
3	cups grated Monterey Jack cheese

Commercial salsa
Sour cream

Combine beans, broth, garlic, and half the onion in a Dutch oven. Bring to boil. Reduce heat; simmer for 3 hours, until beans are soft. Add more broth if necessary. In a skillet, sauté remaining onions in oil until tender. Add chilies, oregano, cloves, and pepper; mix thoroughly. Stir into beans. Add chicken; simmer 1 hour. Top with cheese, salsa, and sour cream. **Yield: 8-10 servings**

Virginia Brunswick Stew

1	large stewing chicken or 2 fryers, disjointed
2	quarts water
2	slices bacon, cut up
1	large onion, sliced
2	teaspoons salt, divided
3	large tomatoes, peeled and chopped
2	large russet potatoes, peeled and sliced
2	cups lima beans
1	teaspoon granulated sugar
½	teaspoon pepper

Dash red pepper

1½	cups fresh corn kernels
2	tablespoons butter or margarine
2	tablespoons all-purpose flour

Put chicken in a heavy pot; add water, bacon, onion, and 1 teaspoon salt. Cover; bring to a boil; simmer 1 hour. Remove chicken from pot, skin, de-bone, and cut into bite-sized pieces. Return chicken to pot; add tomatoes, potatoes, beans, sugar, 1 teaspoon salt, pepper, and red pepper. Simmer 30 minutes. Add corn; simmer 30 minutes more. Add butter and flour; cook an additional 30 minutes. Stir frequently. **Yield: 10 servings**

Pedernales River Chili

Contributed by Lyndon Johnson's cook, this originally
appeared in Parade Magazine.

4	pounds ground chuck
1	large onion, chopped
2	cloves garlic, crushed
2	tablespoons chili powder
2	teaspoons salt
1	teaspoon ground oregano
1	teaspoon cumin seed
2	(16-ounce) cans tomatoes
2	cups hot water

Brown chuck, onion, and garlic in a Dutch oven; drain excess drippings. Add chili powder, salt, oregano, cumin, tomatoes, and water. Break up tomatoes with back of spoon. Simmer for 1 hour. **Yield: 10 servings**

❡ Never let a soup or stew boil; it should barely simmer.

Italian Minestrone Soup

1½	pounds lean ground beef
¾	cup chopped onion
3	(10¾-ounce) cans minestrone soup
1	(10¾-ounce) can tomato soup
1	(16-ounce) can pork and beans
1½	cups chopped celery (optional)
1	tablespoon Worcestershire sauce
½	teaspoon oregano
1	teaspoon garlic powder
4	cups water

Brown beef and onion in a Dutch oven; drain excess grease. Add soups, pork and beans, celery, Worcestershire sauce, oregano, garlic powder, and water. Stir and heat until steaming. **Yield: 8 servings**

❡ Bones from smoked ham (such as hocks) can be used for a tasty stock for navy bean, lentil, or split-pea soup.

Meatball Minestrone

2½	pounds extra lean ground beef
2	cups chopped onion, divided
5	tablespoons beef bouillon granules, divided
8	cups water
2	(16-ounce) cans stewed tomatoes
1½	teaspoons thyme
¼	teaspoon pepper
2	cups shredded cabbage
4	ounces thin spaghetti, broken

Grated Parmesan cheese
Fresh parsley

In large bowl, combine beef, 1 cup onion, and 2 tablespoons bouillon. Mix well; shape into ½" meatballs. Place on ungreased cookie sheet; bake at 350° for 18-20 minutes or until browned. Drain on paper towels; put in Dutch oven. Add remaining onion, remaining bouillon, water, tomatoes, thyme, and pepper. Bring to a boil; reduce heat, cover, and simmer for 1 hour. Add cabbage and spaghetti; simmer for 15 minutes more. Serve hot, garnished with cheese and parsley. **Yield: 12 servings**

Cabbage Patch Stew

1	pound ground beef
1	cup chopped onion
1½	cups chopped cabbage
½	cup chopped celery
1	(16-ounce) can whole tomatoes, chopped
1	(15½-ounce) can kidney beans
1½	teaspoons salt
⅛	teaspoon pepper
1	teaspoon butter or margarine

Brown ground beef and onions in Dutch oven; drain excess grease. Add cabbage and celery; cook and stir until vegetables are lightly browned. Stir in tomatoes, beans, salt, pepper, and butter. Cover and simmer 30 minutes. **Yield: 4-6 servings**

Many Vegetable Beef Soup

1	pound beef stew meat, cubed
2½	cups tomato juice
⅓	cup chopped onion
4	teaspoons salt
¼	teaspoon chili powder
2	bay leaves
2	teaspoons Worcestershire sauce
6	cups water
1	(16-ounce) can tomatoes, chopped
1	cup diced celery
1	cup white shoepeg corn
2	cups sliced, peeled carrots
2	cups diced, peeled russet potatoes
1	(10-ounce) package frozen tiny lima beans
1	cup chopped cabbage

Combine meat, tomato juice, onion, salt, chili powder, bay leaves, Worcestershire sauce, and water in a soup kettle. Cover and simmer 2 hours. Add tomatoes, celery, corn, carrots, potatoes, lima beans, and cabbage. Cover and simmer for 1 additional hour. Remove bay leaves before serving. **Yield: 15-20 servings**

Squirrel Island Stew

From Squirrel Island, Maine

1	(16-ounce) can whole tomatoes, undrained
¾	cup chopped onion
⅓	cup instant tapioca
½	cup red wine
2	pounds beef chuck, cubed
1	(8½-ounce) can tiny green peas, undrained
4	carrots, peeled and cut in 1" lengths
3	medium russet potatoes, peeled and coarsely chopped

In large ovenproof Dutch oven or crock pot, break up tomatoes. Add onion, tapioca, wine, beef, peas, and carrots. Cover tightly; bake at 250° for a total of 5 hours. Depending upon time frame, add parboiled potatoes just before serving or add raw potatoes about 2 hours before baking time is up. **Yield: 5-6 servings**

Hearty Texas Soup

1   cup chopped onion
¼   cup butter or margarine, melted
5   cups boiling water
½   cups instant potato flakes
1   (1-pound) link Italian sausage
½   Jalapeño pepper
1   medium head cabbage, shredded
Salt, pepper to taste

Sauté onion in butter until transparent. Stir onion and potato flakes into water. Skin and slice sausage into ¼" rounds; add to soup stock. Bring to a boil, then simmer for 30 minutes. Add pepper and cabbage; simmer for an additional 30 minutes. Season with salt and pepper.
Yield: 8 servings

Sausage Bean Chowder

1   pound bulk pork sausage
2   (16-ounce) cans kidney beans, undrained
2   (16-ounce) can tomatoes
1   quart water
1   bay leaf
1   large onion, chopped
1½   teaspoons salt
½   teaspoon garlic salt
½   teaspoon thyme
⅛   teaspoon pepper
1   cup diced potatoes
½   cup chopped green pepper

Cook sausage, breaking up. Pour off fat. Combine beans, tomatoes, water and bay leaf, onion, salt, garlic salt, thyme, and pepper. Add sausage and simmer, covered, for 1 hour. Add potatoes and chopped green pepper. Cook, covered, 15 to 20 minutes. **Yield: 8-10 servings**

Clam Chowder

3   slices bacon
6   russet potatoes, peeled and cubed
1   large onion, chopped
2   stalks celery, diced
Salt, pepper to taste
3   (6½-ounce) cans chopped clams, drained
1   (15-ounce) can tomato sauce
1   bay leaf, crumbled

Fry bacon until crisp; crumble and set aside; reserve drippings. Cook potatoes, onion, and celery in boiling water to cover. When almost done, add salt, pepper, reserved drippings, clams, tomato sauce, and bay leaf. Cook over low heat for 20 minutes. Add a little flour to thicken broth. Top each serving with crumbled bacon. **Yield: 6 servings**

Crabmeat Soup

1   (11¼-ounce) can green pea soup
1   (10¾-ounce) can cream of tomato soup
1   cup sour cream
1   cup half-and-half
½   cup water
Dash hot pepper sauce
1   teaspoon granulated sugar
2   teaspoons Worcestershire sauce
5   teaspoons Sherry
2   (6½-ounce) cans crabmeat
Salt, pepper to taste

In large saucepan, combine soups, sour cream, half-and-half, water, hot pepper sauce, sugar, Worcestershire sauce, Sherry, and crabmeat. Season with salt and pepper. Cook, stirring, over medium heat, until hot; do *not* boil. *May substitute 1 pound fresh crabmeat for canned.* **Yield: 6 servings**

Crab Soup

Delicious, quick, easy!

2	(10½-ounce) cans cream of celery soup
2	soup cans whole milk
1	pound crabmeat

Salt, pepper to taste
Sherry to taste

Combine soup, milk, and crabmeat in saucepan and heat. Taste for seasoning and add Sherry before serving. **Yield: 6-8 servings**

Shrimp Soup

1	6" stalk celery
1	small onion
1	cup milk
3	cups half-and-half
½	cup butter or margarine
½	pound shrimp, cleaned, cooked, and ground

Salt, pepper, paprika to taste

Combine celery, onion, and milk in top of double boiler. Cook for 1 hour over simmering water. Strain vegetables off. Add half-and-half, butter, and shrimp. Season with salt, pepper, and paprika; cook for about 20 minutes. **Yield: 8 servings**

Oyster Stew

¼	cup butter or margarine
¼	cup all-purpose flour
1	quart half-and-half
1	quart oysters
2	tablespoons minced celery
2	very thin slices onion
1-2	tablespoons Sherry
1	teaspoon Worcestershire sauce

Salt, pepper to taste

In a saucepan, make a cream sauce of butter, flour, and half-and-half. In another saucepan, cook the oysters, celery, and onion over low heat in oyster liquor until gills curl. Gently stir the oysters into the cream sauce. Add Sherry and Worcestershire sauce; heat thoroughly. Serve very hot. *For a thinner soup, decrease amount of flour.* **Yield: 4-6 servings**

The Creamery Seafood Chowder

The chef at The Creamery, a small, intimate
restaurant in Wisconsin, created this for us
one cold winter's night.

4-5	cups chicken broth
1	small onion, chopped
2-3	carrots, thinly sliced
1	large turnip, peeled and diced
½	teaspoon grated lemon rind
1	(8-12-ounce) salmon fillet, skinned, boned, and broken up
1	pound medium shrimp, cleaned, shelled, and deveined
1	cup heavy cream
3	tablespoons parsley

Bring broth to a boil in large stock pot. Add onion, carrots, turnips, and lemon rind; simmer until carrots are barely tender. Then add salmon and shrimp; season with salt and pepper. Simmer for 5 minutes or until fish is done. Just before serving, add cream and parsley; heat through, stirring gently. Do *not* boil. **Yield: 6 servings**

Seafood Soup

You'll find it's difficult to recognize the "secret"
ingredient in this soup.

¼	cup chopped onion
1	small clove garlic, mashed
1	tablespoon butter or margarine
1	(10¾-ounce) can New England clam chowder
1	(10¾-ounce) can tomato-rice soup
2	cups water
1	(6½-ounce) can tuna, drained and flaked
2	tablespoons parsley

Salt, pepper to taste
Dry Sherry to taste

In large saucepan, sauté onion and garlic in butter until transparent. Add soups and water. Stir in tuna, parsley, salt, and pepper. Heat slowly, stirring to prevent sticking. Just before serving, add Sherry to taste. *Six recipes will serve 22.* **Yield: 4-6 servings**

76

the quantity, then take it from the fire and set it over water that is kept constantly boiling, this being an even heat and not apt to burn to the veffel ; in this manner let it evaporate, ftirring it often, till it becomes when cold, as hard a fubftnce as glue, then let it dry by a gentle warmth and kept from moifture.

When you ufe it, pour boiling water upon it. It makes an excellent broth, either ftrong or fmall according to the quantity you put in. It will keep good at leaft twelve months

To make a green Peas Soup.

Take a neck of mutton and a knuckle of veal, make of them fome good gravy ; then take half a peck of the fineft young peas, boil and beat them to a pulp ; then put to them fome of the gravy, ftrain them through a hair fieve to take out the pulp, put all together with fome falt and whole pepper, then boil it a little, and if the foup is not green enough, boil a handful of fpinage very tender, rub it through a hair fieve and put it into the foup, with one handful of wheat flour to keep it from running ; you muft not let it boil after the fpinage is put in, it will cifcolour it, then cut white bread in diamonds, fry them in butter till crifp, and put it into a difh with a few whole peas. Garnifh with creed rice and red beet root.

You may make afparagus foup the fame way, only add tops of afparagus inftead of whole peas.

A good Sauce for roafted Meat.

Wafh an anchovy very clean, and put to it a glafs of red wine, fome gravy or ftrong broth, fome nutmeg, one fhalot fliced and the juice of a Seville orange ; ftew thefe together a little, and pour it to the gravy that runs from the meat.

A good Gravy for any Ufe.

Take two ounces of butter, and burn it in a frying pan till it is brown, but not black, put in two pounds of coarfe lean beef, two quarts of water, and half a pint of wine, either red or white as you would have the colour ; put in three or four fhalots, fix mufhrooms, cloves, mace, whol- pepper, and five anchovies, let it ftew an hour over a gentle fire, and then ftrain it for ufe.

JELLIES

Jamestown Church (ruins)
JAMESTOWN, VIRGINIA
CIRCA 1676

THE FIRST RECORDED ministry of Jamestown Church dates back to 1644. At that time, its membership probably included legacies of the original Jamestown settlers. Historians believe that the ruins pictured above were of a church that was constructed immediately after Bacon's Rebellion in 1675. Led by planter Nathaniel Bacon, this rebellion against the Indians resulted in extensive destruction of buildings and property in the area, including the first Jamestown Church, built around 1639. These ruins are all that is left of the reconstructed church (1676-1690), from which a communion plate, dated 1694, has survived.

Creamy Broccoli Soup

3	bunches broccoli, cut into small pieces
4	tablespoons butter or margarine
⅔	cup chopped onion
4	tablespoons all-purpose flour
2	cups chicken broth
1½	cups light cream or milk
½	teaspoon Worcestershire sauce
¾	teaspoon salt
1½	cups grated Cheddar cheese

Chopped chives or parsley

Cook broccoli in boiling salted water for 10-12 minutes. Drain, reserving liquid. Melt butter in large saucepan. Add onion and cook until soft. Blend in flour. Add broth and cook, stirring constantly, until mixture boils. Stir in ½ cup liquid drained from broccoli, cream, Worcestershire sauce, and salt. Add broccoli. Heat to boiling. Stir in cheese. Serve sprinkled with chives or parsley. **Yield: 8-10 servings**

Creamy Parmesan and Cauliflower Soup

5	cups chicken or vegetable stock
1	large cauliflower, cut into florets
½	cup pasta bows
⅔	cup light cream or milk

Freshly grated nutmeg

⅛	teaspoon cayenne pepper
4	tablespoons grated Parmesan cheese

Bring stock to a boil and add cauliflower. Simmer about 10 minutes or until cauliflower is very soft. Remove cauliflower with slotted spoon; transfer to food processor. Add pasta to the stock and simmer for 10 minutes or until tender. Drain, reserve pasta; pour the liquid over the cauliflower in food processor. Add the cream or milk, nutmeg and cayenne to the cauliflower. Blend until smooth; strain. Stir in the cooked pasta; reheat the soup; stir in the Parmesan. Taste and adjust the seasoning. Serve hot with melba toast (recipe on page 61). **Yield: 6 servings**

Cheddar Chowder

Easily prepared with common pantry staples

3	cups water
3	chicken bouillon cubes
4	medium russet potatoes, peeled and cubed
1	cup thinly sliced, peeled carrots
½	cup thinly sliced onion
½	cup diced green pepper
⅓	cup butter or margarine, melted
⅓	cup all-purpose flour
3½	cups milk
2	cups grated Cheddar cheese
1	(2-ounce) jar diced pimiento

Dissolve bouillon cubes in boiling water in large saucepan. Add potatoes, carrots, onion, and green pepper; simmer 10-12 minutes. Remove from heat; do not drain. In a separate saucepan, blend flour into melted butter. Gradually add milk; cook over low heat, stirring, until thickened. Add grated cheese and pimientos; stir until cheese melts. Pour cheese sauce into vegetable mixture. Heat thoroughly, but do not boil.
Yield: 8 servings

Mushroom Bisque

4	cups chicken broth
1	pound mushrooms, chopped
½	cup chopped onion
6	tablespoons butter or margarine
6	tablespoons all-purpose flour
3	cups milk
1	cup heavy cream
1	teaspoon salt
	White pepper to taste
	Dash hot pepper sauce, nutmeg
2	tablespoons Sherry

Bring broth to a boil in a large stock pot; add mushrooms and onions. Lower heat and simmer for 30 minutes. Meanwhile, melt butter and add flour. Whisk in milk and heavy cream that have been heated together. Cook and stir until sauce comes to a boil and then stir into mushroom mixture. Season to taste with salt, pepper, hot pepper sauce, nutmeg, and Sherry. Cook and stir until thoroughly heated. *Do not freeze.*
Yield: 8-10 servings

French Onion Soup with Cheese

This comes from an old French recipe.

5 medium Vidalia or white onions, chopped
5 tablespoons butter or margarine, divided
4 (10¾-ounce) cans beef bouillon
½ teaspoon salt
⅛ teaspoon freshly ground black pepper
6 slices French bread, toasted on one side
½ cup grated Gruyère or white Cheddar cheese

In Dutch oven, sauté onions in 3 tablespoons butter until golden. Stir in bouillon, salt, and pepper. Heat to boiling. Pour into tureen or 6 individual serving bowls. Meanwhile, spread untoasted sides of bread with remaining 2 tablespoons butter or margarine. Float bread, buttered side up, on top of soup. Sprinkle cheese over. **Yield: 6 servings**

Vegetarian Chili

From the Richmond Hill Notebook

1 large onion, chopped
1 large green pepper, chopped
1 tablespoon olive oil
1 cup water
2-3 (16-ounce) cans whole tomatoes
1 (16-ounce) can tomato sauce
1 (1-quart) can kidney beans, drained
2 (16-ounce) cans black beans, drained
2 (15-ounce) cans garbanzo beans, drained
1-3 tablespoons chili powder
3-5 cloves garlic, pressed or chopped fine
2-3 teaspoons cumin
1 (10-ounce) jar sliced green olives

In covered pot, sauté onion and green pepper in olive oil and water until translucent. Add tomatoes, sauce, and beans. Season to taste with chili powder, garlic and cumin. Bring to a boil, reduce heat, and simmer. Add olives before serving. Great served with sour cream, grated cheese, rice, salad, and cornbread or chips. *Freezes well.* **Yield: 15-20 servings**

❡ *Do not add salt to dried beans until they are tender because they will not soften after salt has been added.*

Portuguese White Bean Soup

1	cup chopped onion
1	garlic clove, minced
2	tablespoons olive oil
1	bay leaf

Pinch of salt

½	teaspoon ground fennel
1	medium red or yellow bell pepper, chopped
1	medium potato, cubed
2	tablespoons dry Sherry
1	tablespoon fresh lemon juice
2	cups vegetable stock or water
1	(16-ounce) can white beans, undrained

Ground pepper to taste
Chopped parsley

In a soup pot, sauté onions and garlic in olive oil until softened, about 5 minutes. Add bay leaf, salt, fennel, and peppers to pot; continue cooking for 5 minutes, stirring often. Add potato, Sherry, lemon juice, and stock. Cover ; simmer for 10-15 minutes or until the potatoes are tender. Stir in beans; gently reheat. Add pepper. Garnish with parsley; serve immediately. **Yield: 4 servings**

Black Bean Soup

*An adaptation from the original recipe
from Gourmet for Richmond Hill*

2	large onions, chopped
4-6	cloves garlic, minced
2	tablespoons olive oil
6-8	carrots, cleaned, scraped and chopped
8-10	(15-ounce) cans black beans, drained
4-6	(14-ounce) cans vegetable broth *or*
8-10	cups water, divided
2-4	tablespoons ground cumin
½-1	teaspoon cayenne to taste
1½-4	teaspoons ground coriander
½-1	cup dry Sherry (optional)

Sauté onion and garlic in oil until onions are translucent. May add 1 cup water at this point. Add carrots; cook for 10-25 minutes. Add beans, water or vegetable broth, and cumin, cayenne, and coriander. Cook until very thick and beans are soft. You may prefer to puree 6-10 cups of soup, then add back in to thicken soup. *Serve with rice, sour cream, chopped onions, and grated cheese.* **Yield: 20-30 servings**

Buttermilk Vichyssoise

½   cup skim milk, scalded
1   (10½-ounce) can cream of celery soup
1   cucumber, peeled and sliced
1   green pepper, chopped
1   medium onion, chopped
2-3   dashes lemon pepper or other seasoning
1   cup buttermilk

Blend milk with soup. Place soup mixture, cucumber, green pepper, onion, and lemon pepper in blender or food processor; process until smooth. Pour mixture into bowl; stir in buttermilk. Refrigerate for several hours before serving. **Yield: 4 servings**

Cantaloupe-Amaretto Soup

This is gorgeous in August!

1   fresh ripe cantaloupe, peeled, seeded, and cubed
2   fresh ripe peaches, peeled, pitted and chopped
1   teaspoon almond extract
2   cups heavy cream (or half-and-half)
¼   cup amaretto
2   tablespoons fresh lemon juice
Pinch nutmeg or cinnamon

In a blender, purée small amounts of the cantaloupe and peaches with the liquids until all ingredients are used. Stir in nutmeg or cinnamon. Chill for several hours before serving. **Yield: 4-6 servings**

Cauliflower Soup

4   leeks, sliced
2   tablespoons butter or margarine
1   cup chicken broth
1   cup cooked cauliflower
1   cup half-and-half
Salt, pepper to taste
Minced chives

Sauté leeks in butter. Place in blender with broth, cauliflower, and half-and-half. Purée. Taste for seasoning. Chill. Garnish with minced chives when serving. **Variation:** May substitute 1 medium onion for leeks. **Yield: 4 servings**

Minty Cucumber Soup

2	cucumbers, peeled and seeded
3	green onions (white part only)
1	teaspoon minced garlic
1½	cups nonfat yogurt
½	cup sour cream
½	teaspoon salt
¼	teaspoon white pepper
¼	cup minced parsley
4	tablespoons chopped cucumber
4	mint sprigs

Combine cucumber, onions, garlic, yogurt, sour cream, salt, pepper, and parsley in food processor blender. Purée until smooth. Refrigerate. Garnish each serving with 1 tablespoon cucumber and/or a mint sprig. **Yield: 4 servings**

Cucumber-Tomato Soup

1	(10½-ounce) can cream of tomato soup
1	soup can milk
1	medium cucumber, peeled, seeded, and shredded
2	tablespoons sliced green onion
1	teaspoon salt
½	teaspoon Worcestershire sauce
Dash pepper	

Whisk soup and milk together until smooth. Add cucumber, onion, salt, Worcestershire sauce, and pepper. Mix well. Refrigerate for several hours before serving. **Yield: 4-6 servings**

Chilled Zucchini Soup

5-6	small-to-medium zucchini
1	cup thinly sliced onion
1½	teaspoons curry powder
3	cups chicken stock
½	cup milk
1	cup heavy cream
Salt, pepper to taste	
Chopped chives to garnish	

Boil zucchini, onion, and curry powder in stock for 3-4 minutes. Drain; reserve broth. Process drained vegetables in blender. Add milk, cream, salt, and pepper; process again. Mix with cooled broth. Refrigerate several hours. Serve sprinkled with chives. **Yield: 6-8 servings**

Gazpacho Andaluz

2	large tomatoes, peeled, seeded, and divided
1	cucumber, peeled, seeded, and halved
1	medium onion, peeled and halved
1	medium green pepper, seeded and quartered
1	pimiento
3	cups vegetable cocktail juice, divided
⅓	cup olive oil
2	cloves garlic, mashed
¼	cup chopped chives
⅓	cup red wine vinegar
¼	teaspoon hot pepper sauce
⅛	teaspoon pepper

Salt to taste
Croutons

In a blender or food processor, purée one tomato, half the cucumber, half the onion, half the green pepper, the pimiento, and ½ cup juice. Transfer mixture to large bowl; stir in the remaining juice, olive oil, garlic, chives, vinegar, hot pepper sauce, salt, and pepper. Chop remaining tomato, cucumber, onion, and pepper; add to soup. Refrigerate for several hours. Serve in chilled bowls; garnish with croutons. **Yield: 12-16 servings**

Cold Spinach Soup

½	cup minced shallots
3	tablespoons butter or margarine, melted
2	(10-ounce) packages frozen chopped spinach
3	(14½-ounce) cans chicken broth
1	teaspoon salt
⅛	teaspoon pepper

Dash nutmeg

1	(8-ounce) package cream cheese, cubed

Sauté shallots in butter. Add spinach and cook, covered, over low heat about 10 minutes or until spinach thaws. Drain well. Add broth, salt, pepper, and nutmeg. Simmer 5 minutes. Cool slightly. Pour into blender a little at a time and process until smooth. Pour into large saucepan. Add cream cheese; cook and stir until cheese melts. Store in refrigerator in nonmetallic container at least 4 hours before serving. *Be sure to use shallots.* **Yield: 10-12 servings**

❦ *Garnish soups with chopped parsley, sour cream, croutons, grated cheese, lemon slices or popcorn.*

Salads

Contents

Our Thanks

F OR THIS FOOD we are about to receive, may we be truly thankful, O Lord. *Amen.*

T AKE THIS FOOD, O Father, and help it to make our minds bright so that we might know Thee; our hearts sure so that we might love Thee; and our hands strong that we might serve Thee. *Amen.*

Apricot Salad with Pecans

3	cups apricot nectar
2	(3-ounce) packages lemon gelatin
2	(3-ounce) packages cream cheese
2	(16-ounce) cans pitted, light, sweet cherries, drained
¼	teaspoon salt
1	cup chopped pecans

Heat apricot nectar and stir in gelatin. Remove from heat. While mixture is hot, add cream cheese, cut in pieces, stirring until lumps disappear. Add cherries, salt, and nuts and pour into either a 6-cup mold or an 11" x 6" x 2" glass baking dish. Refrigerate until congealed. Slice and serve on lettuce. **Yield: 12 servings**

Apricot Salad

This yummy salad goes well with chicken dishes.

1	(3-ounce) package apricot- or peach-flavored gelatin
¾	cup boiling water
1	cup sour cream
1	(8-ounce) can crushed pineapple, drained
1	(11-ounce) can mandarin oranges, drained

Dissolve gelatin in boiling water; cool slightly. Stir in sour cream, pineapple, and oranges. Spoon into 6-7 individual molds lightly sprayed with non-stick vegetable spray. Refrigerate until congealed. Unmold and serve on lettuce leaves. **Yield: 6-7 servings**

Ambrosia Mold

1	(3-ounce) package orange-flavored gelatin
1	tablespoon granulated sugar
1	cup boiling water
¾	cup cold water
1	cup frozen whipped topping, thawed
1	(11-ounce) can mandarin orange sections, drained
⅔	cup flaked coconut
1	banana, sliced

Dissolve gelatin and sugar in boiling water; add cold water. Refrigerate until slightly thickened. Fold in whipped topping, oranges, coconut, and banana. Spoon into a 6-cup mold. Refrigerate until firm. **Yield: 8 servings**

Blueberry Salad

2   (3-ounce) packages grape- or blackberry-flavored
        gelatin
2   cups boiling water
1   (20-ounce) can crushed pineapple in juice, undrained
1   (21-ounce) can blueberry pie filling
1   cup sour cream
1   (8-ounce) package cream cheese, at room temperature
½   cup granulated sugar
1   teaspoon vanilla
½   cup chopped nuts

Dissolve gelatin in boiling water; stir in pineapple and pie filling. Pour into 13" x 9" x 2" rectangular glass pan and refrigerate until firm. Combine sour cream, cream cheese, sugar, and vanilla. Spread on top of congealed salad. Sprinkle nuts on top. **Yield: 12 servings**

Cola Salad

1   (16-ounce) can pitted dark sweet cherries
1   (3-ounce) package cherry-flavored gelatin
1   cup cola-flavored carbonated drink
2   tablespoons lemon juice
1   (3-ounce) package cream cheese, at room temperature
½   cup coarsely chopped pecans or walnuts

Drain cherries and reserve juice. Set cherries aside. In a saucepan, bring ¾ cup cherry juice to a boil. Add gelatin; stir until dissolved. Remove from heat; stir in cola drink and lemon juice. Chill until mixture mounds slightly when dropped from a spoon. Cut cream cheese into very small pieces; fold into gelatin with cherries and nuts. Pour into 7 lightly oiled individual molds. Refrigerate until set. Unmold and serve on lettuce. **Yield: 7 servings**

Molded Fruit Salad

1	(16-ounce) can grapefruit sections
1	(16-ounce) can pitted, light, sweet cherries
1	(20-ounce) can pineapple chunks
2	tablespoons unflavored gelatin
½	cup cold water
½	cup chopped pecans
4	tablespoons Sherry

Drain juice from grapefruit, cherries, and pineapple; reserve fruit. Pour juice into saucepan; bring to a boil; remove from heat. Soften gelatin in cold water; add to hot juice. Stir in grapefruit, cherries, pineapple, pecans, and Sherry. Pour into either a 6-cup mold or an 11" x 6" x 2" glass baking dish. Refrigerate until congealed. Slice; serve on lettuce.
Yield: 12 servings

Raspberry Mold

1	(6-ounce) package raspberry flavored-gelatin
1	cup hot water
1	(10-ounce) package frozen raspberries, thawed and undrained
1	(16-ounce) can applesauce

Sauce:

⅓	cup raspberry yogurt
⅓	cup mayonnaise
⅓	cup sour cream

SALAD: Dissolve gelatin in hot water. Stir in raspberries and applesauce. Pour into 6-cup mold; refrigerate until congealed.

SAUCE: Combine yogurt, mayonnaise, and sour cream; refrigerate. Cut salad into servings and top each with sauce. **Yield: 8 servings**

Seafoam Salad

1	(29-ounce) can pear halves
1	(3-ounce) package lime-flavored gelatin
½	cup chopped nuts
1	(12-ounce) carton cottage cheese
1	(8-ounce) carton frozen whipped topping

Drain pears; reserve ½ cup syrup. Mash pears with fork and set aside. Heat syrup and add gelatin, stirring to dissolve. Combine syrup and pears. Fold in nuts, cottage cheese, and topping. Blend well. Pour into 1½-quart dish. Chill until set. **Yield: 8 servings**

Watergate Salad

1	(20-ounce) can crushed pineapple, undrained
1	(3.4-ounce) package instant pistachio pudding mix
½	cup chopped nuts
1	cup miniature marshmallows
1	(9-ounce) carton frozen whipped topping

Combine pineapple and pudding mix. Stir in nuts, marshmallows, and whipped topping. Pour into 11" x 7" x 2" rectangular dish; refrigerate. **Yield: 8-10 servings**

Frozen Fruit Salad

Here's a quick fix for a hot summer day!

2	(17-ounce) cans fruit cocktail
1	(8-ounce) can crushed pineapple
1	(8-ounce) package cream cheese, softened
2	heaping tablespoons mayonnaise
1	cup fresh blueberries (optional)

Drain fruit cocktail and pineapple; reserve juice. Combine cream cheese and mayonnaise. Gently stir in fruit cocktail, pineapple, and blueberries. Add enough reserved juice to achieve a soupy consistency. Spoon into 2 metal ice cube trays (sections removed). Cover and freeze. Slice into sections and serve each on a lettuce leaf. **Yield: 8-10 servings**

Guiltless Waldorf Salad

3	large, firm, tart apples
1	cup chopped pecans
3	stalks celery, finely chopped
1	cup raisins
½	cup fat-free sour cream
½	teaspoon granulated sugar substitute
2	tablespoons lemon juice

Chop unpeeled apples. Mix with pecans, celery, and raisins. In a small bowl, whisk together sour cream, sugar substitute, and lemon juice until well blended. Pour over fruit mixture and mix carefully. Refrigerate. **Yield: 6 servings**

Nutty Apple Salad

2	sweet apples, unpeeled
½	cup sliced celery
½	cup halved seedless grapes
½	cup peanuts, salted or unsalted
½	cup mayonnaise
½	cup sour cream

Core and dice apples. Combine apples, celery, grapes and peanuts. Toss with mayonnaise and sour cream. **Yield: 4 servings**

Grapefruit Salad with Avocado

3	white grapefruit, halved
1	cup grapefruit juice (from grapefruit)
1½	cups boiling water
2	(3-ounce) packages lemon-flavored gelatin
5	tablespoons granulated sugar
2	avocados, peeled and sliced

Scoop out grapefruit sections; drain, reserving enough juice to make 1 cup liquid. If necessary, add enough water to make 1 cup. To 1½ cups boiling water, add gelatin, sugar, and juice. Refrigerate until slightly thickened. Fold in grapefruit; spoon into 13" x 9" x 2" pan. Refrigerate several hours or until congealed. To serve, cut in squares; serve on lettuce leaves garnished with maraschino cherries or avocado slices. **Variation:** Pour salad mixture into hollowed-out grapefruit shells. Refrigerate until congealed. To serve, cut each half in half; garnish as above. **Yield: 12 servings**

Rump of beef a-la-mode.

Bone it, lard it with bacon, make a ftuffing with bread crumbs, parfley and fweet herbs chopped, a little efchalot, nutmeg, pepper, falt, lemon peel grated, fuet chopped, and yolk of egg; ftuff the part where the bone came out, and here and there in the lean; fkewer it and bind it with a tape; bake it, or ftew it with a pint of red wine, a quart of water; take out the meat, fcum the fauce, thicken it with a little flower; add morells, pickled mufhrooms, or lemon juice. It eats very well cold; or may be cut in flices, fried, toffed up in fome of the fauce (thickened with flower) with oyfters and catchup.

A ragout of a rump of beef.

Cut the meat from the bone, flower, and fry it; pour over it a little boiling water, about a pint of fmall beer; add a carrot or two, an onion ftuck with cloves, fome pepper-corns, falt, a piece of lemon peel, a bunch of fweet herbs; let this ftew an hour, then add fome good gravy: when the meat is tender take it out, ftrain the fauce, thicken it with a little flower; add a little celery ready boiled, a little catchup; put in the meat; juft fimmer it up. Or the celery may be omitted, and the ragout enriched by adding mufhrooms frefh or pickled; artichoke bottoms boiled and quartered, and hard yolks of eggs.

Bruton Parish Church
WILLIAMSBURG, VIRGINIA
1712-1715

SEVENTEENTH AND EIGHTEENTH century church vestry books are among the primary sources of church histories. The first vestry book, dated 1674, for Williamsburg churches, notes that Williamsburg citizens who absented themselves from church would be fined a certain number of pounds of tobacco. However, these laws were often violated and not strictly enforced. In 1678, when several Williamsburg churches (probably wooden construction) required extensive repairs, the local vestry decided to replace them with a new church, to be named Bruton Parish. Designed by colonial governor Alexander Spotswood, whose plans called for a cruciform design, this parish church was built of brick in 1712-15. It remains the state's principal representative of the era's ecclesiastical architecture.

Antipasto Salad

1	green pepper, chopped
1	(16-ounce) can garbanzo beans, drained
4	green onions, sliced
1	(6-ounce) can pitted black olives, drained
½	cup commercial Italian salad dressing
1	clove garlic
4	cups romaine lettuce
2	cups iceberg lettuce
½	pound salami, sliced
½	pound mozzarella cheese, cubed
2	tomatoes, each cut into 6 wedges
1	(2-ounce) can anchovies, drained

Combine green pepper, beans, green onions, olives, and salad dressing. Cover; refrigerate 1 hour. Rub salad bowl with garlic. Tear lettuces into bite-sized pieces; place in bowl with salami, cheese, and chilled ingredients. Toss gently. Top with tomatoes and anchovies.
Yield: 6 servings

Chicken Apricot Salad

This wonderful summer dish came from a California orchard.

½	cup mayonnaise
1	cup sour cream
¼	cup milk
2	tablespoons lemon juice
2	teaspoons prepared mustard
1	teaspoon salt
1	cup chopped dried apricots
3	cups chopped, cooked chicken
1	cup chopped celery
⅓	cup minced scallions

In a large bowl, combine mayonnaise, sour cream, milk, lemon juice, mustard, and salt. Gently mix in apricots, chicken, celery, and scallions. Refrigerate. Serve on a bed of crisp lettuce leaves. **Yield: 4 servings**

Chicken Salad with Macadamia Nuts

1	teaspoon tarragon
2	tablespoons white wine
½	cup mayonnaise
½	cup sour cream
2	cups chopped, cooked chicken
¾	cup macadamia nuts, chopped

Salt, pepper to taste

Combine tarragon, wine, mayonnaise, and sour cream. Fold in chicken and nuts. Season to taste with salt and pepper. Refrigerate until serving time. **Yield: 4 servings**

Chinese Chicken Salad

2	ounces Chinese bean threads

Canola oil

1	small head iceberg lettuce, shredded finely
4	green onions, sliced diagonally
3-4	tablespoons slivered almonds, toasted
2	tablespoons sesame seed, toasted
2-3	cups chopped, cooked chicken breast

Dressing:

2	tablespoons granulated sugar
1	teaspoon salt
½	teaspoon white pepper
¼	cup canola oil
3	tablespoons white vinegar
2	teaspoons oriental sesame oil
1	teaspoon soy sauce

Pull bean threads apart as much as possible. Deep-fry bean threads in two batches in 1" of hot canola oil until all are puffed. Drain on paper towels. In large bowl, combine bean threads, lettuce, green onions, almonds, sesame seed, and chicken. Make dressing by whisking together sugar, salt, white pepper, canola oil, vinegar, sesame oil, and soy sauce; pour over salad. Serve immediately. **Yield: 4-6 servings**

Fruity Chicken Salad

2   tablespoons EACH: vegetable oil, orange juice, cider vinegar
1   teaspoon salt
5   cups chopped, cooked chicken
3   cups cooked white rice
1½   cups seedless green grapes, halved
1½   cups diced celery
1   (15-ounce) can chunk pineapple, drained
1   (11-ounce) can mandarin oranges, drained
1   cup slivered almonds, toasted
½   cup mayonnaise

In large bowl, combine oil, orange juice, vinegar, and salt. Add chicken. Let stand for 30 minutes. Add rice, grapes, celery, pineapple, oranges, almonds, and mayonnaise. Toss gently; refrigerate. **Yield: 10-12 servings**

Hawaiian Chicken Fruit Salad

3   large chicken breasts, cooked and diced
¾   cup chopped celery
1   (20-ounce) can pineapple chunks, drained
1   (11-ounce) can mandarin oranges, drained
¼   cup coarsely chopped pecans
⅛   teaspoon salt
3½   tablespoons mayonnaise
Bibb lettuce leaves

Toss chicken with celery, pineapple chunks, mandarin oranges, and all but a few pecans. Gently mix in salt and mayonnaise. Refrigerate. Garnish with remaining pecans; serve on bed of lettuce leaves. **Yield: 8 servings**

Pressed Chicken Salad

1	(4-6 pound) hen
6	hard-boiled eggs, shelled
1	small bottle Spanish olives, undrained
1	cup chopped celery
1	(2-ounce) jar pimiento
1	cup sweet pickle relish
1	cup hot chicken stock
1	(10-ounce) jar mayonnaise-mustard salad dressing
2	packages unflavored gelatin, soaked in ½ cup cold water
1	cup mayonnaise

Boil and debone chicken. Put chicken, eggs, olives, celery, pimiento, and pickle relish into a food processor fitted with chopping blade. Process until mixture is the texture of coarse meal. In a large bowl mix meat with stock, dressing, gelatin, and mayonnaise. Mix well. Pour into individual molds to serve as a luncheon salad or into an 8-10 cup mold to serve with crackers as an appetizer. Refrigerate overnight before unmolding onto a bed of lettuce. **Yield: 8-12 salad servings or 40-60 appetizer servings**

Exotic Luncheon Salad with Turkey

2	quarts chopped, cooked turkey breast
2	(8-ounce) cans sliced water chestnuts, drained
2	pounds seedless green grapes, halved
2	cups sliced celery
2-3	cups toasted slivered almonds, divided
3	cups mayonnaise
1	tablespoon curry powder
2	tablespoons soy sauce
2	tablespoons lemon juice
	Boston, Bibb, or butter lettuce
1	(20-ounce) can litchi nuts, drained or
2	(15-ounce) cans pineapple chunks, drained

Combine turkey, water chestnuts, grapes, celery, and 1½-2 cups of the almonds. Mix the mayonnaise with the curry, soy sauce, and lemon juice. Combine with turkey mixture; chill for several hours. Spoon onto a bed of lettuce leaves arranged on individual serving plates. Sprinkle with remaining almonds and garnish with litchi nuts or pineapple chunks. **Yield: 12 servings**

Mediterranean Salad

½   pound chunky pasta shapes
6   ounces fine green beans
2   large fresh tomatoes
2   ounces fresh basil leaves
1   (6½-ounce) can tuna, packed in oil, drained
2   hard-cooked eggs, shelled and sliced
2   (2-ounce) can anchovies, drained
Capers and black olives

Cook pasta according to package directions; drain. Cool. Trim beans and blanch in boiling water for 3 minutes. Immediately plunge in cold water to stop cooking. Drain. Slice or quarter the tomatoes and arrange on the bottom of a salad bowl. Toss with a little of the dressing and cover with a quarter of the basil leaves. Cover with beans. Toss with a little more dressing; cover with a third of the remaining basil. Cover with pasta tossed in a little more dressing, half the remaining basil, and the roughly flaked tuna. Arrange the eggs on top. Sprinkle with anchovies, capers, and olives. Pour remaining dressing over and garnish with the remaining basil. Serve immediately. Do not chill. **Yield: 4 servings**

Dressing:

6   tablespoons olive oil
2   tablespoons white wine vinegar or lemon juice
2   garlic cloves, crushed
½   teaspoon Dijon mustard
2   tablespoons chopped fresh basil
Salt, pepper to taste

Whisk together olive oil and vinegar; add garlic, mustard, and basil. Season with salt and pepper. Leave to infuse while preparing salad.

Seafood Pasta Salad

1	(12-ounce) package twist trio pasta
3	large tomatoes, seeded and chopped
2	green peppers, diced
2	red bell peppers, diced
½	cup EACH: sliced green, black olives
1	large cucumber, peeled and thinly chopped
1-2	yellow squash, thinly sliced
1-2	zucchini, thinly sliced
1	cup chopped celery
½	cup minced sweet onion
1	pound shrimp, cleaned, cooked, and chopped
½	pound sea legs, cut into small pieces

Dressing:

1	(16-ounce) bottle ranch dressing
1	tablespoon red wine vinegar
1	teaspoon dill or basil

Celery salt, garlic salt, salt, and pepper to taste

Cook pasta according to package directions; drain. When cool, add tomatoes, peppers, olives, cucumber, squash, zucchini, celery, and onion. Whisk dressing with vinegar, dill or basil. Season as desired with celery salt, garlic salt, salt and pepper. Stir shrimp and sea legs. Refrigerate 3-4 hours before serving. Add dressing just before serving. *This recipe doubles or triples with ease.* **Yield: 12 servings**

Shrimp and Rice Salad

1	(10-ounce) package frozen green peas
3	cups cooked long-grain white rice
1	pound medium or large shrimp, cleaned, deveined, and cooked
1	cup mayonnaise
¾	cup celery slices
2	tablespoons finely chopped onion

Salt, white pepper to taste

Thaw green peas in colander. Combine all ingredients except salt and pepper, mixing lightly. Season to taste. Chill in refrigerator. Serve on a lettuce-lined platter surrounded by tomato wedges. **Yield: 4-6 servings**

Taco Salad

1	head iceberg lettuce, torn into bite-sized pieces
2	green onions, chopped
1	cup canned kidney beans, rinsed and drained
1	hard-cooked egg, chopped
1	cup shredded medium Cheddar
¼	cup chopped black olives
1½	cups broken tortilla chips

In a large bowl, combine, onions, beans, egg, cheese, olives, and chips. Toss lightly. Top with cooled Taco Sauce (recipe below) and serve. Yield: 8-10 servings

Taco Sauce:

½	pound ground beef
1	tablespoon vegetable oil
1	(8-ounce) can tomato sauce
1	cup beef broth
¼	cup red wine
1	tablespoon minced onion
⅛	teaspoon garlic powder
⅛	teaspoon cumin
⅛	teaspoon black pepper
1	teaspoon chili powder
1	teaspoon salt

In a skillet, brown ground beef in oil; drain. Add tomato sauce, broth, wine, onion, garlic powder, cumin, pepper, chili powder, and salt. Simmer for 20 minutes. Cool for 10 minutes.

Marinated Green Beans

2	(16-ounce) cans cut green beans, drained
½	clove garlic
1	medium-sized mild onion, thinly sliced
2	tablespoons granulated sugar
½	teaspoon paprika
¼	teaspoon salt
⅛	teaspoon pepper
⅛	teaspoon oregano
2	teaspoons parsley
½	teaspoon prepared mustard
5	tablespoons cider vinegar
4	tablespoons vegetable oil, divided

Rub salad bowl with garlic. Add beans and onion to prepared bowl. In small bowl, combine sugar, paprika, salt, pepper, oregano, parsley, and mustard. Whisk in vinegar and oil, 1 tablespoon at a time. Pour over bean mixture; toss gently. Cover; refrigerate overnight. **Yield: 8-10 servings**

Broccoli Salad with Bacon

This salad is a mainstay at our family reunions.

1½	pounds fresh broccoli
8-10	slices bacon
½	cup raisins
½	cup chopped onion
1	cup mayonnaise
¼	cup granulated sugar
2	tablespoons white vinegar

Rinse broccoli and cut into florets. Pan fry bacon, drain excess grease, and crumble. Toss broccoli with bacon, raisins, and onion. Meanwhile, prepare dressing by combining mayonnaise with sugar and vinegar. Mix dressing with broccoli mixture. **Yield: 6 servings**

Ritter's Carrottes Rapées

2	tablespoons olive oil
2	tablespoons vegetable oil
1½	tablespoons tarragon vinegar
1	tablespoon lemon juice
¾	teaspoon Dijon mustard
¼	teaspoon salt

White pepper to taste

2½	cups grated carrots

Whisk together oils, vinegar, lemon juice, mustard, salt and pepper. Toss with carrots. *This dish is best made ahead of time.* **Yield: 4 servings**

Marinated Green Pea Salad

1	(16-ounce) can tiny green peas, drained
1	(16-ounce) can French green beans, drained
4	stalks celery, diced
1	small onion, minced
1	medium green pepper, diced
1	(2-ounce) jar diced pimiento

Dressing:

¼	cup vegetable oil
½	teaspoon salt
1	cup granulated sugar
½	cup cider vinegar
1	tablespoon water

Generous dash paprika

Combine peas, beans, celery, onion, pepper, and pimiento in a large bowl. Shake dressing ingredients together in jar. Pour dressing over and refrigerate overnight. Before serving, drain salad in colander. Serve on lettuce leaves. **Yield: 8 servings**

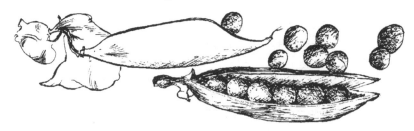

Pea and Peanut Salad

1	(10-ounce) package frozen peas, cooked 4 minutes, drained and cooled
¼	cup chopped onion
½	cup chopped celery
¼	teaspoon garlic powder
1	teaspoon Worcestershire sauce
⅓	cup sour cream
½	cup mayonnaise
1	cup Spanish peanuts

Carefully fold together all ingredients, except Spanish peanuts. Just before serving time, add the peanuts and mix well. **Variation:** This can also be used as an hors d'oeuvre, served with crackers of your choice. **Yield: 6 servings**

Seven Layer Salad

Make ahead for lunch, picnic, potluck for a crowd.

11	ounces fresh or chopped, frozen spinach, thawed and drained
	Salt, pepper, granulated sugar
1	pound bacon, cooked, drained and crumbled
6	hard boiled eggs, chopped
1	(10-ounce) package frozen peas, thawed
1	medium onion, thinly sliced
1	cup prepared mayonnaise-type salad dressing
1	cup mayonnaise
2	cups grated Swiss cheese

In a 13" x 9" x 2" glass baking dish, layer spinach and sprinkle with salt, pepper, and sugar. Top with bacon and sprinkle with salt, pepper, and sugar. Next add eggs and sprinkle with salt, pepper, and sugar. Top with peas and onion. Combine salad dressing and mayonnaise; spread on top. Sprinkle grated cheese over layered ingredients. Cover; refrigerate overnight. **Yield: 8 or more servings**

Sweet and Sour Potato Salad

2½	cups sliced, cooked russet potatoes, still warm
1¼	teaspoons salt
1	teaspoon granulated sugar
1½	teaspoons celery seed
1	tablespoon white vinegar
½	cup chopped onion
¾	cup mayonnaise
2	hard-boiled eggs, sliced

Sprinkle warm potato slices with salt, sugar, celery seed, and vinegar. Add onion. Fold in mayonnaise; toss gently to mix. Finally, add eggs. Chill thoroughly before serving. **Yield: 4 servings**

Russian Salad

3	large russet potatoes, peeled
4	carrots, peeled
½	cup chopped celery
1	(8½-ounce) can tiny peas, drained
1	(8¼-ounce) can diced beets, drained
2	hard-boiled eggs, chopped
½	cup finely chopped, peeled apple
¼	cup minced sour pickle
¼	pound baked ham, diced
¾	cup mayonnaise
2	teaspoons prepared mustard
1½	tablespoons lemon juice

Parboil potatoes, carrots, and celery until barely done; drain, cool, and cube. In large bowl, combine potatoes, carrots, celery, peas, beets, eggs, apple, pickle, and ham. Combine mayonnaise, mustard, and lemon juice; pour over vegetable-ham mixture and mix gently. Add additional mayonnaise if necessary. Refrigerate overnight and stir again to mix well before serving. **Variation:** Can be used as sandwich filling or as cocktail food (fill hollowed-out cherry tomatoes) or a luncheon entrée (fill large ripe tomato). **Yield: 12 servings**

❧ *Slow toasting of bread insures that croutons will stay crunchy when tossed with greens and dressing. Cubes should be dry enough to float on water.*

Suzanne's Pea Salad

1	(15-ounce) can chick peas, drained
1	(15-ounce) can black-eyed peas, drained
½	cup chopped onion
½	cup diced celery
6	ounces country ham, cut into ¼" dice
1	medium tomato, seeded and chopped
⅓	cup mayonnaise

Salt, pepper to taste

Combine chick peas, black-eyed peas, onion, celery, ham, tomato, and mayonnaise. Season with salt and pepper. Refrigerate for several hours to develop flavors. **Yield: 6 servings**

Carrie's Salad

12	lettuce leaves
4-6	cauliflorets, cut up
½	cup chopped celery
16	Spanish olives, sliced
1	ounce crumbled blue cheese

Toss lettuce with cauliflower, celery, olives, and blue cheese in a large bowl. Toss salad ingredients with dressing to taste. Serve in individual bowls or plates. **Yield: 6 servings**

Dressing:

1	cup olive oil
¼	cup cider vinegar
¼	cup granulated sugar
1	teaspoon salt
1	teaspoon paprika
1	teaspoon dry mustard
1	tablespoon grated onion

In a jar, shake together oil, vinegar, sugar, salt, paprika, mustard, and onion to make dressing. Refrigerate.

Luzette's Hearts of Palm Salad

Dressing:

	Pinch each of tarragon, thyme, basil
2	tablespoons cider vinegar
⅓	cup olive oil
½	teaspoon salt
½	teaspoon pepper
1	tablespoon Dijon mustard
1	clove garlic, crushed

Greens:

1	(15-ounce) can hearts of palm, drained and sliced
2	cups watercress
2	cups torn romaine
1	cup torn iceberg lettuce

Soak herbs in vinegar for 1 hour. Whisk in oil, salt, pepper, mustard and garlic. Combine hearts of palm with greens in a large bowl. Add only enough dressing to barely moisten each piece. **Yield: 8 servings**

Caesar Salad

½	teaspoon salt
¼	teaspoon pepper
2	cloves garlic
1	(2-ounce) can anchovies, drained
2	tablespoons capers, drained
1½	tablespoons Dijon mustard
⅛	teaspoon Worcestershire sauce
2	dashes hot pepper sauce
2	raw egg yolks
¾	cup olive oil
1	head Romaine lettuce, washed, dried, and torn into bite-sized pieces
1½	tablespoons lemon juice
2	tablespoons bacon bits
2	tablespoons grated Parmesan cheese
½	cup croutons

Put salt and pepper in large salad bowl. Add garlic; mash with back of wooden spoon. Add anchovies; mash. Add capers; mash. Mix in mustard, Worcestershire sauce, hot pepper sauce, and egg yolks. Add olive oil; mix thoroughly. Add lettuce; toss gently. Add lemon juice. Serve with bacon bits, Parmesan, and croutons on cold salad plates. **Yield: 4 servings**

Bill's Spinach Salad

1	pound fresh spinach, rinsed, stemmed, and torn
6-8	spring onions, sliced
¼	pound fresh mushrooms, sliced
2	ounces Chinese bean sprouts
3-4	eggs, hard-boiled and sliced
1	(8-ounce) can sliced water chestnuts, drained
¼	pound bacon slices, cooked and crumbled

In a large bowl, combine spinach, onions, mushrooms, bean sprouts, eggs, water chestnuts, and bacon. Add dressing (recipe below); toss with salad mixture to coat evenly. **Yield: 6 servings**

Dressing:

¾	cup vegetable oil
⅔	cup granulated sugar
⅓	cup ketchup
½	cup cider vinegar

Combine oil, sugar, ketchup, and vinegar in jar; shake well.

A Honey of a Salad

4-6	cups romaine lettuce, torn into bite-sized pieces
1	(11-ounce) can mandarin oranges, drained
⅓	cup sliced almonds or pine nuts

Toss lettuce gently with oranges and nuts in a large bowl. Divide into sixths and mound onto individual salad plates. Drizzle dressing (recipe below) over each. **Yield: 6 servings**

Honey-Poppy Seed Dressing:

⅓	cup honey
1	teaspoon salt
2	tablespoons cider vinegar
1	tablespoon prepared mustard
¾	cup vegetable oil
1	tablespoon finely chopped onion
2-3	tablespoons poppy seed

In a jar, shake together honey, salt, vinegar, mustard, oil, onion and poppy seed to make dressing. Refrigerate.

Blue Cheese Aspic

1	envelope unflavored gelatin
1½	cups tomato juice, divided
½	teaspoon garlic salt
½	teaspoon celery salt
½	cup blue cheese (Roquefort) salad dressing
1	large avocado
Salad greens	
Mayonnaise	

Soften gelatin in ½ cup tomato juice. Heat remaining juice; add softened gelatin and stir to dissolve. Season with garlic and celery salts. Add dressing. Refrigerate until aspic is the consistency of unbeaten egg white. Peel and cube avocado and fold into aspic. Pour into 3-cup mold or 6 individual molds. Refrigerate until congealed. Unmold and serve on salad greens; garnish with mayonnaise. **Yield: 6 servings**

Shrimp and Tomato Aspic

1½	teaspoons unflavored gelatin
1	(3-ounce) package lemon-flavored gelatin
1	cup hot vegetable cocktail juice
¾	cup cold vegetable cocktail juice
¼	cup prepared horseradish, drained
¾	cup minced green pepper
¾	cup chopped celery
1	cup cooked, chopped shrimp
1	tablespoon Worcestershire sauce

Dissolve unflavored gelatin and lemon gelatin in hot vegetable cocktail juice. Add cold juice; refrigerate until the consistency of egg white. Add horseradish, green pepper, celery, shrimp, and Worcestershire sauce. Pour into 6-cup ring mold; chill until firm. Serve with the following dressing. **Yield: 6 servings**

Dressing:

1	(3-ounce) package cream cheese, softened
2	tablespoons crumbled blue cheese
1-2	tablespoons milk

Whip cream cheese, blue cheese, and mix together until creamy. Add milk to achieve desired consistency. Refrigerate.

Easy Tomato Aspic

1   (14½-ounce) can stewed tomatoes with onions, celery, and green pepper
1   tablespoon cider vinegar
1   (3-ounce) package lemon-flavored gelatin
Lettuce leaves
Mayonnaise

Mix tomatoes with vinegar in small saucepan; bring to a boil. Stir in gelatin; cook and stir until gelatin dissolves. Pour into 2-cup mold. Refrigerate until set. Unmold and serve on lettuce leaves with mayonnaise. **Yield: 4 servings**

GR-R-R-EAT Vinaigrette

½   cup olive oil
2   tablespoons white wine vinegar
2   tablespoons fresh lemon juice
1   teaspoon salt
½   teaspoon pepper
¼   teaspoon granulated sugar
2   teaspoons minced garlic
1   tablespoon parsley
1   teaspoon basil

Combine oil, vinegar, lemon juice, salt, pepper, sugar, garlic, parsley, and basil in small bowl and whisk together until blended. Store in refrigerator. Serve over fresh tomatoes or garden salads. **Yield: 1 cup**

❧ *Cut a thin slice from stem end of a red or green bell pepper, remove seeds, and use as a container for mayonnaise.*

Piquant Salad Dressing

½   cup cider vinegar
2   teaspoon salt
1   teaspoon granulated sugar
½   teaspoon pepper
1   teaspoon paprika
1   teaspoon dry mustard
1   cup vegetable oil
2   teaspoons prepared mustard
1   teaspoon Worcestershire sauce
8   drops hot pepper sauce
½   small onion

Combine vinegar, salt, sugar, pepper, paprika, and dry mustard in pint jar. Shake well. Add oil, prepared mustard, Worcestershire sauce, and hot pepper sauce; shake again. Add onion to jar; refrigerate. **Yield: 2 cups**

Spinach Salad Dressing

¾   cup granulated sugar
¼   cup vegetable oil
¼   cup cider vinegar
1   cup mayonnaise
Dash   salt

Combine sugar, oil, vinegar, mayonnaise, and salt in container of blender or food processor. Process until smooth. Store in refrigerator for several months. Serve over spinach salads. **Yield: 2½ cups**

Tips for Successful Salads

Dry salad greens well after rinsing since dressing sticks better to dry greens.

Wrapping washed and dried lettuce leaves in towels and refrigerating them helps to retain crispness. Always break or tear leaves, never cut, or they may assume an unattractive brown edge.

Don't add salt to a green salad until just before serving. Salt wilts and toughens salad greens.

Entrées

Contents

Beef à la Mode

Here's a French dish from Liverpool, England.

1	(4-pound) pot roast (rump, sirloin, round, or chuck)
4	cups red wine, divided
1	cup chopped onion, divided
2	cloves garlic, minced
1	bay leaf
½	teaspoon freshly ground pepper
2	teaspoons salt
⅛	teaspoon nutmeg
¼	cup all-purpose flour
Salt and pepper to taste	
2	cups beef bouillon
8	small carrots
8	baby onions

Marinate beef at least 3-4 hours or overnight in a marinade made of 2 cups red wine, ½ cup chopped onion, garlic, bay leaf, pepper, salt and nutmeg. Drain and wipe beef. Strain marinade and reserve. Dredge roast in flour seasoned with salt and pepper. Brown in hot vegetable oil in Dutch oven. Pour off oil; add 2 cups red wine, reserved marinade, bouillon, and remaining chopped onion. Cover tightly and bake at 325° for 3½ hours. Skim off fat. Add carrots and onions and return to oven for 45 additional minutes. Thicken juices with flour to make gravy. **Yield: 8 servings**

Beef Marinade

2	tablespoons sugar
¼	cup Sherry
¼	cup soy sauce
2	tablespoons honey
2	teaspoons seasoned salt flavor enhancer
2	teaspoons salt
1	cup Worcestershire sauce
¾	cup brown sugar
1	cup lemon juice
2	pounds top round steak

Combine sugar, Sherry, soy sauce, honey, seasoned salt flavor enhancer, salt, Worcestershire sauce, brown sugar, and lemon juice. Pour over steak in shallow dish. Cover; refrigerate 24 hours. Grill over medium-hot coals; refrigerate overnight before slicing thinly to serve. **Yield: 4-6 servings**

Beef Tenderloin with Horseradish Sauce

1	whole beef tenderloin
2	teaspoons seasoning salt
½	teaspoon pepper
1	tablespoon seasoned salt flavor enhancer
1	tablespoon soy sauce

Preheat oven broiler; brown tenderloin on each side. Place tenderloin on a sheet of heavy-duty foil. Mix together seasoning salt, pepper, flavor enhancer, and soy sauce; rub over meat. Wrap meat in foil and return to oven, reducing temperature to 350°. Bake for an additional 45 minutes. Excellent served with horseradish sauce. **Yield: 10-12 servings**

Horseradish Sauce:

1	(5-ounce) jar prepared horseradish
1	cup French onion dip
½	teaspoon Worcestershire sauce
1	tablespoon hot sauce

Combine horseradish, dip, Worcestershire sauce, and hot sauce.
Yield: 1½ cups

❧ *Look for flecks of fat within the lean in beef; this marbling increases juiciness, flavor, and tenderness.*

Grilled Steak with Lime Marinade

Here's an easy cook-out food—great with rice pilaf and fruit salad.

⅓	cup fresh lime juice
¼	cup vegetable oil
¼	cup molasses
2	tablespoons prepared mustard
1	teaspoon grated lime zest
1	teaspoon garlic powder
½	teaspoon salt
2	pounds top round or sirloin steak

Whisk together lime juice, oil, molasses, mustard, zest, garlic powder, and salt. Transfer to a large zip-lock plastic bag, add steak and seal tightly. Refrigerate 4-8 hours, turning occasionally. Bring steak to room temperature before grilling over medium-hot coals. Slice diagonally to serve.
Yield: 4-6 servings

Easy Sherried Beef

3	pounds stew beef
1	(4-ounce) can mushrooms *or*
½	pound fresh mushrooms, sliced
1	(8-ounce) can sliced water chestnuts
2	(10¾-ounce) cans golden mushroom soup
1	cup Sherry
1	(1-ounce) package onion soup mix
Hot cooked noodles or rice	

Cut beef into 1½" cubes. Mix beef, mushrooms, water chestnuts, mushroom soup, Sherry, and onion soup mix in 3-quart casserole. Cover tightly and bake at 325° for 4 hours. *May be prepared in a crock pot and/ or baked at a lower temperature for a longer period of time.* Serve over noodles or rice. **Yield: 6-8 servings**

Pot au Feu

1½	pounds beef chuck roast with bone
Water	
4	leeks, ends trimmed, whole or sliced
4-5	whole carrots
4	turnips, halved
6	medium boiling potatoes
1	small curly cabbage, quartered
1	large onion studded with 6-8 whole cloves
1	bouquet garni
1	clove garlic
4	marrow bones
Rock salt, pepper to taste	
French bread, sliced	

Place beef in Dutch oven; cover with water; bring to a boil. Reduce heat; simmer 1½ hours. Add leeks, carrots, turnips, potatoes, cabbage, onion, bouquet garni, and garlic; cook for 20 minutes. Add bones; cook for 15-20 minutes or until beef is tender. To serve, place meat in center of a large bowl; surround with vegetables; pour pot liquor over. Serve the marrow bones in a separate dish; extract marrow with knife and spread on French bread. Sprinkle with rock salt and pepper. *Suggested condiments: Dijon mustard and sour pickles.* **Yield: 4-5 servings**

❡ *Meat will brown better if you blot any surface moisture with a paper towel. Dusting the meat with flour will also contribute to browning.*

Goldie's Pot Roast

1	(3-pound) chuck roast
3	tablespoons shortening
2	onions, chopped
1	cup water
½	cup ketchup
1	teaspoon salt
⅛	teaspoon pepper
½	teaspoon garlic powder
1	teaspoon pickling spices, tied in bag
5	carrots, pared and halved
1	(16-ounce) can lima beans, drained

Brown meat in shortening in Dutch oven over medium heat. Remove meat and sauté onion in drippings. Return roast to pan; add water, ketchup, salt, pepper, garlic powder, and spices. Bake, covered, at 350° for about 2½ hours. Add carrots and limas; bake for an additional half hour. **Yield: 5-6 servings**

Marinated Flank Steak

1	(1-pound) flank steak
	Meat tenderizer
¼	cup vinegar
¼	cup vegetable oil
¼	cup ketchup
¼	cup molasses
1	teaspoon salt
½	teaspoon pepper
½	teaspoon garlic salt

Treat steak with tenderizer. Place in a shallow dish or in a heavy-duty zip-lock plastic bag. In a jar, shake vinegar, oil, ketchup, molasses, salt, pepper, and garlic salt. Pour over steak, turning to coat. Cover or seal; marinate steak in refrigerator 8-12 hours, turning occasionally. Remove steak from marinade, discarding marinade. Grill, uncovered, over hot coals (400°-500°) 10-12 minutes on each side or to desired degree of doneness. To serve, cut steak diagonally across grain into thin slices. **Yield: 4 servings**

Sirloin Shish Kebab

½   cup red wine
1   teaspoon Worcestershire sauce
½   cup olive or vegetable oil
2   tablespoons ketchup
1   teaspoon granulated sugar
1   tablespoon vinegar
1   teaspoon marjoram
1   teaspoon rosemary, crushed
2   pounds sirloin steak, cut in 1½" cubes
Whole fresh mushrooms
Green pepper chunks
Whole cherry tomatoes
Sweet onion chunks

Combine wine, Worcestershire sauce, oil, ketchup, sugar, vinegar, marjoram, and rosemary in a shallow bowl to form a marinade. Cut steak into 1½" cubes and add with mushrooms (stems removed, lightly rinsed, and dried) to marinade. Refrigerate at least 4 hours, turning meat and mushrooms occasionally. On metal skewers alternate beef cubes with mushroom caps, green pepper chunks, cherry tomatoes, and onion chunks. Grill over glowing coals for about 20 minutes, turning frequently and basting with marinade. **Yield: 4-5 servings**

Spiced Beef

We always slice this after church on Christmas morning.

2   ounces saltpeter
1¾   cup salt
1   (¾-ounce) package ground allspice
1   (1⅛-ounce) package ground cloves
1   (1⅛-ounce) package ground cinnamon
1   (15-pound) top round roast, bone-in
1   quart sorghum molasses

Combine saltpeter, salt, allspice, cloves, and cinnamon and rub into meat. Place in large bowl and coat with molasses. Cover and refrigerate one day for each pound of beef. Turn meat daily and baste with juices that form in the bowl. Put meat into large Dutch oven and cover with water. Bring to a boil and let simmer gently for 3 hours, making sure that beef is always covered with water. Remove from heat; allow to cool in cooking liquid. Trim excess fat and then wrap meat with damp cloth and aluminum foil. Store in refrigerator. Slice thinly for serving. *This may be frozen and refrozen.* **Yield: 50-60 servings**

Vidalia Onion and Beef Strudel

¾   cup shredded mozzarella cheese
¼   cup grated Parmesan cheese
¼   cup light margarine
1½   cups thinly sliced Vidalia onions
6   ounces beef tenderloin, cut into ⅛" slices
1   teaspoon all-purpose flour
1   teaspoon light brown sugar
½   teaspoon cumin
¼   teaspoon each salt, pepper
½   cup beef broth
1   (8-ounce) can refrigerated crescent rolls
2   tablespoons grated Parmesan cheese
½   cup light sour cream

In a small bowl, combine mozzarella cheese and ¼ cup Parmesan cheese; set aside. Melt margarine in skillet and add onions. Cook and stir for 15-20 minutes until onions are browned and caramelized. Remove from skillet and add beef slices. Cook and stir for 2-3 minutes. Return onions and any juice to skillet. Add flour, brown sugar, cumin, salt, pepper and beef broth. Cook and stir for about 3 minutes or until almost all liquid is absorbed.

Separate dough into 8 triangles. Slightly overlap long sides of 2 triangles to make one larger triangle; press edges to seal. Repeat with remaining triangles. Place triangles in a row on greased cookie sheet, overlapping center points. Evenly spoon meat mixture down center of triangles in a 1½" wide strip, beginning and ending 1" from ends. Sprinkle cheese mixture over beef filling. Bring side points over filling, crossing one another to make a braided appearance. Seal ends. Sprinkle 2 tablespoons Parmesan cheese over all. Bake at 375° for 15-20 minutes. Slice and serve with dollops of sour cream. **Yield: 4 servings**

Beef Burritos

½   cup rice
½   pound lean ground beef
1   large green pepper, diced
1   small onion, chopped
2   teaspoons chili powder
Salt to taste
1   (16-ounce) can black beans, drained
1   (14½-ounce) can Mexican-style stewed tomatoes
1   (8-ounce) can whole kernel corn, drained
8   (10") flour tortillas
1   cup light sour cream
½   cup commercial salsa

Cook rice as directed on package; set aside. Meanwhile cook beef, green pepper, and onion in skillet; drain excess grease. Stir in chili powder and salt; cook and stir for 1 minute. Add beans, tomatoes, corn, and cooked rice. Soften tortillas briefly in microwave. Spoon about 4 tablespoons filling onto each tortilla. Fold to enclose filling. Arrange burritos seam-side down in lightly greased 13" x 9" x 2" rectangular baking dish. Bake at 400° for about 10 minutes or until tortillas start to brown. Top each with a dollop of sour cream and spoon salsa over. **Yield: 8 servings**

English Cottage Pie

2   pounds ground beef
1   large onion, finely chopped
3   large carrots, pared and thinly sliced
2   tablespoons ketchup
1   tablespoons parsley
½   teaspoon each sage, thyme, chervil
1   bay leaf, crumbled
⅔   cup beef broth
⅓   cup dry red wine
Salt and pepper to taste
4   cups hot mashed potatoes
½   cup grated sharp Cheddar cheese

Brown beef and onion; drain excess grease. Stir in carrots, ketchup, herbs, broth, wine, salt, and pepper. Simmer gently 30 minutes, or until carrots are done. Spoon meat mixture into a greased 2-quart casserole, adding enough cooking liquid to moisten meat well. Spread with hot mashed potatoes, sprinkle with cheese, and bake at 375° for 8-10 minutes until cheese is melted and golden. **Yield: 6-8 servings**

Hachis Parmentier

From a French cooking class

1   medium onion, chopped
1   tablespoon minced parsley
4   tablespoons butter or margarine, divided
1   pound ground beef
Salt, pepper to taste
½   cup veal or beef bouillon
2   pounds boiling potatoes
⅓   cup boiling milk
¼   cup buttered bread crumbs
1   tablespoon grated Parmesan cheese

Sauté onion and parsley in 2 tablespoons melted butter. Add ground beef and cook until browned. Season with salt and pepper. Stir in bouillon and simmer for 5 minutes. Peel and boil potatoes until done; drain. Mash potatoes; add 2 tablespoons butter and boiling milk. Season with additional salt and pepper. Place a layer of meat in the bottom of a greased deep-dish pie plate. Spread with creamed potatoes. Repeat layers until all is used. Sprinkle with bread crumbs and cheese. Broil until golden brown. **Yield: 6 servings**

Texas Surprise

This is an original from Cooking Capers.

2   pounds ground beef
1   clove garlic, minced
1   green pepper, finely chopped
1   (16½-ounce) can cream-style corn
2   (6-ounce) cans tomato paste
2   (8-ounce) cans tomato sauce
1   (2-ounce) jar chopped pimiento
2   teaspoons chili powder
2   (8-ounce) bags medium noodles, cooked and drained
½   pound Cheddar cheese, grated

In a large skillet, brown beef, garlic, and green pepper. Drain excess grease. Add corn, tomato paste, tomato sauce, pimiento, and chili powder. Simmer. Line a lightly greased 13" x 9" x 2" glass baking dish with noodles and pour sauce over top. Top with grated cheese. Bake in 350° oven for 20-30 minutes until heated thoroughly. Top with grated cheese and bake for an additional 10 minutes. **Yield: 12 servings**

Grenadin de Veau Elizabeth

This is an original from Country Capers.

½   pound mushrooms, rinsed and sliced
4   tablespoons butter or margarine, divided
½   cup chicken bouillon
1   pound veal scallops
½   cup all-purpose flour
Salt, pepper to taste
2   tablespoons dry Sherry
4   tablespoons heavy cream
Minced fresh parsley

Sauté mushrooms in 2 tablespoons melted butter; when partially cooked, stir in chicken bouillon and cook until lightly browned. Set aside. Dredge veal scallops in flour seasoned with salt and pepper. Sauté in remaining butter until golden. Add Sherry, which will flare immediately. Then stir in mushrooms and cream which will form a creamy sauce. Sprinkle with parsley before serving. **Yield: 2-3 servings**

Veal Roast

2-3   pound veal roast
2   tablespoons all-purpose flour seasoned with salt, pepper
2   tablespoons bacon fat
1   tablespoon lemon zest
1   tablespoon lemon juice
¼-⅓   cup white wine
Salt, pepper to taste
2   slices bacon, cut in half
5   fresh mushrooms, sliced

Dredge roast in seasoned flour. Brown in hot bacon fat. Transfer to roasting pan fitted with baking rack. Top with lemon zest, juice, and wine. Season with salt and pepper. Lay bacon strips over top of roast and add mushrooms to pan. Bake, uncovered, at 325° for 1¾-2½ hours or until meat thermometer reads 170°. **Yield: 6-10 servings**

Baked Stuffed Pork Tenderloin

2	tablespoons minced onion
⅓	cup chopped green pepper
6	tablespoons melted butter or margarine, divided
2	cups fresh bread crumbs, toasted
1	egg, beaten
⅛	teaspoon sage
¾	cup diced Muenster cheese
1	cup cooked pork sausage, crumbled
2	(¾-1 pound) boneless pork tenderloins
Salt, pepper to taste	
¾	cup hot chicken bouillon

Sauté onion and green pepper in 4 tablespoons butter. Add bread crumbs, egg, sage, cheese, and sausage. Split the tenderloins lengthwise, cutting within ½" of other side. Open meat and spread bread mixture over top. Close and tie with string. Arrange in lightly greased 11" x 7" x 2" rectangular baking dish. Pour remaining butter over meat; season with salt and pepper. Add bouillon to pan. Bake at 400° for 1 hour. **Yield: 6 servings**

Easy Baked Pork Tenderloin

3	tablespoons Dijon mustard
3	tablespoons light soy sauce
2	(¾-1 pound) boneless pork tenderloins
½	cup water

Combine mustard and soy sauce and coat meat with this mixture. Place in baking pan and add water. Bake, uncovered, at 350° for 45-50 minutes. To serve, slice and pour pan juices over meat. **Yield: 4-6 servings**

Grilled Pork Tenderloin

1	cup soy sauce
1	cup white wine
1	clove garlic, mashed
1	teaspoon ginger
¼	cup vegetable oil
1	cup chopped onion
2	(¾-1 pound) boneless pork tenderloins

Whisk together soy sauce, wine, garlic, ginger, oil, and onion. Transfer to a large zip-lock plastic bag. Add tenderloins; seal tightly. Refrigerate 1 hour before grilling. **Yield: 4-6 servings**

Herbed Pork Tenderloin with Roasted Potatoes

⅓	cup olive oil
2	garlic cloves, minced
2	teaspoons dried rosemary, crushed
2	teaspoons dried thyme, crushed
½	teaspoon salt
¼	teaspoon freshly ground pepper
2	(¾-1 pound) boneless pork tenderloins
2½	pounds red-skinned potatoes, quartered

Combine oil, garlic, rosemary, thyme, salt, and pepper; coat meat with 3 tablespoons of mixture. Place meat in large roasting pan. Toss potatoes with remaining seasoning mixture; arrange around meat in pan. Bake at 375° for 45-50 minutes. Broil on top rack of oven for 5 minutes to brown. Let stand 5 minutes before slicing. **Yield: 6 servings**

Roast Pork Loin with Orange Glaze

1	(3-pound) pork loin roast, boned, rolled, and tied
Olive oil	
Pepper	
1	orange (juice and rind)
¾	cup honey
½	cup brown sugar

Rub roast with oil and sprinkle with pepper. Place on rack and bake at 325° for 25 minutes per pound. Meanwhile, grate orange rind and set aside. Juice the orange and combine juice with reserved rind, honey, and sugar. Mix well. Remove roast from oven 25 minutes before done. Prick with fork and coat with orange glaze. Return to oven; continue baking. Heat remaining glaze in small saucepan. When roast is done, remove from oven, brush again with glaze, and let stand 10 minutes before slicing into ¼" slices; serve any remaining glaze on the side. **Yield: 8 servings**

 Fresh pork should be cooked to an internal temperature of 170°.

 To serve fully cooked hams hot, heat to an internal temperature of 140°.

Smothered Pork Chops

All this needs to complete the meal is a green salad or vegetable.

⅓   cup all-purpose flour
Salt, pepper to taste
4-5   pork chops
2   tablespoons vegetable oil
3-4   baking potatoes, peeled and sliced
¼   cup chopped onion
Water
Bottled brown bouquet sauce

Combine flour, salt, and pepper. Dredge pork chops in seasoned flour and brown quickly in hot oil in skillet. Remove from pan. Add potatoes, onion, and enough water to barely cover potatoes. Place chops on top. Cover pan and simmer gently until potatoes are done. If necessary, add thickening to make a smooth gravy. Add a dash of bouquet sauce for color. **Yield: 4 servings**

Grilled Sausages with Milwaukee Marinade

1   cup beer
¼   cup brown sugar
¼   cup cider vinegar
¼   cup vegetable oil
½   teaspoon red pepper flakes
½   teaspoon paprika
½   teaspoon thyme
2   teaspoons Dijon mustard
Salt, pepper to taste
2   pounds large sausage links

In a blender, combine beer, sugar, vinegar, oil, red pepper, paprika, thyme, mustard, salt, and pepper; process. Transfer to a large zip-lock plastic bag. Pierce sausages with a fork, add to bag, and seal tightly. Refrigerate at least 4 hours or overnight. Remove sausage from marinade. Grill 8-10 minutes over medium-hot charcoal fire. **Yield: 6 servings**

For extra crisp sausage patties, dip them in flour before frying.

Grilled Butterflied Leg of Lamb

3	cups dry red wine
½	cup olive oil
2	carrots, peeled and grated
2	onions, thinly sliced
1	tablespoon thyme
6	sprigs parsley
2	bay leaves, crumbled
2	teaspoons salt
½	teaspoon pepper
1	(7-pound) leg of lamb, boned and pounded to an even thickness by butcher

Combine wine, oil, carrots, onion, thyme, parsley, bay leaves, salt, and pepper and pour over lamb in large shallow glass dish. Cover; refrigerate 1-2 days, turning frequently. Grill over medium-hot coals for 45-60 minutes, basting occasionally with reserved marinade. Slice diagonally to serve. Warm remaining marinade to serve with grilled lamb.
Yield: 6-8 servings

Rack of Lamb Dijonnaise

This is fabulous for a small dinner party.

4	(14-ounce) lamb racks
Vegetable oil (to coat lamb)	
Salt, pepper to taste	
4	tablespoons minced shallots
4	tablespoons minced garlic
4	tablespoons chopped cilantro
1	cup melted butter
4	cups fresh bread crumbs
8	tablespoons Dijon mustard
Fresh mint leaves	

Trim and remove all visible fat from lamb. Rub with oil and season with salt and pepper. Sear meat on both sides in a hot skillet. Combine shallots, garlic, cilantro, butter, and bread crumbs. Spread lamb with Dijon mustard and seasoned bread crumbs. Bake at 500° for approximately 15 minutes for medium-rare lamb. Let meat rest after removing from the oven. Slice and arrange in a crown and garnish with fresh mint.
Yield: 4 servings

✻ *Quality lamb will have fine-textured meat with very little marbling.*

Roast Leg of Lamb with Mustard

1	(6-7 pound) leg of lamb
3	tablespoons dry mustard
2	tablespoons cider vinegar
1	tablespoon Worcestershire sauce
1	teaspoon garlic powder
1	cup water

Preheat oven to 450°. Roast lamb on rack in a shallow pan for 30 minutes. Meanwhile, combine mustard, vinegar, Worcestershire sauce, and garlic powder. Remove lamb from oven. Pierce all over with a sharp knife; spread with mustard mixture. Add water to pan and lower oven temperature to 325°. Roast for 3-4 hours, basting occasionally, until lamb is cooked to desired doneness. **Yield: 8 servings**

Braised Lamb Shanks

6	(1-pound) lamb shanks
3	tablespoons olive oil, divided
4	medium onions, thinly sliced
3	cloves garlic, minced
1	(28-ounce) can whole tomatoes, undrained and chopped
4	cups water
1	bay leaf
2	cinnamon sticks
¼	teaspoon allspice
¾	teaspoon dried orange peel
2	teaspoons salt
Pepper to taste	
1	(2-pound) rutabaga, peeled and cut into 1" pieces
6	carrots, peeled and cut into 1" pieces

Brown lamb shanks, one at a time, in 2 tablespoons hot oil; transfer to large overdrove kettle. Pour off fat from skillet; sauté onion in remaining olive oil until golden. Add garlic; cook briefly; add to lamb shanks. Then add tomatoes, water, bay leaf, cinnamon, allspice, orange peel, salt, and pepper. Bring to a boil. Cover and transfer to oven; bake at 350° for 1¾ hours. Stir in rutabaga and carrots; cover; bake an additional 30 minutes. *Lamb shanks improve in flavor if made 1 day ahead. Cool mixture, uncovered, and refrigerate, covered.* Skim fat, discarding it; re-heat over medium heat. Transfer lamb and vegetables with slotted spoon to serving platter. Boil braising liquid until reduced to 3 cups. Return meat and vegetable to kettle; simmer, covered, until heated through. Discard bay leaf. Serve with rice. **Yield: 6 servings**

Baked Chicken Reuben

4   chicken breast halves
¼   teaspoon salt
⅛   teaspoon pepper
1   (16-ounce) can sauerkraut, drained
4   (4" x 6") slices natural Swiss cheese
1¼   cups commercial Thousand Island salad dressing
1   tablespoon chopped parsley

Place chicken in a greased 13" x 9" x 2" baking dish. Season with salt and pepper. Spoon sauerkraut over chicken and top each piece with a slice of cheese. Drizzle dressing over all. Cover pan with aluminum foil and bake at 325° for about 1½ hours or until fork-tender. Sprinkle with parsley before serving. **Yield: 4 servings**

Chicken Breasts with Lime Butter

Here's a $10,000 winner!

6   chicken breast halves, boned and skinned
½   teaspoon salt
½   teaspoon pepper
⅓   cup vegetable oil
2   tablespoons lime juice
½   cup butter (no substitute)
½   teaspoon chives
½   teaspoon dill weed

Season chicken with salt and pepper. Heat oil in skillet over medium-high heat; add chicken and sauté for 4 minutes or until lightly browned. Turn, cover, and reduce heat to low. Cook for 10 minutes more or until fork tender. Remove chicken from pan and keep warm on serving platter. Drain off oil in skillet; add lime juice and cook over low heat until juice begins to bubble. Add butter, and cook, stirring, until butter becomes opaque and sauce thickens. Stir in chives and dill. Spoon over chicken. *This is great with rice.* **Yield: 3-6 servings**

Chicken Florentine

6   boneless, skinless chicken breast halves
1   (10-ounce) package frozen, chopped spinach, thawed,
      and squeezed dry
1   (2½-ounce) jar chopped mushrooms, drained
½   cup chopped onion
½   cup grated mozzarella cheese
½   cup ricotta cheese
Pepper to taste

Lightly grease a 13" x 9" x 2" baking dish. Flatten chicken. In a small bowl, combine spinach, mushrooms, onion, cheeses, and pepper. Divide mixture into sixths; spoon a portion onto each piece of chicken. Wrap chicken around stuffing and secure with wooden picks. Cover and bake at 350° for about 1 hour or until chicken is done. **Yield: 6 servings**

Chicken George

This is an original from Country Capers.

5   chicken breast halves, boned
Salt, pepper to taste
Thyme, parsley, paprika to taste
1   (10¾-ounce) can cream of mushroom soup
½   cup Sauterne wine
1   (4-ounce) can mushrooms, drained
Hot cooked rice

Place chicken pieces in ungreased 13" x 9" x 2" rectangular baking dish. Season chicken with salt, pepper, thyme, parsley, and paprika. Combine undiluted soup, wine and mushrooms and pour over chicken. Bake at 350° for about 1½ hours or until browned. Serve over rice.
Yield: 5 servings

❡ *Each chicken piece* must be dried throughly before breading or coating.

❡ *When fried chicken* is greasy, the temperature of the cooking oil is too low.

Coq au Vin de Bourguignon

This makes a great Sunday dinner dish.

2   tablespoons butter or margarine
2   tablespoons olive oil
2   thick slices bacon
12   small onions or shallots
1   carrot, peeled and sliced
5   pounds chicken pieces
⅜   cup all-purpose flour
1   bottle Burgundy wine
Bouquet garni to taste
2   cloves garlic, minced
Salt, pepper to taste

Heat butter and oil together in Dutch oven. Add bacon, onions, and carrot and cook until lightly browned. Remove from pan and keep warm. Lightly brown chicken pieces on all sides in Dutch oven. Sprinkle with flour and continue cooking until golden brown. Pour wine over chicken and bring to a boil. Add the bouquet garni, garlic, salt, pepper, and reserved onion mixture. Cover and simmer gently for 1½ hours. This dish can be made a day ahead. Separate chicken and sauce after cooking. Cool; de glaze (remove fat) sauce. Skin and bone chicken. Return chicken to sauce and heat before serving. **Yield: 8 servings**

English Country Chicken

8   chicken breast halves or thighs, skinned and boned
2   cups orange marmalade
⅓   cup prepared mustard
1   teaspoon curry powder
½   teaspoon salt
2   tablespoons lemon juice
1   lemon, thinly sliced
½   cup water
2   tablespoons cornstarch

Place chicken pieces in lightly greased 13" x 9" x 2" baking dish. Combine marmalade, mustard, curry powder, and salt; heat until marmalade melts. Add lemon juice; pour over chicken. Cover tightly with foil. Bake at 375° for 45 minutes. Remove foil, baste chicken; top each piece with a lemon slice. Return to oven; bake, uncovered, for 30 minutes more. Place chicken pieces on serving platter. Pour sauce from baking pan into a small saucepan; add water and cornstarch. Blend well. Cook, stirring, until thickened. Pour over chicken. **Yield: 4-6 servings**

French Country Chicken

8	boneless, skinless chicken breast halves
1	(4-ounce) package dried chipped beef
8	strips bacon
1	(10¾-ounce) can cream of chicken or mushroom soup
1	cup sour cream

Wash and dry chicken; set aside. Separate chipped beef slices; spread in bottom of lightly greased 13" x 9" x 2" glass baking dish. Wrap each chicken breast with bacon slice; arrange over chipped beef. Combine soup and sour cream; spoon over chicken pieces. Bake, uncovered, at 300° for 2½ hours. **Yield: 6-8 servings**

Fabulous Fried Chicken

4	boneless, skinless chicken breast halves
Salt, pepper to taste	
2	eggs
1	teaspoon vegetable oil
½	cup all-purpose flour
2	cups fresh white bread crumbs
½	cup real butter

Flatten chicken breasts. Wipe with paper towels. Season with salt and pepper. In pie plate, beat eggs with vegetable oil. Dip chicken pieces in flour, then egg, and finally coat with bread crumbs. Refrigerate for at least 30 minutes. Meanwhile, clarify butter by cutting into small pieces and cooking in small saucepan over medium heat until solids separate and liquids can be strained into frying pan. Heat frying pan to medium-hot (325°) and sauté chicken for 8 to 10 minutes on each side or until golden brown. Serve hot. **Yield: 4 servings**

Jane's Tailgate Chicken

Non-stick vegetable spray
2   chickens, cut-up
Cracked black pepper
Garlic salt
½   cup Chablis or Sauterne wine

Coat large baking pan with non-stick vegetable spray. Arrange chicken in pan skin side down. Crack pepper over chicken and sprinkle with garlic salt. Place pan on highest oven shelf and broil near heat source for 10-15 minutes. Move oven rack to next lower notch; turn broiler down. Add wine to pan and broil for an additional 10-15 minutes. Remove pan from oven. Turn chicken pieces over. Generously season with more black pepper and garlic salt. If desired, add more wine to pan. Return rack to highest shelf; turn broiler back to high and broil for 10 more minutes. **Yield: 10-14 servings**

Ricky Chicky

6   tablespoons lemon juice
6   tablespoons gin
¾   teaspoon oregano
1½   teaspoons salt
1½   teaspoons sugar
½   cup vegetable oil
4   boneless, skinless chicken breast halves
3-4   cups thinly sliced mild white onions

Whisk together the lemon juice, gin, oregano, salt, sugar, and vegetable oil. Transfer to a large zip-lock plastic bag, add chicken, and seal tightly. Refrigerate 30-45 minutes. Grill the chicken, reserving marinade, for 7 minutes on each side. While the chicken is grilling, in a heavy skillet combine the reserved marinade and onions and sauté until the onions are lightly browned. Serve onions over chicken. **Yield: 2-4 servings**

Sicilian Skillet Chicken

4	boneless, skinless chicken breast halves
6	tablespoons grated Parmesan cheese, divided
3	tablespoons all-purpose flour
Salt, pepper to taste	
2	tablespoons olive oil
1	cup sliced fresh mushrooms
½	onion, finely chopped
½	teaspoon rosemary, crushed
1	(14½-ounce) can Italian-style stewed tomatoes
¾	pound pasta

Flatten chicken slightly. Coat with 4 tablespoons cheese and then flour. Season to taste with salt and pepper. In a skillet, cook chicken in oil over medium high heat until done. Remove to serving dish; keep warm. In same skillet, sauté mushrooms, onion, and rosemary until soft. Add tomatoes; cook uncovered over medium-high heat until thickened. Meanwhile, boil water for pasta, timing cooking to coincide with chicken and sauce. Serve chicken and sauce over pasta. Top with remaining cheese. **Yield: 4 servings**

Stuffed Chicken Breasts

Prepare everything but sauce ahead of time; cover and refrigerate until baking time. Leftovers can be frozen.

1	(6-ounce) package chicken-flavored stuffing mix
8	boneless chicken breast halves, with skin
Salt, pepper, paprika to taste	
¼	cup butter or margarine

Sauce:

1	(10¾-ounce) can cream of chicken soup
½	cup cooking sherry
Water	

Prepare stuffing mix according to package directions; divide in eighths. Place mounds of stuffing in a greased 13" x 9" x 2" baking dish and cover each mound with a piece of chicken. Season to taste with salt, pepper, and paprika. Dot each breast with butter. Bake, uncovered, at 325° for 30 minutes or until chicken is lightly browned. Meanwhile mix soup, sherry, and enough water together to achieve a gravy-like consistency. Spoon sauce over chicken and return to oven for an additional 15 minutes, or until bubbly. **Yield: 8 servings**

Asheville Chicken Strata

8   slices day-old bread, cubed into 1" pieces
2   cups chopped cooked chicken
½   cup mayonnaise
Salt, pepper to taste
⅓   cup chopped celery
⅓   cup sliced Spanish olives
½   cup sliced almonds or water chestnuts
2   eggs, beaten
1½   cups milk
1   (10¾-ounce) can cream of chicken soup
⅓   cup buttered bread crumbs
½   cup shredded sharp Cheddar cheese

Put half the bread into a greased 13" x 9" x 2" baking dish. Cover with chicken, mayonnaise, salt and pepper. Top with remaining bread. Combine celery, olives, almonds or water chestnuts, eggs, and milk; pour over bread. Cover and refrigerate 1-24 hours. Before baking, spoon undiluted soup over casserole; top with bread crumbs. Bake at 325° for 45 minutes. Sprinkle with cheese; return to oven briefly to melt.
Yield: 6-8 servings

Chicken with Wild Rice Casserole

4   chicken breast halves
1   cup dry Sherry
1   cup water
½   cup chopped celery
¼   cup chopped onion
1½   teaspoons salt
1   (6-ounce) package wild and long-grain rice mix
1   pound mushrooms, sliced
½   cup butter or margarine, melted
1   cup sour cream
1   (10¾-ounce) can cream of mushroom soup, undiluted
½   cup slivered almonds

Combine chicken, Sherry, water, celery, onion, and salt in Dutch oven and bring to a boil; simmer 1 hour. Skin, bone, and cut chicken into bite-sized pieces. Strain cooking liquid and use instead of water to cook rice according to package directions. Sauté mushrooms in butter; combine with sour cream and soup. Add rice and chicken pieces and spoon into a lightly greased 3-quart casserole. Sprinkle with almonds and bake at 350° for 1 hour. **Yield: 6-8 servings**

Easy Gourmet Chicken

4	boneless, skinless chicken breasts
2	medium baking potatoes, peeled and thinly sliced
1	(4-ounce) can sliced mushrooms
1	small chopped onion
½	teaspoon garlic powder
½	teaspoon salt
¼	teaspoon pepper
1	(10¾-ounce) can cream of mushroom or chicken soup

Place chicken in bottom of a 9" x 9" x 2" greased baking dish. Layer over chicken in this order: potatoes, mushrooms, and onions. Season with garlic powder, salt, and pepper. Pour soup over all. Bake, uncovered, at 350° for 45 minutes. **Yield: 4 servings**

Garden Club Chicken Casserole

1	(4-pound) chicken
10	cups water
1	cup chopped green pepper
1	cup chopped onion
½	cup butter or margarine
2	cups grated sharp Cheddar cheese
1	(6-ounce) bottle Spanish olives, sliced
6	ounces sliced mushrooms
1	(8-ounce) can sliced water chestnuts
1	(8-ounce) package spinach noodles
1	(10¾-ounce) can cream of mushroom soup
1	teaspoon Greek seasoning

Boil chicken in water until done; reserve stock. Cut chicken in bite-sized pieces; set aside. Sauté green pepper and onion in butter. Stir in cheese, olives, mushrooms, water chestnuts, and chicken. Using 3 cups reserved chicken stock, boil noodles until stock is absorbed. Stir in soup and chicken mixture. Spoon into greased 3-quart casserole and sprinkle top with Greek seasoning. Bake at 350° for 45 minutes until hot and bubbly. *Save some stock to moisten while baking.* May be prepared ahead of time and frozen; bake after thawing. Add reserved stock. **Yield: 15 servings**

Lucille's Chicken Casserole

Absolutely, the best!

1   (4-pound) fryer
1   (10¾-ounce) can cream of mushroom soup
1   (10¾-ounce) can Cheddar cheese soup
1   (6-ounce) roll garlic cheese
2   (16-ounce) cans whole green beans, drained
1   (8-ounce) can sliced water chestnuts
1   (16-ounce) can Chinese vegetables, drained
1   (3-ounce) can French-fried onion rings

In a large pot, boil chicken until done. Bone, skin, and cut into bite-sized pieces; set aside. In saucepan, heat together soups and cheese until cheese melts. Add green beans, water chestnuts, Chinese vegetables, and reserved chicken. Spoon into greased 3-quart casserole. Bake at 350° for 30 minutes. Top with onion rings; bake 10 minutes more. **Yield: 12 servings**

Savory Chicken Casserole

1   cup sour cream
1   (8-ounce) package cream cheese, softened
1   (10¾-ounce) can cream of mushroom soup
1   soup can milk
¼   cup minced onion
½   teaspoon garlic salt
½   teaspoon curry powder
½   teaspoon Worcestershire sauce
4-6   ounces medium noodles, cooked
4   chicken breast halves, cooked, skinned, boned, and chopped
Paprika

Combine sour cream, cream cheese, soup, and milk; stir until smooth. Add onion, garlic salt, curry, and Worcestershire sauce. Stir in noodles and chicken. Spoon into greased 2-quart casserole; sprinkle top with paprika. Bake, uncovered, at 350° for 30 minutes. *Doubles easily.* **Yield: 6 servings**

Tudor Grove Roast Turkey and Stuffing

¾   cup chopped onion
⅓   cup chopped celery
½   cup butter or margarine, melted
2   tart apples, cored and unpeeled
½   cup chopped pecans
1   (16-ounce) package stuffing mix
1   cup orange juice
1   (13-16 pound) turkey, rinsed; liver reserved
Softened butter or margarine
Salt, pepper, paprika to taste

Sauté onion and celery in butter until translucent and golden. Add apples and pecans; toss well. Remove from heat; stir in stuffing mix. Stir until all butter is absorbed. Add enough orange juice to dampen, but not soak mixture; set aside.

Spray a large roasting pan with non-stick vegetable spray. Tear a piece of heavy-duty aluminum foil long enough to wrap around the turkey end-to-end; place over pan. Tear another piece of foil long enough to wrap around the turkey side-to-side; lay over first piece of foil. Spray foil with vegetable spray. Fill turkey with stuffing, but do not pack. Smear skin surfaces with butter; sprinkle with salt, pepper, and paprika. Wrap turkey airtight in foil. Insert meat thermometer through foil into thigh joint.

Bake at 500° for about 2½ hours. Check thermometer reading to determine doneness. When close to 185°, remove pan from oven, peel back foil, and tear off at pan edge. Reduce heat to 375°; return turkey to oven; continue baking for 20-30 minutes or until skin is crisp and brown.
Yield: 10 servings

Gravy:

   Turkey drippings
   Reserved turkey liver, chopped
   2   tablespoons all-purpose flour
   1   cup orange juice
   1   tablespoon soy sauce (optional)

Open foil; pour juices off into saucepan. Add liver; simmer 20-30 minutes. Transfer to blender; process. Add flour and orange juice; process again. Pour back into saucepan; bring to a boil. Cook, stirring, until thickened. Thin to proper consistency with additional orange juice, if necessary. Add soy sauce, if desired.

Smoked Turkey

1	10-to-15 pound turkey
1	clove garlic
½	lemon
¼	teaspoon salt
¼	teaspoon pepper
1	cooking apple, cored and quartered
2	carrots, cut into thirds
1	stalk celery, cut into thirds
1	small onion, quartered
2	tablespoons melted butter or margarine

Mesquite chunks

Remove giblets and neck from turkey; reserve for other uses. Rinse turkey with cold water; pat dry. Rub cavity with garlic and lemon. Sprinkle with salt and pepper. Place apple, carrots, celery, and onion in cavity of turkey; close cavity with skewers. Tie ends of legs to tail with cord; lift wing tips up and over back so they are tucked under bird. Baste with butter.

Prepare charcoal fire in smoker, and let burn 15-20 minutes. Soak mesquite chunks in water at least 15 minutes. Place mesquite on coals. Place water pan in smoker, and fill with water. Place turkey on food rack that has been treated with non-stick vegetable spray. Cover with smoker lid; cook turkey 8-12 hours or until meat thermometer reaches 185° when inserted in breast or meaty portion of thigh. Refill water pan with boiling water and add additional charcoal (started on the side) as needed. *May substitute hickory nuts that have been presoaked in water for the mesquite.* **Yield: 14-18 servings**

If a shoulder, baste it with cream till half done, then flour it and baste it with butter.

The breast must be roasted with the caul on till it is enough, and the sweetbread skewered on the backside of the breast. When it is nigh enough, take off the caul, baste it and dredge it with flour. All these are to be sent to table with some melted butter, and garnished with sliced lemon.

If a Loin or Fillet not stuffed, be sure to paper the fat, that as little may be lost as possible. All joints are to be laid at a distance from the fire, till soaked, then near the fire. When you lay it down baste it with good butter, (except it be the shoulder, and that may be done the same if you chuse it) when it is near enough baste it again, and dredge it with flour.

How to roast a Pig.

First wipe it dry with a cloth, then take a piece of butter and some crumbs of bread, of each about a quarter of a pound, some sage, thyme, sweet marjoram, pepper, salt, and nutmeg, the yolks of two eggs, mix these together and sew it up in the belly. Flour it very thick, then spit it, and put it to the fire, taking care that your fire burns well at both ends, then hang a flat iron in the middle of the grate. Continue flouring it 'till the eyes drop out, or you find the crackling hard, then wipe it with a cloth, wet it in salt and water and baste it with butter. When the gravy begins to run put basons in the dripping pan to receive it. When you perceive it is enough, take a quarter of a pound of butter, put it into a coarse cloth, and having made a brisk fire, rub the pig over with it, till the crackling is crisp, and then take it from the fire. Cut off the head, and cut the pig in two down the back, where take out the spit. Then cut the ears off and place one at each end, and also the under jaw in two and placed one at each side, make the sauce thus :

Take some good butter, melt it, mix it with the gravy received in the basons, and the brains bruised, some dried sage shred small, pour these into the dish and serve it up.

How to roast Pork.

The best way to roast a leg is first to parboil it, then skin and roast it, baste it with butter, then take some sage, shred

it

Christ Church
LANCASTER COUNTY (IRVINGTON), VIRGINIA
CIRCA 1732

INFORMATION UNCOVERED FROM early vestry books indicates that the first Christ Church was erected about 1654. Leading vestry men were John Carter and his sons, John and Robert "King" Carter, who were among the earliest settlers, land agents, and landholders in Virginia. Built around 1732 by wealthy planter Robert "King" Carter, the present Christ Church replaced the first church. The walls are three feet thick and large slabs of freestone pave the aisles. Highback pews offered privacy, with the largest family pew belonging to the Carters in front, having damask curtains for additional privacy. This well-preserved church is a monument and burial ground for the Carter family and their descendants.

Cypress Banks Barbecued Duck

2   large or 4 small ducks
Salt, pepper, paprika to taste
2½   teaspoons prepared mustard
2   tablespoons ketchup
½   cup water
2   tablespoons Worcestershire sauce
4   tablespoons port wine
2   tablespoons butter or margarine
Wild rice

Remove breasts from bone cutting meat closely to bone with sharp knife. Season with salt, pepper, and paprika. Blend mustard and ketchup. Add water, Worcestershire sauce, wine and butter. In small saucepan warm ingredients over low heat. Line broiler pan with heavy-duty aluminum foil and place meat on top. Broil for 10 minutes. Remove from heat and baste with sauce. Broil for an additional 5 minutes. Move basted meat to outdoor grill and cook until hot and browned. Do not overcook. Serve with wild rice. **Yield: 4 servings**

Heavenly Hanover Dove

This recipe can be used for other game birds.

12-16 dove breasts, cleaned
1   tablespoon each salt, pepper
½   teaspoon paprika
All-purpose flour
⅓   cup vegetable oil
1   tablespoon soy sauce
1   cup chicken broth
⅔   cup dry Sherry or Burgundy, divided
2   cups sour cream
Fresh parsley to garnish

Soak dove breasts in salted water overnight in refrigerator. The next day, dry them before rolling in a mixture of the salt, pepper, and paprika. Coat each piece in flour and brown in hot oil. Remove the meat from the pan. Add soy sauce, broth, and half the Sherry to the drippings and mix well. Return meat to the pan, cover, simmer until done. Transfer meat to serving platter and keep warm. Add sour cream and remaining Sherry. Blend and heat thoroughly, but do not boil. Pour sauce over meat and garnish with parsley. *Wild rice is a super accompaniment.* **Yield: 4-6 servings**

Island Farm Doves

12   doves
Salt, pepper to taste
3-4   tablespoons vegetable oil
2   medium onions, chopped
6   strips bacon
1   (10¾-ounce) can cream of celery soup
1   (10¾-ounce) can cream of mushroom soup
2   cups beer
1   (4-ounce) can sliced mushrooms
2   tablespoons dried parsley
½   lemon, sliced
Hot cooked rice

Remove dove breasts from bones by cutting meat closely to breast bones. Sprinkle with salt and pepper. Brown slightly in skillet in hot oil. Remove meat from skillet and set aside. In same skillet, sauté onions and bacon until onions are transparent. Drain. Place meat, onions, and bacon in greased 13" x 9" x 2" rectangular baking dish. Combine soups and beer; spread over meat mixture. Top with mushrooms, parsley, and lemon slices. Cover with aluminum foil. Bake at 325° for 2 hours, or until doves are tender. Serve over rice. **Yield: 4-6 servings**

Quail

A Christmas tradition; great with grits!

6-8   quail, cleaned
Salt, pepper to taste
½   cup butter or margarine
1   medium onion, finely chopped
2   tablespoons flour
½   cup white wine
1   cup chicken broth

Remove quail wings and necks, if desired. Season to taste with salt and pepper. In a skillet, sauté onion in melted butter until transparent. Remove onion; set aside. Brown birds, remove from skillet; place in greased baking dish. Stir flour into remaining drippings; brown; 1 minute. Stir in wine and broth; cook, stirring, until mixture boils. Pour sauce over birds; top with sautéed onion. Cover. Bake at 275° for 90 minutes, turning birds every 30 minutes. **Yield: 4 servings**

Roasted Quail

8	quail, cleaned
8	slices bacon
2	tablespoons butter or margarine
¼	cup water
1	tablespoon lemon juice
4-8	ounces currant jelly

Wrap each bird with a slice of bacon. Place in roasting pan, cover, and roast at 350° for 30 minutes. Remove cover and continue roasting until bacon is crisp. Put birds on an oven-proof serving platter. Meanwhile, put bacon drippings from roasting pan into a small saucepan. Add butter, water, lemon juice, and 4 ounces jelly. Cook and stir until jelly melts and sauce is hot. Add additional jelly, if desired. Serve sauce with quail.
Yield: 4 servings

Tuckahoe Vermouth Venison

2	pounds venison
2-3	tablespoons vegetable oil
2	(10¾-ounce) cans cream of mushroom soup
1	(1-ounce) package dehydrated onion soup mix
½	cup dry Vermouth or white wine
1	pound fresh mushrooms, sliced
3	tablespoons butter or margarine, melted

Hot cooked rice

Cube venison and remove all white membrane. Brown meat in oil in large skillet. Combine mushroom soup, onion soup mix, and Vermouth or wine. Place meat in greased 2½-quart casserole and pour soup mixture over top. Cover and bake at 350° for 2½ hours. Sauté mushrooms in melted butter; pour over meat and continue baking for an additional 30 minutes. **Yield: 4-6 servings**

Bluefish "Crab" Cakes

1	pound poached bluefish fillets, skinned and flaked (white meat only)
½	teaspoon seafood seasoning
1	tablespoon minced green pepper
2	tablespoons minced onion
2	eggs, beaten
½	cup finely crushed cracker crumbs
4	tablespoons mayonnaise
2	tablespoons Dijon mustard

Salt, pepper to taste
Tartar sauce

Mix together bluefish, seasoning, green pepper, onion, eggs, crumbs, mayonnaise, mustard, salt, and pepper. Shape into 4 large or 8 small cakes. Fry in hot shortening until lightly browned. Serve with tartar sauce (recipe below). **Yield: 4 servings**

Tartar Sauce for Dill Lovers

1	cup mayonnaise
¼	cup grated dill pickle, juice reserved
2	teaspoons grated onion
1	teaspoon parsley
2	teaspoons cream of tartar

Combine mayonnaise, pickle, onion, parsley, and cream of tartar. Thin sauce to desired consistency with reserved pickle juice. Adjust amount of cream of tartar to taste. *Covered and refrigerated, this will keep for weeks.* **Yield: 1½ cups**

Grouper Fillets

1½-2	pounds grouper fillets
¼	cup melted butter or margarine
1	tablespoon fresh lemon juice
1	teaspoon salt
½	teaspoon dill weed
Dash	pepper

Wash fillets and pat dry with paper towels. Place in lightly greased 13" x 9" x 2" glass baking dish. Combine butter or margarine, lemon juice, salt, dill weed, and pepper and pour over fillets. Bake at 350° for about 20 minutes or until fish flakes easily. **Variation:** This method works equally well with orange roughy fillets. **Yield: 4 servings**

Grilled Salmon Diable

⅓   cup butter or margarine, softened
2   tablespoons lemon juice
2   teaspoons Dijon mustard
⅛   teaspoon cayenne pepper
1   tablespoon parsley
6   salmon steaks, 1" thick (about 2½ pounds)
2   tablespoons olive oil
Salt, pepper to taste

In small bowl, beat butter. Gradually add lemon juice, mustard, cayenne, and parsley. If made ahead, refrigerate but bring to room temperature before using. Wipe salmon with paper towels; brush with oil and season with salt and pepper. Grill over medium hot coals for about 4-5 minutes on each side or until thickest part of fish flakes easily. Top each steak with a spoonful of butter mixture. **Yield: 6 servings**

Simple Salmon

1   pound salmon fillets
2   tablespoons lemon juice
Salt, pepper to taste
2   teaspoons dill weed

Dill sauce:

1   cup sour cream
3   tablespoons lemon juice
2   green onions, chopped
½   teaspoon dill weed

Place salmon fillets on a large sheet of buttered aluminum foil. Add lemon juice, salt, pepper, and dill. Seal foil. Bake at 350° for 20-25 minutes or until fish flakes easily. Remove from oven and place on serving platter. While salmon bakes, combine sour cream, lemon juice, green onion, and dill in a small saucepan; warm gently. Spoon sauce over baked fish. **Yield: 2 servings**

Salmon Quiche

1   cup whipping cream
2   eggs
1   (7¾-ounce) can red salmon, drained
2   tablespoons minced onion
4   tablespoons chopped Spanish olives
1   tablespoon lemon juice
¼   teaspoon salt
⅛   teaspoon pepper
1   9" pastry shell, unbaked

In a large bowl, beat cream and eggs together; set aside. In another bowl, combine salmon, onion, olives, lemon juice, salt, and pepper. Add to cream mixture. Pour into pastry shell. Bake at 375° for 30-35 minutes. **Yield: 4-6 servings**

Grilled Tuna with Orange Sauce

6   tablespoons unsalted butter, softened
Zest and juice from 1 orange
1   tablespoon chopped Italian flat-leaf parsley
1½   pounds fresh yellowfin tuna
Orange slices

Combine butter and orange zest. Slowly add juice and parsley. Treat grill with non-stick vegetable spray. Brush tuna with orange butter; grill over hot coals 3-4 minutes on each side or until desired degree of doneness is reached. Continue brushing with orange sauce while grilling. Garnish with orange slices; serve hot. **Yield: 4 servings**

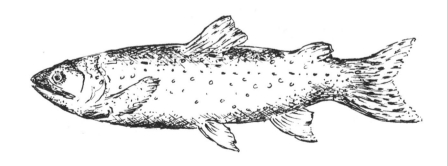

Tuna Casserole

*This was a regular item on the menu when
my children were growing up.*

6   ounces fettucine, cooked *al dente*
½   teaspoon thyme
¼   teaspoon salt
1   (10½-ounce) can cream of celery soup
½   cup milk
2   (7-ounce) cans solid white tuna, drained and flaked
½   cup chopped celery
½   cup chopped green pepper
½   cup chopped onion
½   cup chopped water chestnuts
½   cup mayonnaise
1   cup grated sharp Cheddar cheese, divided
¼   cup chopped almonds, toasted

In a lightly greased 2-quart casserole, combine fettucine, thyme, and salt.
In a saucepan, combine soup and milk and stir together until smooth.
Add tuna, celery, green pepper, onion, water chestnuts, mayonnaise, and
half the cheese. Cook and stir until cheese melts. Pour sauce over fettucine
and mix until combined; add almonds. Sprinkle with remaining cheese.
Bake at 425° for 20 minutes or until bubbly and lightly browned.
Yield: 6 servings

Maryland Crab Cakes I

Absolutely, the best!

2   slices whole wheat bread, crusts removed
2   eggs, beaten
2   tablespoons minced fresh parsley
3   tablespoons prepared mustard
1   tablespoon cider vinegar
1-2   teaspoons Worcestershire sauce
1   pound lump crabmeat, picked over
Salt, pepper to taste
Rendered bacon fat

Tear bread into small pieces. Soak at least 10 minutes in a combination
of eggs, parsley, mustard, vinegar, and Worcestershire sauce. Gently add
crabmeat to egg-bread mixture. Season with salt and pepper. Cover and
refrigerate until ready to shape into 6 or 7 cakes. Using bacon fat, fry in
sauté pan until browned. **Yield: 4-6 servings**

Maryland Crab Cakes II

1	pound backfin crabmeat
2	eggs
2	tablespoons mayonnaise
2	tablespoons horseradish mustard
¼	teaspoon salt
⅛	teaspoon pepper

Dash hot pepper sauce
1	tablespoon minced parsley
1	cup finely crushed saltine crackers

Tartar sauce

Pick over crabmeat, discarding any bits of shell. To this, *gently* stir in eggs, mayonnaise, horseradish mustard, salt, pepper, hot pepper sauce, and parsley and mix lightly. Do not pack ingredients. Shape into 6 cakes. Pat cracker crumbs on both sides of cakes and fry in hot vegetable oil until golden brown. Serve with tartar sauce. **Yield: 6 servings**

Fancy Deviled Crab

2	pounds fresh crabmeat
2½	cups mayonnaise
2	eggs, beaten
2	eggs, hard boiled and chopped
3-4	slices white bread, toasted and cubed
¼	cup grated onion
½	teaspoon curry
¼	teaspoon dry mustard

Lemon pepper, celery salt to taste
Salt to taste
Grated Parmesan cheese
Chopped parsley

Combine crabmeat, mayonnaise, eggs, bread, onion, curry, and mustard. Taste and season with lemon pepper, celery salt, and salt. Spoon into scallop-shaped baking shells. Sprinkle each with Parmesan and parsley. Put shells on baking sheet. Bake at 350° for 20 minutes or until bubbly and browned. *May be prepared 6-8 hours before baking; refrigerate.* **Yield: 12-14 servings**

Crabmeat-Artichoke Casserole

½   pound sliced fresh mushrooms
7   tablespoons melted butter or margarine, divided
2½   tablespoons all-purpose flour
1   cup milk
1   teaspoon Worcestershire sauce
Salt, pepper to taste
¼   cup dry white wine
1   (14-ounce) can artichoke hearts, drained and sliced
1   pound backfin crabmeat
¼   cup grated Parmesan cheese
Paprika, chopped parsley

Sauté mushrooms in 3 tablespoons melted butter; set aside. In saucepan, combine 4 tablespoons melted butter and flour; cook for 1 minute. Whisk in milk, Worcestershire sauce, salt, and pepper; cook, stirring, until sauce thickens. Remove from heat and add wine; set aside. Lightly grease an 8" x 8" x 2" baking dish. Cover bottom with artichokes. Add crabmeat, then mushrooms. Pour white sauce over mushrooms; sprinkle with cheese. Bake at 375° for 20-30 minutes. Sprinkle with paprika and parsley before serving. **Yield: 6 servings**

Crab Commonwealth

A tradition at the Commonwealth Club

1   tablespoon mustard-mayonnaise sauce
1   tablespoon Worcestershire sauce
3   tablespoons mayonnaise
1   pound backfin crabmeat
1   cup cracker crumbs
4   tablespoons paprika
3   tablespoons melted butter

Combine mustard-mayonnaise sauce, Worcestershire sauce, and mayonnaise. Gently fold in crabmeat, taking care not to break up lumps. Spoon into 4 seafood shells or ramekins. Mix cracker crumbs with paprika; pat mixture on top of crabmeat. Drizzle with melted butter. Bake at 350° for 15-20 minutes. If crumbs are not browned, adjust oven to broiler setting for a few seconds. **Yield: 4 servings**

California Crab Supreme

*The original version calls for Dungeness crabmeat,
available in California; however, it's just as good
prepared with East Coast lump crabmeat.*

6	tablespoons butter, divided
2	tablespoons all-purpose flour
1	cup light cream
½	teaspoon Worcestershire sauce
½	teaspoon grated onion
½	cup dry sack or other Sherry
1	pound lump crabmeat
½	cup fine fresh bread crumbs
Dash	paprika
4	slices lemon

Melt 2 tablespoons butter in saucepan until foamy. Add flour and, stirring constantly, cook for 3 minutes. Slowly add cream, Worcestershire sauce, and onion; cook and stir until thoroughly blended and mixture thickens. Remove from heat. Thin sauce to taste with small amounts of sherry. Gently fold in crabmeat. Spoon mixture into 4 shell ramekins. Sprinkle tops with bread crumbs and paprika; crown each with a lemon slice. Dot with remaining butter. Bake at 425° for 15 minutes or until bubbly. **Yield: 4 servings**

Crab and Cheese Supreme

6-8	thin slices white bread, lightly toasted
2	cups crabmeat, flaked
½	pound Swiss cheese, grated
3	eggs
1	cup light cream
1	cup milk
Salt, pepper, paprika to taste	

Line a greased 13" x 9" x 2" rectangular baking dish with toasted bread; cover with crabmeat. Sprinkle with cheese. Beat eggs until light; combine with cream and milk. Pour over contents of dish. Bake at 325° for 25 minutes. **Yield: 8 servings**

Oh-So-Good Oysters

I had this recipe for years before I finally tried it—I haven't
fixed oysters any other way since!

1	quart oysters, drained
2	tablespoons Worcestershire sauce
1-2	tablespoons lemon juice
¼-½	cup cracker crumbs
2	tablespoons fresh parsley
4	slices bacon, fried, drained, and crumbled

Spray a 1-quart casserole with non-stick vegetable spray. Combine oysters, Worcestershire sauce, lemon juice, ¼ cup cracker crumbs, and parsley. Spoon into prepared casserole. Bake at 375° for 30 minutes or more. When done, add remaining crumbs, if necessary, to absorb liquid and top with crumbled bacon. **Yield: 4 servings**

Scalloped Oysters I

2	tablespoons minced green onion
3	tablespoons butter or margarine
1¼	cup fresh white bread crumbs
Salt, pepper to taste	
2	tablespoons minced parsley
6	oysters, drained

Sauté green onion in butter until transparent. Add bread crumbs, stirring to mix with butter and to brown slightly. Add salt and pepper; fold in parsley. Spread half the crumbs in a 4" round baking cup. Arrange oysters on top; then cover with the remaining crumbs. If desired, dot top with butter. Cover; refrigerate if not baking immediately. Place dish on a baking sheet and bake in 450° oven for 8-10 minutes or until lightly browned. *Multiply ingredients to reflect total number of desired servings.* **Yield: 1 serving**

Scalloped Oysters II

1	cup saltine cracker crumbs
1	pint oysters, drained
¾	cup diced celery, parboiled
1	cup grated Cheddar cheese
2	eggs
1	cup milk
½	teaspoon dry mustard
¼	teaspoon paprika
1	teaspoon salt

Dash pepper

Line a lightly greased 1-quart baking dish with crumbs. Next layer half the oysters, half the celery, and half the cheese. Repeat. Beat eggs together with milk, mustard, paprika, salt, and pepper. Pour over oysters and bake at 325° for 1 hour. **Yield: 4-5 servings**

Wilmington Club Oysters

1	quart oysters
½	cup finely chopped celery
½	cup butter or margarine
2	tablespoons Worcestershire sauce
½	cup Sherry

Drain oysters, reserving juice. Set oysters aside. Cook celery in reserved juice over medium heat until tender. Add oysters and butter and cook until edges begin to curl. Stir in Worcestershire sauce and Sherry. **Yield: 4-6 servings**

Scallops à la Jenny

¼	cup melted butter or margarine, divided
1	pound scallops
⅓	cup seasoned bread crumbs
⅛	teaspoon each: garlic salt, dry mustard, paprika
2	tablespoons Sherry
4	lemon wedges

Put 2-3 tablespoons butter in 11" x 7" x 2" baking dish; add scallops. Combine crumbs, garlic salt, mustard, and paprika with remaining butter; sprinkle over scallops. Bake at 350° for 8-10 minutes. Drizzle Sherry over scallops; broil briefly. Serve with lemon wedges. **Yield: 4 servings**

Scallop Casserole

¼   cup finely chopped onion
½   teaspoon pepper
12   medium mushrooms, sliced
6   tablespoons melted butter
1   tablespoon lemon juice
1   tablespoon sherry
2   pounds scallops
8   slices tomato
6   wedges avocado
6   tablespoons Parmesan cheese

Sauté onion, pepper, and sliced mushrooms in melted butter. Add lemon juice, sherry, and scallops. Turn into lightly greased 11" x 7" x 2" rectangular baking dish. Cover with tomato slices and avocado and sprinkle with Parmesan cheese. Bake at 350° for 10 minutes. **Yield: 4 servings**

Bahamian Shrimp

Many years ago, we watched as this wonderful dish was prepared table side for us in a Zurich restaurant.

¾   pound shrimp, cleaned, deveined, and cooked
½   cup butter or margarine, melted
¼   cup minced onion
1   tablespoon minced red bell pepper
¾   cup heavy cream
⅛   teaspoon curry powder
⅛   teaspoon pepper
Salt to taste
⅓   cup drained crushed pineapple
¾   cup sour cream
1   large banana, thinly sliced

Briefly sauté shrimp in melted butter over low heat for about 2 minutes. Stir in onion and red peppers; sauté for another minute. Stir in cream, curry, pepper, salt, and pineapple, and heat, stirring. Stir in sour cream and cook slowly for another 2 minutes. Fold in banana and heat briefly. Serve over hot, cooked rice. **Yield: 4 servings**

Grilled Shrimp

¼	cup lemon juice
¼	cup soy sauce
3	tablespoons brown sugar
1	teaspoon canola oil
1	teaspoon garlic salt
20-40	medium green shrimp, cleaned and peeled

Combine lemon juice, soy sauce, brown sugar, oil, and garlic salt in small saucepan and bring to a boil; reduce heat and simmer 5 minutes. Cool slightly. Pour over shrimp in shallow dish, cover, and marinate in refrigerator for 30 minutes. Thread shrimp on skewers and grill over hot coals for 4 minutes on each side. **Yield: 2-4 servings**

Asparagus Shrimp Casserole

2	(10-ounce) packages frozen asparagus
1	pound medium shrimp, steamed and peeled
¼	cup butter
4	tablespoons all-purpose flour
½	cup half-and-half
¾	cup milk
2	eggs, beaten
½	cup white wine
Salt, pepper to taste	
4	drops hot pepper sauce
½	cup grated Parmesan cheese

Cook asparagus according to package directions; drain; set aside to cool. Layer shrimp and asparagus in a lightly greased 11" x 7" x 2" rectangular baking dish. In a saucepan over medium heat, melt butter and add flour. Whisk in cream and milk; cook, stirring, until sauce thickens. Remove from stove; add eggs a little at a time. Stir in wine, salt, pepper, and hot pepper sauce. Pour sauce over shrimp and asparagus and cover with cheese. Bake at 350° for 20-25 minutes. **Yield: 4-6 servings**

Shrimp Jambalaya

3	slices bacon
3	tablespoons chopped onion
1	rib celery, chopped
3	tablespoons chopped green pepper
1	tablespoon all-purpose flour
1	(29-ounce) can whole tomatoes, chopped
2	tablespoons parsley
Cayenne pepper to taste	
1	teaspoon chili powder
¾	cup cooked rice
2	cups raw shrimp, cleaned, peeled, and deveined

Pan-fry bacon and reserve drippings; crumble bacon and set aside. In drippings sauté onion, celery, and green pepper. Add flour and cook, stirring, until lightly browned. Add tomatoes, parsley, cayenne, and chili powder and simmer until mixture thickens slightly. Add rice and shrimp and cook until shrimp are done (pink). Stir in bacon, taste for seasoning, and serve hot. **Yield: 4 servings**

Twice-Baked Potatoes with Shrimp

8	large baking potatoes
4-5	tablespoons chopped onion
¾	cup butter or margarine
2	cups sour cream
¾-1	cup half-and-half
1½	cups grated sharp Cheddar cheese
1½	pounds shrimp, steamed, peeled, and coarsely chopped
Salt, pepper to taste	
Old Bay seasoning to taste	
Paprika, chopped parsley	

Bake potatoes. When potatoes are done, cool slightly; halve and scoop out pulp. Reserve shells. Mash pulp; beat in onion, butter, sour cream, half-and-half, and cheese. Stir in shrimp; correct seasoning with salt, pepper, and Old Bay. Divide filling among the shells. Sprinkle with paprika and parsley. Freeze on cookie sheet; then bag. Before serving, thaw in refrigerator and bake at 425° for 15 minutes. **Variation:** Substitute small salad shrimp for shrimp described above. **Yield: 16 servings**

Shrimp and Chicken Casserole

1	(2-3 pound) broiler-fryer
1	teaspoon salt
2	(16-ounce) bags frozen broccoli cuts, thawed and well drained
1	cup mayonnaise or salad dressing
1	(10¾-ounce) can cream of chicken soup, undiluted
1	(10¾-ounce) can cream of celery soup, undiluted
3	tablespoons lemon juice
¼	teaspoon white pepper
1	pound medium-sized shrimp, steamed and peeled
1	cup shredded Cheddar cheese
1	tablespoon melted butter or margarine
½	cup soft bread crumbs
	Paprika
	Shrimp, parsley sprigs to garnish

Combine chicken and salt in a Dutch oven; add enough water to cover, and bring to a boil. Reduce heat and simmer until tender. Bone chicken and cut into bite-sized pieces; set aside. Spread broccoli in lightly greased 13" x 9" x 2" rectangular baking dish; set aside.

Combine mayonnaise, soups, lemon juice, and white pepper; spread one third of this sauce over broccoli. Mix shrimp and chicken together; spread over casserole dish. Top with remaining sauce; cover.

Bake at 350° for 30 minutes. Remove cover; sprinkle with cheese. Combine bread crumbs and melted butter; sprinkle over cheese. Return to oven for an additional 15 minutes. Before serving, sprinkle with paprika; garnish with reserved shrimp and parsley sprigs. *To prepare ahead of time, cover, and refrigerate up to 8 hours. Remove from refrigerator and let stand at room temperature for 30 minutes before baking.* **Yield: 10 servings**

English Muffin Delight

Super entrée for brunch or lunch!

8	ounces cooked shrimp, coarsely chopped
1½	cups diced cooked chicken breast
½	cup finely chopped celery
½	cup light mayonnaise
¼	teaspoon salt
⅛	teaspoon white pepper
6	English muffins
3	tablespoons butter or margarine
12	slices process American cheese

Combine shrimp, chicken, celery, mayonnaise, salt, and pepper. Split muffins, butter sparingly, and toast lightly. Mound 2 tablespoons shrimp salad on each muffin. Bake at 350° for 10 minutes. Top each with a slice of cheese; return to oven long enough to melt cheese. **Yield: 12 servings**

Seafood Casserole

8	slices white bread, crusts removed and cubed
2	cups crabmeat
2	cups lobster chunks
2	cups chopped shrimp
⅓	cup chopped onion
¼	cup chopped green pepper
1	cup chopped celery
½	cup mayonnaise
3⅓	cups milk, divided
4	eggs, beaten
1	(10¾-ounce) can cream of mushroom soup, undiluted
1	cup grated Cheddar cheese
Paprika	

Spread half of bread cubes in bottom of greased 13" x 9" x 2" rectangular baking dish; set aside. Combine crabmeat, lobster, shrimp, onion, green pepper, celery, and mayonnaise. Spread over bread in casserole. Top with remaining bread. Combine 3 cups milk and eggs; pour over casserole, cover, and refrigerate overnight. Before baking, dilute soup with remaining ⅓ cup milk; pour over bread. Sprinkle with cheese and paprika. Bake, uncovered, at 350° for 30-40 minutes. **Yield: 8-10 servings**

Lasagna

Here's an old family favorite that freezes well.

1	clove garlic, minced
1	large onion, chopped
1	medium carrot, pared and chopped
1	teaspoon basil
1	teaspoon parsley
¼-⅓	cup olive oil
1	(16-ounce) can tomatoes, chopped
1	(6-ounce) can tomato paste
½-¾	cup water
1	teaspoon salt

Pepper to taste

1	pound ground beef, browned and drained
9	lasagna noodles
1	(6-ounce) package sliced mozzarella cheese

Cheese sauce:

4	tablespoons butter or margarine
1	small onion, chopped
3	tablespoons all-purpose flour
¾	cup grated Parmesan cheese

Dash salt

2	cups milk
2	egg yolks

Sauté garlic, onion, carrot, basil, and parsley in olive oil. Add tomatoes and tomato paste mixed with water; season with salt and pepper. Stir in beef. Cover and simmer over low heat for at least 45 minutes. Meanwhile, cook lasagna noodles according to package directions, drain, and set aside.

CHEESE SAUCE: Sauté onion in butter; stir in flour. Add cheese and salt. Stir in milk gradually; cook over low heat until smooth and thick. Add egg yolks a little at a time to prevent curdling. Cook and stir over low heat for 10 minutes.

In the bottom of a greased 13" x 9" x 2" rectangular baking dish, layer one third of the noodles with half of the meat sauce, mozzarella cheese, and cheese sauce. Repeat, ending with noodles. Top with dots of butter and sprinkle with additional Parmesan cheese. Bake at 375° for 45 minutes. **Yield: 10-12 servings**

Vegetarian Lasagna

¼	cup chopped onion
2	teaspoons vegetable oil
½	cup grated carrots
1	cup sliced fresh mushrooms
1	(8-ounce) can tomato sauce
1	(6-ounce) can tomato paste
½	cup chopped black olives
¾	teaspoon oregano
6	lasagna noodles, cooked and drained
1	cup cottage cheese
1	(10-ounce) package frozen chopped spinach, cooked and drained
4	ounces sliced Monterey Jack cheese
¼	cup grated Parmesan cheese

Sauté onions in oil until soft. Add carrots and mushrooms; cook until tender. Stir in tomato sauce, tomato paste, olives, and oregano. Set aside. Lightly grease a 13" x 9" x 2" rectangular baking dish. Layer one half each noodles, cottage cheese, spinach, and tomato sauce mixture. Top with one third of the Monterey Jack cheese. Repeat. Top with remaining Monterey Jack cheese and Parmesan. Bake at 375° for 30 minutes. Cool 10 minutes before cutting. **Yield: 4-6 servings**

Pasta with Pesto Sauce

2	cloves garlic
Salt to taste	
½	cup pine nuts
1	cup fresh basil
⅔	cup mild olive oil
4	tablespoons butter or margarine
Pepper to taste	
4	tablespoons grated Parmesan cheese
1	pound spaghetti

Peel the garlic and process in food processor with a little salt and the pine nuts until broken up. Add the basil; continue processing to a paste. Dribble olive oil in a little at a time until the mixture is creamy and thick. Mix in butter; season with pepper. Add cheese. Store the pesto in a jar. Pour a little olive oil on top to exclude the air. Refrigerate. Cook the pasta according to package directions; drain well. Toss the pasta with half the pesto; serve with the remaining pesto spooned on top. **Yield: 4 servings**

Pasta with Shrimp and Feta Cheese

1	pound medium raw shrimp, cleaned and shelled
4	tablespoons butter or margarine, melted
6	scallions, chopped
½	pound feta cheese, cut in ½" cubes

Salt, pepper to taste
Small bunch fresh chives, cut into 1" lengths, and divided
1   pound pasta (penne or rigatoni)

Sauté shrimp in butter until pink. Stir in scallions. Stir feta into shrimp mixture; season with salt and plenty of pepper. Add half the chives to shrimp. Cook pasta according to the package directions; drain well and transfer to serving dish. Spoon sauce over and garnish with reserved chives.
Yield: 4 servings

Pasta with Tomatoes and Basil

4-6	large ripe summer tomatoes, peeled and cubed
1	pound Brie cheese, rind removed and cut into chunks
1	cup fresh basil, rinsed, dried, and chopped
3	cloves garlic, minced
1	cup olive oil
2	teaspoons salt, divided
½	teaspoon pepper
1½	pounds pasta (spaghetti or linguine)

Grated Parmesan cheese

At least 2 hours prior to serving, combine tomatoes, Brie, basil, garlic, oil, ½ teaspoon salt, and pepper in a large serving bowl. Cover and set aside at room temperature. When ready to serve, cook pasta with 1½ teaspoons salt in boiling water according to package directions; drain well. Toss with tomato sauce. Serve immediately with cheese. **Yield: 6 servings**

Baked Eggs Florentine

*Baking eggs in small individual soufflé dishes achieves
an effect similar to coddling.*

1   large bunch fresh spinach, washed and stemmed
8   tablespoons unsalted butter, softened
Salt and freshly ground pepper
8   fresh eggs
¼   cup heavy cream
¼   cup grated sharp Cheddar cheese

In a large saucepan, bring lightly salted water to a boil. Drop in the spinach leaves; parboil for about 30 seconds. Drain; rinse with cold water. Dry spinach on paper toweling. Bring saucepan of water to a boil. Divide melted butter among 4 small soufflé dishes; coarsely chop the cooked spinach and divide among the dishes. Season with salt and pepper. Carefully break 2 eggs into each dish, keeping yolks intact. Drizzle cream over the eggs and sprinkle with cheese. Place dishes in baking pan; pour enough boiling water into the pan to come half way up sides of dishes. Bake at 375° for 10 minutes or until the egg whites are set. **Yield: 4 servings**

Egg and Chipped Beef Brunch

4   slices bacon, diced
½   pound chipped beef, coarsely shredded
½   cup butter or margarine, divided
1   (8-ounce) can sliced mushrooms, drained and divided
½   cup all-purpose flour
Pepper to taste
4   cups milk
16   eggs
¼   teaspoon salt
1   cup evaporated milk

Saute bacon in skillet; add beef, ¼ cup butter, and ½ cup mushrooms. Sprinkle flour over bacon mixture; season with pepper. Gradually add milk. Cook and stir over medium heat until thickened; set aside. Beat eggs with salt and evaporated milk. Melt remaining butter in another skillet; pour in eggs. Cook, stirring, until scrambled. In lightly greased 13" x 9" x 2" glass baking dish, make 2 layers each of eggs and chipped beef sauce, ending with sauce. Garnish with remaining mushrooms. Cover tightly with aluminum foil; bake at 275° for 1 hour. *This can be prepared 1 day ahead, refrigerated, and then baked as directed above.*
Yield: 12 servings

Special Egg Casserole

12	slices bacon
1½	tablespoons butter or margarine
1½	tablespoons all-purpose flour
1	cup milk

Salt, pepper to taste

1	cup grated sharp Cheddar cheese
12	eggs
1	(4-ounce) can mushroom pieces, drained

Buttered bread crumbs

Fry bacon in skillet; reserve 2 tablespoons drippings. Drain and crumble cooked bacon. Make a white sauce with butter, flour, and milk. Season with salt and pepper. Add cheese and stir until melted. Scramble eggs in reserved bacon drippings until soft-set. Combine bacon, cheese sauce, eggs, and mushrooms and spoon into a lightly greased 1½-quart casserole. Top with buttered bread crumbs. Bake at 350° for 20-30 minutes. **Yield: 8 servings**

Mexican Green Chili Strata

Great as an appetizer or brunch entrée, served hot or cold

6	thick slices white bread

Butter or margarine

2	cups shredded sharp Cheddar cheese
2	cups shredded Monterey Jack cheese
1	(4-ounce) can chopped green chilies
1½	cups mild salsa
6	eggs
2	cups milk
2	teaspoons garlic salt
1	teaspoon cumin
1	teaspoon chili powder
½	teaspoon pepper

Butter bread; place buttered side down in a greased 13" x 9" x 2" rectangular baking dish. Sprinkle cheeses over bread. Spoon chilies and salsa over cheese. In a bowl, beat together eggs, milk, garlic salt, cumin, chili powder and pepper; pour over casserole dish. Cover; refrigerate overnight. Bake, uncovered, at 325° for 50 minutes or until top is browned. Serve accompanied by additional salsa for more spice. **Yield: 8 servings**

Cheesy Spinach Quiche

This makes a nice lunch served with a slice of cantaloupe and a muffin.

1	9" unbaked deep-dish pastry shell
1	(10-ounce) package frozen chopped spinach
1	(8-ounce) package Swiss cheese slices
2	tablespoons all-purpose flour
3	eggs, beaten
1	cup heavy cream
½	teaspoon salt

Dash pepper

Liberally prick bottom and sides of pie shell with fork. Bake at 375° for 10-12 minutes. Cool on rack. Cook spinach according to package directions; drain well. Cut cheese into ½" slices; toss with flour; set aside. Combine eggs, cream, salt, and pepper. Stir in spinach and cheese. Spoon into pie shell. Bake at 350° for 1 hour. **Yield: 4-6 servings**

Blake's Never Fail Rarebit

This recipe evokes a memory from Castine, Maine, of lunch with Don and Thisbe in their log cottage by the sea.

½	cup all-purpose flour
2	teaspoons dry mustard
2	teaspoons paprika
1½	teaspoons salt
½	cup butter or margarine
18	ounces full-flavored beer
12	ounces grated sharp Cheddar cheese
4-6	slices hot, buttered toast

Freshly ground black pepper

In a measuring cup, mix the flour with mustard, paprika, and salt. In a 2-quart saucepan, melt butter; stir in dry ingredients and cook for 1 minute. Stirring constantly, add enough beer to prevent excessive thickening. When mixture no longer thickens, add cheese, stirring until smooth. Serve rarebit over toast with a sprinkle of pepper. *Goes great with bacon.* **Yield: 4-6 servings**

Delicious Cheese Soufflé

Delicious and easy!

1   (10¾-ounce) can condensed Cheddar cheese soup
6   eggs, separated

In a saucepan, stirring, heat soup. Remove from heat. In a small bowl, beat egg yolks until thick and lemon-colored. Stir into soup. In another large bowl, using a clean egg beater, whip egg whites until stiff. With a spatula, gently fold soup mixture into egg whites. Pour into a greased 2-quart casserole dish. Bake at 300° for 60-75 minutes or at 400° for 30 minutes. Serve immediately. **Yield: 4 servings**

Stuffed Baked French Toast

10-12 slices bread (white, raisin, cinnamon, egg)
4   eggs, divided
2   cups half-and-half
2   teaspoons vanilla, divided
¾   cup granulated sugar, divided
1   (8-ounce) package cream cheese (regular or light)
Nutmeg
Maple or fruit syrup

Trim crusts from bread. Arrange half the slices in the bottom of a lightly greased 11" x 7" x 2" rectangular baking dish so that bread covers the bottom of the dish. In a bowl beat together 3 eggs, half-and-half, 1 teaspoon vanilla, and ½ cup sugar. Pour half over bread. In a separate bowl, combine cream cheese, 1 teaspoon vanilla, 1 egg, and ¼ cup sugar; pour over moistened bread. Arrange other half of bread over top of filling; pour rest of egg mixture over bread. Sprinkle with nutmeg. Cover with foil; let stand in refrigerator overnight. Bake in covered dish at 350° for 30 minutes. Remove foil; bake an additional 30 minutes or until puffy. Let stand for 10 minutes before cutting. Serve with warmed maple or fruit syrup. *Ingredients may be doubled to fill a 3-quart casserole.* **Yield: 6 servings**

❡ *About eggs. . . Store fresh eggs in their carton to help prevent them from absorbing refrigerator odors. Store with large ends up to help keep yolks in the center.*

Serbian Prisnac

This is great for brunch served with sausage links and fresh fruit.

1	pound Monterey Jack cheese, cubed
4	ounces cream cheese
6	tablespoons butter or margarine, cut up
6	eggs, beaten
1	teaspoon baking powder
½	cup all-purpose flour
1	cup milk
1	teaspoon salt
2	teaspoons sugar

Use hands to mix cheeses and butter. Stir in eggs. Combine baking powder and flour; sift into egg mixture. Stir in milk, salt, and sugar. Spoon into greased 13" x 9" x 2" rectangular baking dish, cover; refrigerate overnight. Bake at 350° for 45-55 minutes. **Yield: 8-10 servings**

Tomato Phyllo Pizza

7	17" x 12" sheets phyllo dough
5	tablespoons melted butter or margarine
7	tablespoons grated fresh Parmesan cheese
1	cup coarsely grated mozzarella cheese
1	cup thinly sliced onion
2	pounds tomatoes, sliced ¼" thick
½	teaspoon oregano
¼	teaspoon thyme

Salt, pepper to taste

Stack phyllo between 2 sheets of waxed paper and cover with a dampened paper towel. Brush a baking sheet lightly with some of the butter, lay 1 sheet of phyllo on the butter, and brush lightly again with butter. Sprinkle with 1 tablespoon of the Parmesan, lay another sheet of phyllo on top, and press so that the second layer adheres to the bottom layer. Butter, sprinkle with 1 tablespoon Parmesan, and layer the remaining phyllo in the same manner, ending with   sheet of phyllo and reserving the remaining 1 tablespoon Parmesan. Sprinkle the top layer with mozzarella, and scatter the onion evenly on top. Arrange the tomatoes in one layer over the onion. Sprinkle the pizza with the reserved 1 tablespoon Parmesan, oregano, thyme, salt, and pepper. Bake at 375° for 30-35 minutes.
Yield: 4-5 servings

Side Dishes

Contents

Our Thanks

FOR FOOD AND all Thy gifts of love, we give Thee thanks and praise. Look down, O Father from above, and bless us all our days. *Amen.*

Green Beans with Raspberry Vinegar

1½	pounds fresh green beans
4	slices bacon
1	large onion, thinly sliced
4	tablespoons raspberry vinegar
¾	teaspoon salt
¼	teaspoon pepper

String, snap beans; then cook in boiling water until crisp-tender; drain. Fry bacon until crisp; drain, reserving drippings in skillet. Crumble bacon; set aside. Sauté onion in reserved drippings until transparent. Add green beans, vinegar, salt, and pepper; simmer 10 minutes. Turn into serving dish; top with crumbled bacon. **Yield: 6-8 servings**

Special Green Beans

2½	pounds fresh green beans
3	cups water
1	cup sliced fresh mushrooms
⅓	cup chopped onion
3	cloves garlic, crushed
1	(8-ounce) can sliced water chestnuts, drained
½	teaspoon salt
½	teaspoon freshly ground pepper
½	teaspoon basil
1	teaspoon Italian seasoning
⅓	cup olive oil
¼	cup grated Parmesan cheese

Wash green beans; trim ends and remove strings. Combine beans and water in Dutch oven. Bring to a boil; cover, reduce heat, and simmer 6-8 minutes or until crisp-tender. Drain; set aside. Sauté mushrooms, onion, garlic, water chestnuts, salt, pepper, basil, and Italian seasoning in olive oil in Dutch oven. Stir in beans; cook until thoroughly heated. Sprinkle with Parmesan. **Variation:** Substitute 2 (16-ounce) cans whole green beans for fresh. **Yield: 8-10 servings**

Tangy Green Beans

Even if company isn't coming for dinner, you can dress down with this recipe and still have a taste of gourmet.

4	cups fresh green beans
2	tablespoons prepared mustard
2	tablespoons granulated sugar
⅓	cup butter or margarine
2	tablespoons cider vinegar
2	tablespoons lemon juice
½	teaspoon salt

Cook beans, uncovered, in boiling salted water 2-3 minutes; then cover; cook 20-30 minutes more. Drain; set aside. Combine mustard, sugar, and butter; cook over low heat until butter melts. Stir in vinegar, juice, and salt; add green beans and heat thoroughly. **Yield: 6 servings**

Lima Beans in Sour Cream

This is an original from Cooking Capers.

½	cup finely chopped onion
2	tablespoons butter or margarine, melted
1	(2-ounce) jar diced pimiento
1	(10-ounce) package frozen lima beans, cooked and drained
1	cup sour cream

Salt, pepper to taste

Sauté onion in butter or margarine; stir in pimiento and limas. Gently add sour cream. Season with salt, pepper. Cook over low heat until thoroughly heated and bubbly. **Yield: 4 servings**

Broccoli Casserole

1	cup sour cream
1	cup mayonnaise
½	cup finely chopped onion
4	cups cooked broccoli, drained
2	cups shredded Cheddar cheese
1	(8-ounce) can sliced water chestnuts, drained
¾	cup herb-seasoned stuffing crumbs

In a large bowl, combine sour cream, mayonnaise, onion, broccoli, cheese, and water chestnuts; mix together gently. Spoon into greased 2-quart casserole dish; top with crumbs. Bake at 375° for 35-40 minutes. **Yield: 8 servings**

Honey Mustard Brussels Sprouts

1	pound fresh Brussels sprouts
1½	cups water
½	teaspoon salt
2	tablespoons honey
2	teaspoons prepared mustard
2	teaspoons lemon juice

Cook Brussels sprouts in salted boiling water until tender; drain. In a small bowl, combine honey, mustard, and lemon juice. Pour over hot sprouts; toss to coat. **Variation:** May substitute 1 (10-ounce) package frozen Brussels sprouts if fresh ones are unavailable. **Yield: 6 servings**

Skillet Cabbage

4	cups shredded cabbage
½	cup minced green pepper
2	cups diced celery
2	large onions, sliced
2	medium tomatoes, peeled and chopped
¼	cup bacon drippings
2	teaspoons granulated sugar

Salt, pepper to taste

Combine cabbage, green pepper, celery, onion, tomatoes, and sugar in a large skillet. Quickly bring to a boil, reduce heat to medium, cover, and steam for 10 minutes. **Yield: 6 servings**

Golden Grated Carrots

1	pound carrots, scraped and shredded
2	tablespoons Chablis or other dry white wine
1	tablespoon butter or margarine
1	tablespoon honey
2	teaspoons lemon juice
⅓	cup golden raisins
1½	teaspoons brown sugar
1	teaspoon curry powder

Place carrots in a lightly greased 1½-quart casserole. Add wine, butter, honey, and lemon juice. Cover with heavy-duty plastic wrap; microwave on high for 5-6 minutes or until crisp-tender. Stir in raisins, brown sugar, and curry. Cover; microwave on high for 1-2 minutes more or until thoroughly heated. Let stand, covered, 2 minutes. Stir well; serve immediately. **Yield: 6 servings**

Sweet and Sour Carrots

10	carrots, peeled and cut in strips
1	teaspoon salt
1	tablespoon butter or margarine
½	cup white vinegar
¾	cup granulated sugar
Minced parsley to garnish	

Cook carrots in enough salted water to cover until barely tender. Drain. Combine butter, vinegar, and sugar in saucepan. Cook and stir over low heat for 20 minutes. Pour over carrots. Remove carrots from sauce before serving; sprinkle with parsley. **Yield: 6 servings**

Far East Celery

4	cups celery stalks, cut in 1" pieces
1	(8-ounce) can sliced water chestnuts
1	(10½-ounce) can cream of chicken soup
1	(2-ounce) jar diced pimiento
½	cup soft bread crumbs
¼	cup slivered almonds, toasted
1	tablespoon butter or margarine, melted

Cook celery in boiling water for about 8 minutes; drain. Combine with water chestnuts, soup, and pimiento; spoon into a lightly greased 1-quart casserole. Toss bread crumbs and almonds with butter; sprinkle over top. Bake at 350° for 35 minutes. **Yield: 4-6 servings**

Corn Pudding

1	(8½-ounce) package corn muffin mix
1	(16½-ounce) can cream-style corn
½	cup milk or sour cream
3	eggs, beaten
1	teaspoon salt
1	teaspoon sugar

Combine mix, corn, milk, eggs, salt, and sugar; blend well. Pour into a greased 1½-quart casserole. Bake at 350° for 30 minutes.
Yield: 6-8 servings

Tangier Island Corn Pudding

This recipe is virtually failure-proof!

¼	cup margarine or butter
½	cup sugar
3	tablespoons cornstarch
Dash salt	
2	eggs, slightly beaten
1	(12-ounce) can evaporated milk
1	(15-ounce) can white cream-style corn

Preheat oven to 350°. While oven is heating, put butter in 9" x 9"x 2" glass baking dish; place in oven to melt. In mixing bowl, combine sugar, cornstarch, and salt. Then stir in eggs, milk, and corn. Pour in melted butter; stir. Pour mixture back into baking dish. Bake for 1 hour.
Yield: 6-8 servings

Baked Eggplant

1	medium eggplant, peeled and sliced
3	tablespoons butter or margarine
2	tablespoons all-purpose flour
1	cup milk
½	cup grated cheese
¾	cup soft bread crumbs
2	teaspoons grated onion
1	tablespoon ketchup
⅛	teaspoon pepper
3	eggs, separated

Cook eggplant in hot water until tender, about 15 minutes; drain and mash. Make a thick cream sauce with butter, flour, and milk. Add eggplant, cheese, bread crumbs, onion, ketchup, and pepper. Beat yolks and whites separately. Add yolks; then fold in stiffly beaten egg whites. Pour in mixture into a greased 1½-quart casserole. Set in pan of hot water. Bake at 375° for 30 minutes, then lower heat to 350° for an additional 30 minutes. **Yield: 6 servings**

Baked Onions

This is an original from Cooking Capers.

3	tablespoons butter or margarine
3	tablespoons all-purpose flour
1	cup cream of mushroom soup, undiluted
½	cup white wine
Salt, pepper to taste	
1	(16-ounce) jar small, whole onions, rinsed and drained
½	cup slivered almonds, toasted
½	cup grated sharp Cheddar cheese

Melt butter; stir in flour, soup, and wine. Cook, stirring constantly until thickened and smooth. Season to taste. Add onions and almonds. Spoon into lightly greased 1-quart casserole; sprinkle with cheese. Bake at 375° for 20 minutes or until hot and bubbly. **Yield: 4-5 servings**

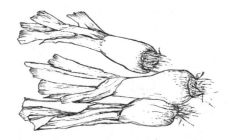

Festive Black-Eyed Peas

2　(14-ounce) cans black-eyed peas
1　medium onion, chopped
2　(14-ounce) cans Italian-style stewed tomatoes, chopped
2　dashes hot pepper sauce
½　cup granulated sugar
Salt, pepper to taste

Combine peas, onion, tomatoes, hot pepper sauce, sugar, salt, and pepper in a saucepan. Cook over low heat, stirring continually so that sugar does not stick. Serve hot. **Yield: 6-8 servings**

Green Peas Parisienne

2　cups shelled green peas
3　tablespoons butter or margarine, divided
¼　cup water
½　teaspoon granulated sugar
Parsley sprigs
½　medium onion, sliced
2-3　tender lettuce leaves
Salt, pepper to taste

Combine peas, 2 tablespoons butter, water, sugar, parsley, onion, and lettuce leaves in saucepan. Cover; cook until peas are tender, about 10-20 minutes. Add additional water only if necessary to keep peas from burning. When done, remove parsley and onion slices. Season with salt and pepper; add remaining butter. **Yield: 4 servings**

Cooking Tips for Vegetables

To retain nutrients, cook vegetables until barely done.

Store mushrooms in the refrigerator in a brown paper bag.

Peel tomatoes easily by dipping them in boiling water for a few seconds.

Vegetables grown underground should be covered during cooking. Vegetables grown above ground should be uncovered during cooking.

Party Peas

1	(10-ounce) package frozen green peas
2	tablespoons butter or margarine
1	cup sliced celery
2	tablespoons finely chopped onion
1	(4-ounce) can sliced mushrooms, drained
3	tablespoons chopped pimiento
¼	teaspoon salt
¼	teaspoon fines herbs

Freshly ground pepper

Cook peas according to package directions; drain and set aside. Melt butter in a medium saucepan; add celery, onion, mushrooms, pimiento, salt, herbs, and pepper; cook until celery is crisp-tender. Add peas; heat thoroughly. **Yield: 4 servings**

Easy Baked Potatoes

2	tablespoons olive or vegetable oil
1	(1.25-ounce) package dehydrated onion soup mix
4-6	red-skinned potatoes, sliced

Pour oil into plastic bag; add soup mix. Add potato slices; shake until potatoes are evenly coated. Spoon into 11" x 7" x 2" rectangular baking dish. Bake at 350° for 25-30 minutes. **Yield: 4 servings**

Company Scalloped Potatoes

1	cup thinly sliced onion
1½	tablespoons butter or margarine, melted
1½	pounds russet potatoes, peeled and thinly sliced
½	teaspoon salt
¼	teaspoon pepper
1½	cups heavy cream
⅓	cup buttered bread crumbs

In a large skillet, sauté the onion in butter until transparent. Remove from heat. Add potato slices, salt, and pepper; toss gently to mix. Spread evenly in a greased 2-quart baking dish. Pour cream over potato slices. Sprinkle bread crumbs on top. Bake at 400° for 10 minutes. Reduce heat to 350°; continue baking for 45 minutes more. **Yield: 6 servings**

❧ *A slice of raw potato is handy for removing vegetable stains.*

Gourmet Cheese Potatoes

1½	pounds all-purpose potatoes
1	quart water
2	cups shredded Muenster cheese
1	cup sour cream
⅓	cup butter or margarine, melted
⅓	cup minced onion
½	teaspoon salt
¼	teaspoon pepper

Paprika

In a large saucepan, bring potatoes and water to a boil over high heat. Reduce heat to medium, cover; cook until potatoes are fork-tender, about 20 minutes. Drain; cool 15 minutes. Peel and shred potatoes into a bowl. Combine cheese, sour cream, butter, onion, salt, and pepper. Fold in potatoes. Spoon mixture into a lightly greased 2-quart casserole; sprinkle top with paprika. Bake at 350° for 30 minutes or until golden brown. *This may be prepared in advance and refrigerated until baking time. Increase baking time 10 minutes.* **Yield: 6-8 servings**

Quick and Easy Scalloped Potatoes

5	medium russet potatoes, peeled
1	cup sour cream
½	cup mayonnaise
1	(10¾-ounce) can cream of chicken soup
¼	cup minced onion

Parboil potatoes for 15 minutes; drain, cool, and slice. Place in greased 2-quart casserole. Combine sour cream, mayonnaise, soup, and onion; spoon over potatoes. Bake at 350° for 30 minutes. **Yield: 4-6 servings**

La Truffade

1	pound firm, white potatoes, sliced
¼	pound thick-sliced bacon, cubed
1	tablespoon vegetable oil
¼	pound Cheddar cheese, cubed

Sauté potatoes and bacon in hot oil in covered heavy skillet. From time to time, flatten mixture with spatula. When the potato mixture is barely done, add cheese. Turn with spatula until cheese begins to thread. Flatten top again with spatula; cover and cook until bottom is brown. Invert on serving platter. *May be used as an entrée.* **Yield: 3-4 servings**

THE ORIGIN OF BRUNSWICK STEW

Brncfwick ftew, taking its name from the county in which it firft faw the light, is, moft diftinctively, a Virginia delicacy. The exact origin of this choice concoction lies veiled in the paft; even its component elements form a bafis for hotly contefted arguments; although all agree that the one ingredient is fquirrel. A ftory runs that once upon a time an amply provifioned hunting party made camp in the woods during fquirrel feafon. On a certain day the hunters went out leaving one of their number to prepare dinner againft their return. The difgruntled fportfman, not difposed fo to fpend his time while the others were enjoying the pleafures of the fport, fimply toffed into a pot of boiling water fome of every ingredient in the commiffary and allowed the mixture to boil until his companions' return. The provifions in that camp included fquirrel, tomatoes, onions, cabbage, butterbeans, red pepper, bacon, falt and corn. To the furprife of the unwilling chef, for he knew not what had gone into the pot any more than his affociates, he had become the originator of a moft delectable difh.

BRUNSWICK STEW

Stew ten large fquirrels, or fame weight in hens, until the meat leaves the bone. Remove bones and fkin. Then add one quart of butterbeans, three pints of tomatoes, two large onions, one quart of okra, an old ham bone, and fix potatoes. Seafon with falt, red pepper, Worcefterfhire fauce, one-half pound of butter, and add one quart cut corn one-half hour before finifhed. Boil all until it is well done and ferve hot. Takes about fix hours to cook. It fhould be thick like a ftew and not thin like foup.

St. John's Church
RICHMOND, VIRGINIA
CIRCA 1741

HENRICO PARISH, ENCOMPASSING present-day Richmond, was formed in 1611, only four years after the settlement of Jamestown. During the subsequent hundred years, various churches and parishes were established in the surrounding area. St. John's Church was built by Richard Randolph on "Indian Town at Richmond." Two lots donated by William Byrd II, founder of Richmond, now constitute part of the cemetery. The Virginia Convention met here in 1775, at which time Patrick Henry gave his fiery "give me liberty or give me death" speech. Buried in its churchyard are George Wythe and Elizabeth Poe, mother of Edgar Allan Poe.

Sweet Potato Casserole

For several years we have brought this dish to share
at St. Stephen's annual Thanksgiving dinner.

Pudding:
3	cups mashed, cooked sweet potatoes
¾	cup granulated sugar
½	cup butter or margarine
2	eggs, beaten
1	teaspoon vanilla
⅓	cup milk

Topping:

1	cup light brown sugar
½	cup all-purpose flour, sifted
⅓	cup butter or margarine, softened
1	cup chopped pecans

PUDDING: In a large bowl, mix together the potatoes, sugar, butter, eggs, vanilla, and milk. Spoon into greased 10" x 10" x 2" casserole.

TOPPING: In a small bowl, combine brown sugar, flour, butter, and pecans. Sprinkle over potato mixture. Bake at 325° for 25 minutes. **Yield: 6 servings**

Sweet Potato Soufflé

2	cups hot, mashed, cooked sweet potatoes
½	cup butter or margarine
1	cup evaporated milk or light cream
1	cup granulated sugar
½	teaspoon salt
2	eggs, lightly beaten
¼	teaspoon cinnamon
¼	teaspoon nutmeg
2	teaspoons vanilla

Miniature marshmallows, if desired

Combine potatoes, butter, milk, sugar, and salt. Beat well with mixer. Add eggs. Stir in cinnamon, nutmeg, and vanilla. Spoon into a greased 2-quart casserole dish. Bake at 350° for 50 minutes or until set. If desired, top with marshmallows; return to oven for 5-10 minutes to brown marshmallows. **Yield: 8 servings**

Apple-Sweet Potato Casserole

This is delicious—and without fat!

1¼	pounds sweet potatoes
½	cup water
1	pound cooking apples
1	cup apple or orange juice
2	tablespoons cornstarch
3	tablespoons water
¼	cup sugar
½	teaspoon cinnamon

Steam potatoes in water 15-20 minutes, or until tender. Peel and slice lengthwise into ½" thick slices. Place in bottom of an 13" x 9" x 2" baking dish that has been coated with non-stick vegetable spray. Peel, core, and slice apples ½" thick. Place apple slices on top of potatoes. In small saucepan, heat juice to boiling; add cornstarch that has been mixed with 3 tablespoons water. Cook until sauce bubbles and thickens. Add sugar and cinnamon. Spoon sauce over sweet potatoes and apples. Bake at 350° for 30-60 minutes or until apples are tender. **Yield: 6 servings**

Rice Parisienne

This is an original from Cooking Capers.

½	cup long-grain rice
2	tablespoons butter or margarine, melted
1	(10¾-ounce) can onion soup
½	soup can water
1	(4-ounce) can sliced mushrooms, drained

Brown rice in butter. Add soup, water, and mushrooms. Cover and simmer for 55 minutes. **Yield: 4 servings**

Fruit 'n Rice

1	cup mixed brown and wild rice
½	cup chopped dried apricots
½	cup Muscat raisins
⅔	cup mixed nuts and roasted soy beans
Vegetable oil	
½	cup tahini (sesame paste)
Honey	

Cook rice according to package directions. Sauté apricots, raisins, and nut mixture in a small amount of vegetable oil. Stir in tahini and cooked rice. Sweeten with honey to taste. **Yield: 4 servings**

Baked Wild Rice

1	(28-ounce) can whole tomatoes
2	cups uncooked wild rice or wild and brown rice mix
2	cups shredded white Cheddar cheese
12	Spanish olives, sliced
1	(12-ounce) package fresh mushrooms, sliced and sautéed in butter or margarine

Chop tomatoes coarsely; reserve all juice. Add rice, cheese, olives, mushrooms, and reserved juice. Spoon into a lightly greased 13" x 9" x 2" glass baking dish. Cover tightly. Bake at 325° for 1½ hours. **Yield: 12 servings**

Wild Rice Casserole

1	cup wild rice, rinsed and drained
½	cup chopped onion
⅓	cup minced celery
1	teaspoon seasoned salt
½	cup white wine
2	tablespoons butter or margarine, melted
4	cups chicken broth
Salt, pepper to taste	

Combine rice, onion, celery, salt, wine, butter, and broth; pour into greased 2-quart casserole. Cover; bake at 325° for 2 hours or until all liquid is absorbed. *Freezes well. May be prepared ahead of time. Halves successfully.* **Yield: 10-12 servings**

Evelyn's Sweet and Sauerkraut

My mother makes this to go with Thanksgiving turkey.

½   large onion, thinly sliced
1   tablespoon butter or margarine, melted
1   (32-ounce) jar crispy sauerkraut, drained and juice
        reserved
½   cup light brown sugar
1   teaspoon caraway seed
Freshly ground black pepper to taste

Sauté onion in butter until soft and slightly golden. Add sauerkraut and enough reserved juice to keep moist. Sprinkle brown sugar over all; stir to blend well, adding more juice if needed. Taste for sweetness and add additional sugar if needed. Add caraway seed and pepper. Cook, uncovered, over low heat for about 5 minutes or until hot. Allow to sit, covered, at room temperature for 15 minutes. Serve warm or at room temperature. *Also great with pork.* **Yield: 8 servings**

Spinach-Artichoke Supreme

2   (10-ounce) packages frozen chopped spinach
5   tablespoons butter or margarine, softened
1   (8-ounce) package cream cheese
1   (8-ounce) can sliced water chestnuts, drained
1   small onion, chopped
Pepper to taste
1   (15-ounce) can artichoke hearts (not marinated),
        drained
3   tablespoons plain fine bread crumbs
2   tablespoons grated Parmesan cheese

Cook spinach in boiling water to cover; drain and set aside. Combine butter, cream cheese, water chestnuts, onion, and pepper; fold in spinach. Line bottom of greased 2-quart casserole with artichokes. Spoon spinach mixture over artichokes. Mix bread crumbs and Parmesan; sprinkle on top. Bake at 350° for 30 minutes. **Yield: 8-10 servings**

Spinach Parmesan

Guaranteed to appeal even to men, this is an original from Cooking Capers.

3	pounds fresh spinach, washed and drained
6	tablespoons grated Parmesan cheese
6	tablespoons minced onion
6	tablespoons heavy cream
5	tablespoons butter or margarine, melted, and divided
½	cup soft bread crumbs

Cook spinach in boiling water until tender. Drain; chop coarsely. Combine with cheese, onion, cream, and 4 tablespoons butter. Spoon into lightly greased rectangular 11" x 7" x 2" glass baking dish. Toss bread crumbs with remaining butter; sprinkle over spinach. Bake at 350° for 20-25 minutes, or until bubbly and golden. **Yield: 8-10 servings**

Squash Casserole

This is great—leftovers can be frozen.

6	cups sliced yellow or green squash
¼	cup chopped onion
½	cup butter or margarine, melted
1	(8-ounce) package herb-seasoned stuffing
1	cup sour cream
1	(10¾-ounce) can cream of chicken soup
1	cup shredded, peeled carrots

Parboil squash and onion for 5 minutes; drain. Combine butter and stuffing; press half this mixture on the bottom of a greased 9" x 9" x 2" casserole. In a large bowl, combine sour cream and soup. Stir in carrots, squash mixture, and one-fourth of the stuffing mixture. Spread over stuffing in dish. Top with remaining stuffing. Bake at 350° for 30 minutes, or until hot and bubbly. **Yield: 8-10 servings**

❧ *Always have water boiling before putting vegetables in; smart cooks salt the water in which they boil vegetables.*

❧ *Cook vegetables in beef or chicken stock for added flavor.*

Spaghetti Squash and Variations

Here's an extremely versatile veggie with some original ideas for its use after easy microwave cooking.

With a sharp, strong knife, cut 1 spaghetti squash in half lengthwise. Scrape out seeds and discard. Place on microwave-safe dish with about a cup water added to dish. Cover loosely with waxed paper; cook on high for 3-6 minutes; turn over and repeat cooking cycle. Feel for softness to determine doneness. A very large squash will require a longer cooking time. Allow to cool for easy handling. With a fork, scrape out the "spaghetti" strings into a bowl and proceed with one of the variations listed below. **Yield: 8-10 servings**

With string beans:

1	(10-ounce) package frozen green beans
1	cup fresh broccoli florets
½	cup sautéed fresh mushroom slices
1	cup sour cream French onion dip
1	medium spaghetti squash, cooked
Grated Parmesan cheese	

Steam green beans and broccoli until barely done; drain. Combine with mushrooms, dip, and spaghetti squash. Spoon into a greased 2-quart casserole. Top with Parmesan. Bake at 350° for 30 minutes.

Dieter's Delight:

1	(10-ounce) package frozen French green beans or green peas
1	(.7-ounce) envelope Italian dressing seasoning mix
½	cup light mayonnaise or no-fat sour cream
1	medium spaghetti squash, cooked

Steam green beans or peas; drain. Combine dressing mix and mayonnaise (or sour cream); fold in green beans and squash. Spoon into a greased 2-quart casserole. Bake at 350° for 30 minutes.

Variation: May also substitute cooked spaghetti squash for pasta with tomato- or cheese-based sauces or may serve simply with seasonings of choice and butter or margarine.

Green Tomato Casserole

Green tomatoes, peeled and cubed
Granulated sugar, salt, and pepper to taste
Herb-seasoned stuffing crumbs
Butter or margarine

Cover bottom of greased casserole with tomatoes. Sprinkle generously with sugar; season with salt and pepper; top with stuffing crumbs; dot with butter. Repeat. Bake at 325° until well done. *Ingredient amounts depend on the number of tomatoes used.*

Baked Tomatoes Parmesan

Use winter tomatoes for this dish.

4-6	medium-to-large tomatoes, unpeeled
¼	cup vegetable oil
¾	cup grated Parmesan cheese
¼	cup butter or margarine

Slice off stem ends and tops of tomatoes; cut into ½" slices. Brush both sides of slices with oil. Place slices in a single layer in lightly greased 13" x 9" x 2" glass baking dish. Top each tomato slice with 1 tablespoon cheese; dot with butter. Bake at 350° for 20 minutes or until tops are golden brown. **Yield: 6 servings**

Tomato Casserole

3½	cups cubed, peeled tomatoes
1	cup chopped onion
2	teaspoons granulated sugar
½	teaspoon salt
1	cup cheese-flavored (white Cheddar preferable) cracker crumbs
1	cup sour cream
1½	cups seasoned croutons
1	tablespoon melted butter or margarine

Coat a 1½-quart glass casserole dish with non-stick vegetable spray. In this, layer half the tomatoes, half the onion, half the sugar, half the salt, and half the cracker crumbs. Repeat. Bake at 325° for 30 minutes. Remove; add sour cream and croutons; drizzle with butter. Return to oven and bake for 10 minutes more. **Yield: 8 servings**

Summer Delight

¼	cup brown sugar
2	teaspoons salt
½	teaspoon black pepper
½	cup uncooked regular rice
1	small eggplant, peeled and sliced
1	large onion, sliced
3	medium yellow squash, peeled and sliced
3	medium zucchini, sliced
1	large green pepper, seeded and sliced
3	large tomatoes, peeled and sliced
1	cup grated Parmesan cheese
2	tablespoons butter or margarine

Combine brown sugar, salt, and pepper; set aside. Place rice in bottom of lightly greased 13" x 9" x 2" glass baking dish. Next layer eggplant, onion, squash, zucchini, green pepper, and tomato in dish. Sprinkle brown sugar mixture and Parmesan over top. Dot with butter. Cover tightly. Bake at 350° for 1½ hours or until rice and vegetables are tender.
Yield: 10-12 servings

Fettucine Primavera

1	(12-ounce) package fettucine noodles
¼	cup butter or margarine
1	cup broccoli florets
1	cup sliced zucchini
½	cup diced green pepper
½	cup chopped onion
½	teaspoon dried basil
2	medium tomatoes, cut into wedges
½	cup sliced mushrooms
	Grated Parmesan cheese

Cook pasta according to package directions; drain well. Meanwhile, melt butter in skillet over medium heat; add broccoli, zucchini, green pepper, onion, and basil. Cook until vegetables are barely tender. Stir in tomatoes and mushrooms. Toss with hot pasta. Serve with Parmesan.
Yield: 5 servings

❡ *To preserve natural sweetness of carrots, cook with peelings on. The peeling will slip right off when the carrots are plunged into cold water.*

Angelic Primavera Pasta

4	ounces angel hair pasta, uncooked
6	tablespoons melted butter or margarine, divided
½	cup grated Parmesan cheese
1½	teaspoons garlic salt
4	beaten eggs, divided
½	cup chopped onion
1	(2½-ounce) jar chopped mushrooms, drained
1	cup skim milk
1	teaspoon minced garlic
⅛	teaspoon pepper
1	(16-ounce) bag frozen broccoli, carrot, cauliflower medley
1	cup shredded Monterey Jack cheese

Cook pasta according to package directions; drain. In a large bowl, combine pasta, 3 tablespoons butter, Parmesan, and garlic salt. Fold in 2 beaten eggs. Spread in 10" pie plate that has been coated with non-stick cooking spray. Bake at 350° for 12-15 minutes. Meanwhile, melt remaining butter in skillet; sauté onion and mushrooms. Add milk, remaining eggs, garlic, and pepper. Microwave vegetables for 3 minutes; add to sauce. Pour mixture over pasta crust; sprinkle with cheese. Bake at 350° for 20-25 minutes or until bubbly. *May substitute 1 cup 99% egg product for beaten eggs.* **Yield: 6-8 servings**

Vegetables à la Napoli

2	cups sliced zucchini
2	medium onions, sliced
1	(6-ounce) can sliced ripe olives, drained
⅓	cup olive oil
2	(10-ounce) packages frozen chopped broccoli, thawed
1	teaspoon oregano
1½	teaspoons salt
2	cloves garlic, minced
½	teaspoon basil
⅓	cup brandy
1	(16-ounce) can plum tomatoes, puréed
Grated Parmesan cheese	

Combine zucchini, onions, olives, olive oil, broccoli, oregano, salt, garlic, basil, and brandy; spoon into greased 2-quart casserole dish. Pour tomatoes over vegetables. Cover tightly. Bake at 350° for 1 hour. Uncover; sprinkle generously with cheese; bake for 15 minutes more. **Yield: 8-10 servings**

Garden Zucchini Pie

5	medium russet potatoes, peeled
4	beaten eggs, divided
¼	cup chopped onion
¼	cup grated Parmesan cheese
2½	cups thinly sliced zucchini
1	tablespoon butter or margarine
¾	cup shredded Swiss or Cheddar cheese
½	cup milk
½	teaspoon oregano
¼	teaspoon each salt, pepper

Coarsely shred potatoes in food processor; immediately place in a bowl of ice water. Rinse shreds well and drain; squeeze dry with paper towels. In a large bowl, combine potatoes, 1 egg, onion, and Parmesan. Pat mixture into a greased 10" pie plate. Bake at 400° for 35-40 minutes. Cool slightly on rack. In a large skillet, cook zucchini in butter until crisp-tender; arrange atop crust. Combine the remaining eggs, cheese, milk, oregano, salt, and pepper. Pour over zucchini. Bake at 350° for 25-30 minutes or until filling sets. Let stand 10 minutes before serving. **Yield: 8 servings**

Ginger Sauce

Serve this over hot fresh vegetables like broccoli,
Brussels sprouts, asparagus.

1	cup sour cream
1-2	tablespoons finely chopped fresh ginger root
2-3	teaspoons lemon juice

Salt, pepper to taste

Combine sour cream, ginger, lemon juice, salt, and pepper. Store in refrigerator at least 6 hours before serving. **Yield: 1 cup**

Scalloped Apples

⅔   cup granulated sugar
½   cup light brown sugar
3   tablespoons all-purpose flour
½   teaspoon cinnamon
¼   teaspoon nutmeg
¼   teaspoon salt
6-7   medium Macintosh apples, peeled and sliced
3   tablespoons water
¼   cup butter or margarine

In a large bowl, combine sugars, flour, cinnamon, nutmeg, and salt; set aside. Gently mix in apple slices. Spoon mixture into a greased 2-quart casserole dish. Dribble water over top; dot with butter. Bake, uncovered, at 350° for 1 hour. **Variation:**   May substitute Granny Smith or any other variety of tart, firm cooking apple for Macintosh. **Yield: 8 servings**

Pineapple Gratin

Here's an excellent accompaniment to roast pork or ham.

1   cup granulated sugar
⅓   cup all-purpose flour
2   (15½-ounce) cans chunk pineapple, drained; juice reserved
2   cups grated Cheddar cheese
8-10   round buttery crackers
4   tablespoons butter or margarine

Combine sugar and flour. Stir in reserved juice, pineapple, and cheese. Pour into greased 2-quart baking dish. Crumble crackers on top; dot with butter. Bake at 350° for 30 minutes. **Yield: 6-8 servings**

Homestead Fruit Dressing

1	(16-ounce) can cling peaches
1	(16-ounce) can sliced pears
1	(16-ounce) can pineapple chunks
⅓	cup raisins
½	cup chopped walnuts
¾	cup brown sugar, divided
1	teaspoon vanilla
1	(16-ounce) can apricot halves
½	cup butter or margarine, melted
5	slices white bread, toasted

Drain peaches, pears, and pineapple together in colander; transfer to large bowl. Add raisins, walnuts, ½ cup brown sugar, and vanilla. Stir gently, being careful not to break up fruit. Spoon into lightly greased 13" x 9" x 2" glass baking dish. Drain apricots separately and place on top of fruit. Cut toast into ½" squares; scatter over fruit. Mix remaining brown sugar with melted butter; drizzle over top. Bake at 325° for 30 minutes.
Yield: 8-10 servings

Baked Fruit Compote

1	(16-ounce) can apricot halves, drained
1	(16-ounce) can purple plums, drained
1	(16-ounce) can peach halves, drained
3-4	thin orange slices, halved
½	cup orange juice
¼	cup brown sugar
½	teaspoon grated lemon zest
2	tablespoons butter or margarine, melted
½	cup flaked coconut

Arrange apricots and plums in rows in a lightly greased 13" x 9" x 2" glass baking dish. Add peach halves, alternating with orange slices. In a small bowl, combine juice, sugar, and lemon zest. Pour over fruit. Drizzle melted butter over fruit and top with coconut. Bake at 425° for 15 minutes.
Yield: 8 servings

Chutney

*An original from P. S., this relish is simply delicious
and wonderful to sell at bazaars.*

2	ounces garlic
2	pounds onions
8	pounds hard apples or pears, peeled, cored, and coarsely chopped
Cider vinegar	
6	pounds granulated sugar
3	pounds seedless raisins
1	tablespoon dry mustard
1	pound crystallized ginger, chopped

Force garlic and onions through a meat grinder or food processor. Transfer mixture to large stock pot. Stir in fruit and enough vinegar to cover. Bring to a boil and cook to pulp stage. Add sugar and boil for 10 minutes. Add raisins, mustard, and ginger. When chutney boils, reduce heat and simmer for 30 minutes. Seal in sterilized jars.
Yield: 8-10 half-pints

Pear Chutney

6	pounds (or more) ripe pears
5	oranges, peeled, seeded, and chopped
2	cups chopped onion
4	cups cider vinegar
1	cup water
1	(1-pound) package currants or raisins
2	pounds dark brown sugar
2	tablespoons mustard seed
1	teaspoon minced garlic
2	teaspoons red pepper flakes
½	teaspoon ground allspice
1	teaspoon ground cloves
1	teaspoon ground ginger

Combine pears, oranges, onion, vinegar, water, currants, sugar, mustard seed, garlic, red pepper, allspice, cloves, and ginger in large pot. Bring mixture to a boil, stirring. Reduce heat; simmer for 2 hours. Ladle into hot sterilized jars; seal. **Yield: 10 half-pints**

Updated Cranberry Sauce

1¼   cups granulated sugar
½   cup raspberry vinegar
¼   cup water
1   (12-ounce) package fresh cranberries
1   cinnamon stick
1   tablespoon grated orange zest

Combine sugar, vinegar, and water in medium saucepan. Bring to a boil; cook until sugar dissolves. Mix in cranberries, cinnamon stick, and orange zest. Reduce heat, cover partially, and simmer about 10 minutes or until berries burst. Remove from heat. Cool completely. Discard cinnamon stick. Refrigerate up to 2 weeks. **Yield: 2½ cups**

Cranberry Port Jelly

Good with game, roasts of all kinds, and on bread!

3   cups granulated sugar
1   cup cranberry juice
1   cup port wine
3   ounces liquid fruit pectin

In top of a double boiler, over rapidly boiling water, combine sugar, juice, and wine. Mix well; stir until sugar dissolves, about 2 minutes. Remove from heat. Immediately stir in pectin; mix well. Skim off foam. Ladle into sterilized jars and seal with melted paraffin. **Variation:** May replace 1 cup cranberry juice with 1 cup port or may substitute any other sweet wine for port. **Yield: 4 cups**

Pear Honey

8   cups peeled, chopped ripe pears
6   cups granulated sugar
2   cups crushed pineapple
1   lemon, thinly sliced
1   cup grated coconut

Mix pears, sugar, pineapple, and lemon slices in large pot. Bring to a boil, stirring occasionally. Reduce heat and simmer, stirring, for about 30 minutes or until thickened. Remove from heat; stir in coconut. Pour into sterilized jars; seal with melted paraffin. **Yield: 3-4 pints**

Freezer Peach Jam

2	pounds ripe fresh peaches, peeled
	Ascorbic acid
2	tablespoons lemon juice
5½	cups granulated sugar
1	(¾-ounce) package powdered fruit pectin
¾	cup water

Purée peaches in blender; treat with ascorbic acid according to package directions. Measure 2½ cups of pulp; if necessary, add enough water to make 2½ cups. Add lemon juice; stir in sugar. In a small saucepan, combine pectin and ¾ cup water. Bring to a boil. Boil hard for 1 minute, stirring constantly. Stir pectin into fruit mixture. Continue stirring for 3 minutes. Quickly ladle into clean jars; cover and let set for 24 hours. Store for 3 weeks in refrigerator or for 1 year in freezer.
Yield: 7 half-pints

Strawberry Preserves

4	cups strawberries
4	cups granulated sugar
2	tablespoons cider vinegar

Wash, drain, and de-cap strawberries; put in nonmetallic pot; add sugar. Cook, stir, and bring to a boil. As soon as mixture boils, set timer for 18 minutes; continue boiling until time is up. Remove from heat, stir in vinegar, cover; let sit overnight. The next morning, skim off any accumulated foam, and ladle preserves into hot, sterilized jars. Seal with melted paraffin or process in hot water bath. **Yield: 2-4 pints**

Onion Relish

This original from P. S. is great with cold roast beef.

2	cups thinly sliced onions
½	cup water
	Cider vinegar
¼	cup mayonnaise
1½	teaspoons celery seed
	Salt to taste

Place onion slices in shallow dish. Pour water over; add enough vinegar to cover. Cover; refrigerate 3-4 hours. Just before serving, drain onions well and gently mix with mayonnaise, celery seed, and salt.
Yield: 4-6 servings

Bread and Butter Pickles

½   cup salt
4   quarts sliced cucumbers (40-50)
Ice cubes
2   quarts sliced onions (10-12)
5   cups cider vinegar
2   tablespoons celery seed
2   tablespoons ginger
4   cups granulated sugar
2   tablespoons white mustard seed
1   tablespoon turmeric

Gently stir salt into cucumbers. Cover with ice cubes; let stand 2-3 hours or until cucumbers are crisp and cold. Add more ice if it melts. Drain; add onions. In a large pot, combine vinegar, celery seed, ginger, sugar, mustard seed, and turmeric. Bring to a boil and boil for 10 minutes before adding cucumbers and onion. Bring to a boil; pack in hot jars. Adjust lids. Process in boiling water bath (212°) for 30 minutes. **Yield: 8 pints**

Ice Pickles

2   cups slaked lime
2   gallons water
7   pounds pickling cucumbers, sliced ¼" thick
3   tablespoons salt
4   pounds granulated sugar
4   tablespoons mixed whole pickling spice
3   quarts cider vinegar

Combine lime and water in large crock. Add cucumbers and soak in lime solution for 24 hours. Drain off solution, rinse cucumbers well, and soak in clear water for 2 hours; drain. In a large non-aluminum pot, mix salt, sugar, pickling spices, and vinegar; bring to a boil. Add cucumbers and simmer 2½-3 hours. Pack pickles in hot, sterilized jars; reheat syrup to boiling; pour over pickles. Seal at once. Process in boiling water bath (212°) for 5 minutes. **Yield: 8 pints**

Watermelon Rind Pickle

As a surprise for my mother's 65th birthday, we entered these pickles in the 1977 state fair and they won a blue ribbon!

10	pounds watermelon rind from 2 large melons
⅛	cup slaked lime (calcium hydroxide)
1	gallon water
8	pounds granulated sugar
2	quarts cider vinegar
1	(¾-ounce) package whole mixed pickling spice
1	(¾-ounce) package whole cloves, divided
4	sticks cinnamon

Cut watermelons in half; remove flesh and seeds. Scrape rind to remove all traces of pink. Cut rind crosswise into 1" wide strips. Peel green skin from the rind. Cut away any bad spots. Cut rind into 2" lengths. Prepare lime water by mixing slaked lime with water. Agitate mixture vigorously and repeatedly over an hour. After allowing excess solid lime to settle, pour off saturated lime water solution into a second container. Add rind pieces to lime water; soak overnight.

Next morning rinse rind 3 times in fresh, clear water. Put rind into large kettle; cover with salted water. Boil for 20 minutes. Drain off water and then add enough cold water to cover rind. Bring to the boil again; drain; set aside.

Tie pickling spice and half the cloves together in cheesecloth bag. Combine sugar and vinegar in kettle; add cheesecloth bag, reserved cloves, and cinnamon sticks. Bring syrup to a boil; simmer until sugar dissolves. Stir in the reserved rind; simmer for 1 hour. Sterilize jars, lids, and bands. Transfer hot rind to jars; pour hot syrup over rind. Place hot lids on jars; turn screw bands. Process in hot water bath for 10 minutes.
Yield: 10-12 pints

Breads

Contents

Our Thanks

G OD IS GREAT, God is good, let us thank Him for our food. By His hand we all are fed. Give us Lord, our daily bread. *Amen.*

B LESSED ART THOU, O Lord our God, King of the Universe, who bringeth forth bread from the earth. *Amen.*

B E PRESENT AT this table, Lord. Be here and everywhere adored. Please bless this food and grant that we may dwell in paradise with Thee. *Amen.*

Apple Citrus Danish

2	cups finely chopped apples
⅓	cup granulated sugar
2	tablespoons all-purpose flour
1	teaspoon grated orange rind
½	teaspoon cinnamon
3	(4-ounce) cans refrigerator crescent rolls
¾	cup sifted confectioner's sugar
1	tablespoon orange juice

In small bowl, combine apples, sugar, flour, orange rind, and cinnamon. Mix well. Separate crescent rolls; place 1 tablespoon filling in center of each roll. Fold the two points of the triangle over to the square corner. Press edges to seal, leaving diagonal slit unsealed. Bake at 300° for 10-15 minutes until golden brown. Combine confectioner's sugar and orange juice; stir until smooth. Spoon over warm rolls. **Yield: 12 rolls**

Banana Bread

¾	cup butter or margarine
1½	cups granulated sugar
1½	cups mashed ripe bananas
2	eggs, well beaten
1	teaspoon vanilla
2	cups sifted all-purpose flour
1	teaspoon baking soda
¾	teaspoon salt
½	cup buttermilk
¾	cup chopped pecans

Cream butter and sugar thoroughly; blend in bananas, eggs, and vanilla. Sift flour, baking soda, and salt together; add to banana mixture alternately with buttermilk. Mix thoroughly. Fold in pecans. Spoon batter into 2 greased and floured 8½" x 4½" x 2½" loaf pans. Bake at 325° for 1 hour. Cool in pans 10 minutes; invert on wire rack to continue cooling. **Yield: 2 loaves**

Whole Wheat Banana Bread

Only 140 calories per slice and 4 grams of fat!

1¼	cups all-purpose flour
½	cup whole wheat flour
1	teaspoon baking soda
¼	teaspoon salt
½	cup granulated sugar
¼	cup vegetable oil
1	egg
1	cup mashed banana
1	teaspoon vanilla

Mix together white, wheat flours, baking soda, and salt. In a separate bowl, combine sugar and oil; beat with mixer 2 minutes. Add egg to sugar mixture; beat until light and lemon-colored. Alternately add dry ingredients and banana, beginning and ending with flour mixture. Stir in vanilla. Pour into 8" x 4" x 2" loaf pan coated with non-fat cooking spray. Bake at 350° for 45 minutes. Cool in pan on rack 15 minutes; remove from pan to cool completely. **Yield: 16 servings**

Blueberry Bread

3	cups unsifted all-purpose flour
2	teaspoons baking powder
1	teaspoon baking soda
½	teaspoon salt
⅔	cup shortening
1⅓	cups granulated sugar
4	eggs
½	cup milk
1½	teaspoons lemon juice
2	cups fresh blueberries, rinsed and drained

Sift flour with baking powder, soda, and salt; set aside. Cream shortening and sugar together until light and fluffy. Stir in eggs, milk, and lemon juice; add sifted ingredients. Gently fold in blueberries. Spoon batter into 2 greased-and-floured 8½" x 4½" x 2½" loaf pans. Bake at 350° for 40-45 minutes. **Yield: 2 loaves**

Chocolate Chip Scones

3	cups all-purpose flour
1	tablespoon baking powder
1	cup butter or margarine, at room temperature
6	tablespoons granulated sugar
3	eggs
⅓	cup buttermilk
½	cup semi-sweet chocolate chips

Mix flour and baking powder in a bowl. In separate, large bowl, cream butter and sugar together for 3-5 minutes until light and fluffy. Add eggs, one at time, beating after each addition. Add flour mixture and mix just until blended. By hand, fold in chocolate chips. Scoop ⅓-cupfuls of dough onto ungreased cookie sheet, spacing mounds about 2" apart. Bake at 350° for 15 minutes; reduce heat to 325° and bake about 13 minutes longer. **Yield: 1 dozen**

Lemon Bread

Bread:

1¾	cups all-purpose flour
1	teaspoon baking powder
¾	teaspoon baking soda
¼	teaspoon salt
¾	cup granulated sugar
1	tablespoon grated lemon rind
1	egg, beaten
1	cup lemon yogurt
6	tablespoons butter or margarine, melted
1	tablespoon lemon juice

Glaze:

¼	cup granulated sugar
2	teaspoons grated lemon rind
⅓	cup lemon juice

BREAD: Combine flour, baking powder, soda, salt, sugar, and lemon rind in large bowl. Make a well in center; set aside. Combine egg, yogurt, butter, and lemon juice in another bowl. Add to flour mixture, stirring just until moistened. Spoon batter into 8½" x 4½" x 2½" greased loaf pan or 4 mini pans. Bake at 350° for 1 hour or until wooden pick inserted in center comes out clean. GLAZE: Mix sugar, lemon rind and lemon juice until sugar is dissolved. Pour glaze over top while bread is still warm. **Yield: 1 large or 4 mini-loaves**

Monkey Bread

1¼	cups granulated sugar, divided
2	tablespoons cinnamon
3	(10-ounce) cans refrigerated biscuits, quartered
½	cup butter or margarine, melted
1	teaspoon vanilla

Mix ½ cup sugar and cinnamon; toss with biscuit pieces. Layer biscuit pieces in greased 12-cup Bundt pan. In a small saucepan, combine remaining sugar, butter, and vanilla; bring to a boil; pour over biscuit pieces. Bake at 350° for 30 minutes. Invert on serving plate.
Yield: 1 coffee cake

Janet's Pumpkin Bread

3	cups granulated sugar
⅔	cups butter or margarine
1	cup vegetable oil
4	eggs, slightly beaten
3½	cups all-purpose flour
2	teaspoons baking soda
½	teaspoon salt
½	teaspoon baking powder
½	teaspoon ground cloves
½	teaspoon cinnamon
½	teaspoon nutmeg
2	cups cooked pumpkin or winter squash
	Raisins plumped in hot water, or nuts as desired

Cream together sugar, margarine, oil, and eggs; set aside. Sift together flour, baking soda, salt, baking powder, cloves, cinnamon, nutmeg; add alternately with pumpkin to egg mixture. Pour into 4 greased and floured 8" x 4" x 2½" loaf pans or 24 greased muffin cups. Bake at 350° for 45 minutes. **Yield: 4 loaves or 24 muffins**

Breakfast Biscuits

4   cups self-rising flour
1   teaspoon granulated sugar
1   teaspoon baking powder
⅓   cup shortening
2   cups buttermilk
Melted butter or margarine for brushing on tops of biscuits

Mix flour, sugar and baking powder. Cut in shortening until mixture resembles coarse meal. Stir in buttermilk. Knead dough several strokes. Roll out on floured board or counter top; cut with floured biscuit cutter. Bake at 450° for 12 minutes. Brush tops with melted butter.
Yield: 2 dozen

Tips for Successful Bread Making

When biscuits are tough, too much flour or too little shortening may have been the cause.

Use shiny pans and cookie sheets, which reflect heat, for muffins, coffee cakes, and breads.

Grease bottoms only of muffins cups to guarantee that muffins will be nicely shaped and have no rims around the top edges.

Frozen Cheese Biscuits

2   cups sifted all-purpose flour
4   teaspoons baking powder
2   teaspoons granulated sugar
½   teaspoon salt
½   teaspoon cream of tartar
½   cup shortening
⅓   pound grated sharp cheese
⅔   cup milk

Sift flour, baking powder, sugar, salt, and cream of tartar into a bowl. Cut in shortening, then cheese. Add milk, mixing thoroughly. Roll ¾" thick; then cut into rounds. Freeze on cookie sheet; then put into freezer bags until ready to bake. Bake at 300° for 10 minutes and then at 450° for 10 minutes. If not frozen, bake at 425° for 10-12 minutes. **Yield: 2 dozen**

Sweet Potato Biscuits

2	medium-sized sweet potatoes, baked and peeled
¼	cup packed dark brown sugar
3	cups all-purpose flour
1½	tablespoons baking powder
½	teaspoon salt
1	teaspoon ground cinnamon
½	teaspoon ground nutmeg
½	teaspoon ground mace
1	teaspoon grated lemon rind
1	cup unsalted butter or margarine, softened
¼	cup milk

In a blender or food processor, purée sweet potato pulp with the brown sugar until smooth. In a separate bowl, sift together flour, baking powder, salt, cinnamon, nutmeg, and mace. Mix in lemon rind. Cut in butter with a pastry blender until mixture resembles coarse meal. Add sweet potato purée and milk and mix until just blended.

Gather dough into a ball, then turn out onto a lightly floured board, and knead 2-3 times. Flatten to a thickness of ¼". Cut out the biscuits using a 3" round cookie cutter lightly dipped in flour. Prick the tops of each biscuit evenly in three places with a fork. Arrange ½" apart on a ungreased baking sheet. Bake at 450° for 12-15 minutes or until golden brown. *These taste wonderful split with a slice of smoked or country ham. They can be made ahead of time, wrapped in aluminum foil and reheated in warm oven for 10 minutes.* **Yield: 16 biscuits**

Batter Bread

6	eggs
2	cups milk
2	cups buttermilk
1	cup cornmeal
1	teaspoon salt
1	teaspoon baking powder
½	teaspoon baking soda
6	tablespoons butter or margarine, melted

Beat eggs; add milk and buttermilk. Sift in cornmeal, salt, baking powder, and baking soda. Add melted butter. Spoon into greased 2-quart baking dish. Bake at 350° for 30-40 minutes until golden. **Yield: 6 servings**

Sour Cream Cornbread

½	cup butter or margarine
1	cup cream-style corn
1	cup sour cream
1	cup self-rising cornmeal
2	eggs, beaten
¼	cup chopped onion

Put butter in 8" cast iron skillet; put skillet in oven to melt butter. Meanwhile, combine corn, sour cream, cornmeal, eggs, and onion. Stir in butter; pour batter into skillet. Bake at 350° for 35 minutes. **Yield: 6 servings**

Jalapeño Cornbread

2	eggs
1	cup sour cream
1	teaspoon salt
3	teaspoons baking powder
½	cup vegetable oil
1	cup cornmeal
1	(4-ounce) can cream-style corn
1	cup grated Cheddar cheese
1	tablespoon chopped Jalapeño peppers
1	(4½-ounce) can chopped green chilies

Combine eggs, sour cream, salt, baking powder, vegetable oil, and cornmeal. Fold in corn, cheese, peppers, and chilies. Bake in greased 11" x 7" x 2" pan at 350° for 45-50 minutes. **Yield: 6-8 servings**

Southwest Pepperjack Bread

1¾	cups shredded hot pepper Monterey Jack cheese, divided
2½	cups buttermilk biscuit baking mix
½	cup cornmeal
½	cup frozen corn kernels, thawed
1	cup milk

Combine 1½ cups Jack cheese, baking mix, cornmeal, and corn. Add milk; stir until a soft dough forms. Knead lightly 8-10 turns. Shape into a ball and place on a greased cookie sheet. Pat dough into an 8" circle about ¾" thick. Using a sharp knife, cut into 8 wedges. Sprinkle with remaining cheese. Bake at 450° for 15-17 minutes. Remove to wire rack; cool completely. **Yield: 8 servings**

Sesame Horseradish Toast

1½	tablespoons prepared horseradish
1	tablespoon plain nonfat yogurt
1	tablespoon reduced-calorie mayonnaise
1	dash hot sauce
4	(4½-ounce) slices Italian bread
1	teaspoon sesame seeds, toasted

Combine horseradish, yogurt, mayonnaise, and hot sauce in a small bowl. Spread one side of each bread slice with 2 teaspoons horseradish mixture. Sprinkle each slice with ¼ teaspoon sesame seeds. Place slices on baking sheet. Broil 4" to 6" from heat until browned. Cut each slice into quarters and serve immediately. **Yield: 4 servings**

Flour Tortillas

Much tastier than store-bought!

4	cups all-purpose flour
2	teaspoons salt
½	teaspoon baking powder
½	cup shortening
1	cup lukewarm water

Sift flour, salt, and baking powder into bowl. Cut in shortening until well distributed. Add water slowly to make a soft dough. Form into ball and knead for 2 minutes. Let stand 15 minutes. Divide into 12 small balls. Roll balls out on floured surface to resemble thin pancakes. Cook on hot, ungreased griddle, turning once when brown patches appear on cooking side. Do not break bubbles that puff up. Good served with hot refried beans (covered with melted cheese), as a base for huevos rancheros, with 7-layer bean dip, or with salsa or chili sauce. **Yield: 1 dozen**

❡ *Doneness is determined by tapping the crust. The loaf should have a hollow sound when done. Removes loaves immediately; place on wire racks away from drafts to cool.*

❡ *Breads and rolls should be stored in an airtight container in a cool, dry place for 5-7 days. Refrigerate bread only in hot, humid weather.*

Corn Muffins

This is an original from Cooking Capers.

2	cups white or yellow cornmeal
1	teaspoon salt
2	cups boiling water
1	cup cold milk
2	eggs
4	teaspoons baking powder
1	tablespoon melted butter or margarine, melted

Sift meal and salt together. Scald with boiling water. Whisk in milk, stirring to prevent lumps. Add eggs, beating well. Finally, just before baking, fold in baking powder and butter. Spoon into greased muffin tins. Bake at 475° for 15 minutes. **Yield: 1 dozen**

Date Muffins

This recipe comes from a grandmother in Massachusetts.
I like to make these for visitors.

2	cups all-purpose flour
⅓	cup granulated sugar
2	teaspoons baking powder
1	teaspoon baking soda
Dash salt	
½	cup chopped dates
⅓	cup salad oil
1	cup milk
1	egg, slightly beaten

Combine flour, sugar, baking powder, soda, salt, and chopped nuts. In a separate bowl, mix oil, milk, and egg. Combine dry ingredients and egg mixtures, stirring just until blended. Spoon into sprayed, greased, or paper-lined muffin cups. Bake at 400° for 15-20 minutes. **Variation:** Substitute 1 cup whole wheat flour for 1 cup all-purpose flour. **Yield: 1 dozen**

Mini-Muffins

Easy—can be mixed ahead, and baked at the last minute

1	cup sour cream
½	cup butter or margarine, melted
2½	cups buttermilk biscuit baking mix

Combine sour cream, butter, and biscuit baking mix. Spoon into 24 greased mini-muffin cups. Bake at 375° for about 20 minutes. **Yield: 2 dozen**

Raisin Bran Muffins

Also called "Six Week Muffins"

1	(15-ounce) package raisin bran cereal
3	cups all-purpose flour
2	cups whole wheat flour
3	cups granulated sugar
5	teaspoons baking soda
2	teaspoons salt
1	cup canola oil
4	eggs, slightly beaten
1	quart nonfat buttermilk
2	cups raisins

In large bowl, mix together bran cereal, flours, sugar, baking soda and salt; set aside. Blend oil, eggs, and buttermilk; add to dry ingredients. Fold in raisins. Refrigerate in covered container for up to 6 weeks. Spray muffin tins with nonfat cooking spray; fill desired number ¾ full and bake at 400° for 15 minutes. *These taste better when refrigerated overnight before baking.* **Yield: 2-3 dozen**

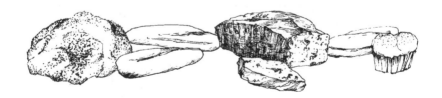

Refrigerator Bran Muffins

2	eggs
1	cup granulated sugar
½	cup butter or margarine, melted
1	cup black coffee
2	cups buttermilk
2½	cups all-purpose flour
2½	teaspoons baking soda
3	cups wheat bran cereal
1	cup currants
Creamy Orange Spread (below)	

Combine eggs, sugar, and butter in a large bowl. Whisk in coffee and buttermilk. Add flour and baking soda. Fold in cereal and currants. Cover; refrigerate batter (up to 2 weeks) until ready to bake. Stir batter before spooning into greased muffin cups. Bake at 375° for 20 minutes. Cool 5 minutes before serving with Creamy Orange Spread. **Variation:** To bake muffins without refrigerating, let mixture stand 20 minutes to soften bran. **Yield: 28**

Creamy Orange Spread:

1	(8-ounce) package regular or light cream cheese, at room temperature
½	cup sweet orange marmalade

With mixer, beat cream cheese and marmalade together until light and fluffy. Refrigerate. **Yield: 1 cup**

Chunky Apple Pancakes

2	cups whole wheat flour
½	teaspoon salt
1	tablespoon baking powder
1	tablespoon brown sugar
2	eggs
3	tablespoons vegetable oil
1⅔	cups milk
2	medium apples, diced

Combine flour, salt, baking powder, and brown sugar; set aside. Beat eggs with oil, add milk; add to dry ingredients. Fold in apples. Bake on preheated oiled griddle until brown. Serve with maple syrup. **Yield: 16-20 pancakes**

BEATEN BISCUIT

*Neither bell nor clock was needed to warn us
of the rifing hour; for when we heard a fteady
thump, thump, thump, we knew Uncle Mofes was
pounding the beaten bifcuit, which, hot and delicious, invariably appeared upon the breakfaft
table.*

One quart of flour, one heaping teafpoonful
of falt, two tablefpoonfuls of butter and lard
mixed, enough milk to make a ftiff dough (about
one cup). Work the dough a little, then beat
on bifcuit block (or bifcuit break) until it
bliſters; roll out to the fize you wifh and cut
with a tin cutter; ftick with a fork.   Bake in
a moderate oven. Serve hot or cold.

It is not beating hard that makes the bifcuit
nice, but the regularity of the motion. Beating
hard, the old cooks fay, kills the dough.

SALLY LUNN

Warm two ounces of butter and two ounces
of lard in a half pint of new milk; add a teafpoonful of falt, a teafpoonful of fugar, and two
and one-half pints of flour, beat thoroughly,
and when the mixture is blood warm, add three
eggs beaten light, and laft of all three tablefpoonfuls of yeaft. Beat hard until the batter
breaks in bliſters. Set it to rife over night. In
the morning turn it into a well-buttered, fhal-
low difh to rife until it is twice as high in the
pan as before. Then bake in a tube pan until
it is a brown and crufty loaf, and eat immediately.

St. Paul's Church
NORFOLK, VIRGINIA
CIRCA 1739 - 1750

CHURCH RECORDS IN Norfolk begin in 1637. The church vestry book (1749) gives a clue to St. Paul's Church origin. This book refers to the fact that bricks and timbers from the *old church* were made available to build a new school house on the property. This *old church* was most likely St. Paul's Church. The minister, a Mr. Smith, received 16,000 weight of tobacco for presiding over the mother church (St. Paul's) and a lesser amount of tobacco for preaching at the several outlying chapels. Tobacco was the coin of the realm in Virginia during the seventeenth and early eighteenth centuries. When Norfolk was destroyed during the Revolutionary War, the church burned; it was restored within its original brick walls and returned to active use in 1786.

Bertie's Baked Pancake

4	tablespoons butter or margarine
½	cup all-purpose flour
Dash	nutmeg or cinnamon
2	eggs
½	cup milk
½	teaspoon vanilla
3-4	tablespoons confectioner's sugar
3-4	tablespoons lemon juice

Put butter in 2-quart round baking or souffle dish; place in oven to melt. Mix flour with nutmeg or cinnamon. In separate bowl, beat eggs; add milk and vanilla. Add slowly to flour mixture; do not overmix. Pour into heated dish. Bake at 425° for 15 minutes. Remove from oven. Sprinkle with confectioner's sugar and lemon juice. Return to oven 1-2 minutes. Serve immediately. *This is great with blueberry syrup or orange marmalade.* **Variation:** May substitute coconut flavoring for vanilla. **Yield: 2 servings**

English Pancakes

English pancakes are slightly different from their American cousins; I like to serve both types on Shrove Tuesday.

1¾	cups all-purpose flour
⅛	teaspoon salt
2	teaspoons granulated sugar
2	eggs
1	egg yolk
1	cup milk
1	cup water
1	teaspoon grated lemon zest
1	tablespoon butter or margarine, melted
Confectioner's sugar	
3	tablespoons lemon juice

Sift flour with salt and sugar. Beat eggs and egg yolk together; add slowly to dry ingredients. Add milk and water; beat until batter is covered with bubbles. Add lemon zest; let batter stand in a cool place at least 1 hour. Stir in melted butter. Bake pancakes on a lightly greased, heated griddle. The finished pancake should be very thin. Sprinkle with confectioner's sugar and lemon juice; roll up to serve. **Yield: 24 (3") pancakes**

Nee Nee's Swedish Pancakes

3	eggs
2	cups milk
4	tablespoons butter or margarine, melted
1	cup all-purpose flour
1	tablespoon granulated sugar
¼	teaspoon salt

Beat eggs well; stir in milk and butter; blend well. Add flour, sugar, and salt. Cover and refrigerate overnight. Bake the next morning on a hot, greased griddle. When pancakes are brown on bottom, turn, adding more butter to the griddle. Serve at once with syrup or jam spooned over. **Variation:** If you intend to use batter the same day, let it stand for 2 hours in the refrigerator. **Yield: 30 small pancakes**

Patrick County Corn Griddle Cakes

My children grew up—fat and sassy—on these griddle cakes!

2	eggs, beaten
2	cups buttermilk
2	cups white cornmeal
1	cup all-purpose flour
2	tablespoons vegetable oil
1	teaspoon salt
1	teaspoon baking soda
1	tablespoon water
3	tablespoons baking powder
1	large ear white corn

In large bowl combine eggs, buttermilk, cornmeal, flour, oil, and salt. In separate bowl, combine soda and water; add to egg mixture. Fold in baking powder. Slit corn kernels lengthwise; then slice into mixture. Bake on griddle over high heat, turning when top is bubbly. Serve hot with lots of butter, syrup, or molasses. **Yield: 12-15 (4") pancakes**

Gourmet French Toast

5   eggs
⅔   cup half-and-half
⅓   cup Triple Sec
2   tablespoons granulated sugar
1   orange peel, zested
2   teaspoons cinnamon
6   tablespoons unsalted butter, divided
6   stale croissants, split lengthwise
Confectioner's sugar

Beat eggs and half-and-half together. Add Triple Sec, sugar, orange zest, and cinnamon. Pour into shallow bowl. Melt a few tablespoons of butter in a skillet over medium heat. Dip each croissant half into egg mixture turning once. Fry on both sides until golden brown in skillet. Sift confectioner's sugar over croissants and serve. **Yield: 6 servings**

Fruit Syrup

½   cup granulated sugar
2   tablespoons cornstarch
1   cup water
1   cup blueberries, divided
1   cup sliced peaches, divided
1   teaspoon lemon juice

Mix sugar and cornstarch in saucepan. Add water and cook over medium-high heat until mixture is transparent and bubbly. Add ½ cup each blueberries and peaches; cook over low heat until fruit is soft. Stir in remaining fruit and lemon juice. **Yield: 3 cups**

Auntie's Ice Box Rolls

2	cups milk, scalded
½	cup granulated sugar
½	cup shortening
1	package active dry yeast
1	egg, beaten
4½	cups all-purpose flour
1½	teaspoons salt
½	teaspoon baking soda
½	teaspoon baking powder

Extra flour for kneading

Combine hot milk, sugar, and shortening. When mixture cools to lukewarm, add yeast, egg, and flour. Beat until smooth. Let rise in a covered bowl for 2 hours. Stir down; add salt, baking soda, baking powder, and enough flour to knead. The dough can be formed into rolls or put into refrigerator until ready to use. Shape into rolls and let rise 2 hours. Bake at 450° for 8-10 minutes. **Yield: 2½ dozen**

French Brioche

This recipe is a variation of one that appeared in the 1932 St. Stephen's cookbook.

1	package dry yeast
¼	cup warm water
¾	cup milk, scalded
¾	cup butter or margarine, divided
½	cup granulated sugar
2	eggs, beaten
4½	cups all-purpose flour
1	teaspoon salt

Granulated sugar

Dissolve yeast in water. Combine hot milk and ½ cup butter; set aside to cool to lukewarm. Add sugar, eggs, flour, and salt. Mix well and turn into large bowl. Cover and let rise until doubled in size. Shape dough into walnut-sized balls and place in greased muffin cups. Melt remaining butter; brush dough with it. Sprinkle lightly with sugar. Cover and let rise again until doubled. Bake at 350° for 20 minutes. **Yield: 24-30**

Potato Refrigerator Rolls

1	cup mashed potatoes
⅔	cup shortening
½	cup granulated sugar
2	eggs
1	teaspoon salt
1	package active dry yeast
½	cup warm (115°) water
1	cup scalded milk, cooled to lukewarm
6-8	cups all-purpose flour
½	cup butter or margarine, melted

Combine mashed potatoes, shortening, sugar, eggs, and salt; beat well. Dissolve yeast in water; mix with milk. Add liquids to potato mixture. Stir in enough sifted flour to make a stiff dough. Toss on floured board and knead well. Put in large bowl and let rise until doubled. Knead lightly. Transfer dough to greased bowl, cover, and refrigerate until 1½ hours before serving. Shape into rolls, place in greased pans, brush with melted butter, cover loosely, and let rise again until light and doubled in size. Bake at 375° for 15-20 minutes. Brush again with melted butter immediately after baking. **Yield: 5 dozen**

Southern Cornmeal Rolls

1	cup white cornmeal
1½	cups boiling water
½	cup milk
½	cup butter or margarine
4¼-5	cups all-purpose flour, divided
¼	cup granulated sugar
2	teaspoons salt
2	packages active dry yeast
1	egg

Combine cornmeal and water in large mixing bowl. Add milk and butter and stir until butter melts. Add 2 cups flour, sugar, salt, yeast, and egg. Blend at lowest speed of mixer; increase speed to medium and beat 3 minutes. Stir in remaining flour to make a soft dough. Knead 3 minutes. Place in greased bowl, turning to grease top. Cover; let rise in warm place until doubled. Shape dough into 24 balls; place in two greased 9" cake pans. Cover and let rise again until light. Bake at 400° for 15-18 minutes. **Yield: 2 dozen**

Sweet Rolls

¾   cup butter or margarine
1   cup scalded milk
2   eggs, beaten
¾   cup granulated sugar
2   teaspoons salt
1   cup cold water
2   packages active dry yeast
½   cup warm water (115°)
7½   cups all-purpose flour, divided

Combine butter and hot milk; set aside while butter melts. Beat eggs with sugar and salt. Add cold water; set aside. Soften the yeast in warm water. In a large mixing bowl, combine the three mixtures. Beat in flour, 2 cups at a time. Turn dough into a large, greased bowl; cover tightly with plastic wrap and refrigerate overnight.

Next morning divide dough in thirds; roll each portion out into an 8" x 16" rectangle ¼" thick. Spread with one of the fillings listed below. Roll lengthwise as for jelly roll; seal edges. Slice into 1" rounds. Place rounds, cut sides down, in four greased 9" cake pans. Cover; let rise until doubled. Bake at 400° for 20 minutes. Frost if desired. **Yield: 4 dozen**

Cinnamon Filling:

1   cup granulated sugar
¾   cup butter or margarine, melted
1½   tablespoons cinnamon
½   cup raisins (optional)

Combine sugar, butter, cinnamon, and raisins.

Orange Filling:

1½   cups granulated sugar
⅓   cup grated fresh orange zest
½   cup currants
⅓   cup butter or margarine, melted

Combine sugar, orange zest, currants, and butter.

Variation: For pan rolls, omit filling(s); shape dough into 1½" balls. place 12-13 balls in each of four greased 9" round cake pans. Cover; let rise until doubled. Bake as directed above.

White Loaf Bread

I used to make this to sell at craft fairs.

2¼	cups milk
¼	cup vegetable oil
5	cups all-purpose flour, divided
¼	cup granulated sugar
2	packages active dry yeast
1	tablespoon salt
1	egg

Heat milk and oil together in saucepan until warm, about 120°-130°. In a large mixing bowl, stir together 1½ cups flour, sugar, yeast, and salt. Add heated milk mixture to dry ingredients and beat well with mixer. Add egg and ½ cup flour and beat at high speed for 3 minutes. Stir in remaining flour to form a soft dough that leaves the sides of the bowl. Turn onto floured surface and knead lightly until smooth ball forms. Place in greased bowl, cover, and let rise until doubled. Punch down, divide, and place in 2 greased 7" x 4" x 3" loaf pans, cover, and let rise again until doubled. Bake at 350° for about 40 minutes or until browned. Yield: 2 loaves

Sally Lunn Bread

2	packages active dry yeast
⅓	cup granulated sugar, divided
½	cup warm water (115°)
½	cup lukewarm milk
½	cup butter or margarine
3	eggs, beaten
4	cups all-purpose flour, sifted
1	teaspoon salt

Dissolve yeast and 1 tablespoon sugar in water; stir in milk; set aside. Cream butter and remaining sugar; blend in eggs. Add liquids to creamed mixture alternately with combined flour and salt, mixing well after each addition. Turn dough into greased bowl. Cover and let rise in warm place until light and doubled in bulk, about 1½ hours. Stir down and spread in well-greased 10" tube pan. Cover and let rise again until light, about 45-60 minutes. Bake at 350° for 45 minutes. Remove from oven and let cool in pan for 10 minutes before inverting on wire rack. *If loaf browns too quickly, cover loosely with aluminum foil during last 20 minutes of baking time.* Yield: 12-14 servings

Sourdough Bread

Starter:

1	cup warm water (115°)
1	package active dry yeast
¾	cup granulated sugar
3	tablespoons instant potato flakes

Combine water, yeast, sugar, and potato flakes. Cover and let stand in warm place 12-18 hours. Then store in refrigerator 3-7 days.

Step 1:

	Starter (above)
¾	cup granulated sugar
3	tablespoons instant potato flakes
1	cup warm water

Combine starter, sugar, potato flakes, and water in quart jar; loosen jar top. Let mixture sit out 10-12 hours. Then remove 1 cup to use. Tighten cap and refrigerate remainder. Feed every 3-5 days. Divide and share starter when it measures 3 cups.

Step 2:

6	cups white bread flour
½	cup canola oil
1	tablespoon salt
1	cup starter
1½	cups warm water

Sift flour into large bowl; make a well in center. In separate bowl, combine oil, starter, and water and pour into well. Mix with hands to make a stiff dough. Knead several times. Grease top of bread. Cover with damp towel and place in large plastic bag. Set out at room temperature all day or overnight.

Step 3:

Knead dough 16-20 strokes. Divide into 2-3 equal parts, depending upon loaf pan size. Place in greased loaf pans; cover. Let rise at least 4-5 hours. Bake at 350° for 30 minutes. Cool 5 minutes in pan before inverting pans on wire racks. Store baked loaves in refrigerator or freezer. **Variation:** Shape into rolls; bake as directed for loaves. **Yield: 2-3 loaves**

Wheat Dilly Bread

Serendipity from a music workshop in Rhode Island

1	package dry yeast
¼	cup lukewarm water
1	cup cottage cheese
1	tablespoon butter or margarine
2	tablespoons granulated sugar
2	tablespoons minced spring onion greens
2	teaspoons dill seeds
1	teaspoon salt
¼	teaspoon soda
1	egg
1	cup wheat flour
1½	cups unbleached flour

Soften yeast in lukewarm water. Heat cottage cheese and butter to lukewarm. In mixing bowl, combine cottage cheese, butter, sugar, onion greens, dill seeds, salt, soda, egg, yeast, and flour. Mix well; knead into a stiff dough. Place in a well-greased 1½-2 quart baking dish. Cover; let rise 50-60 minutes until doubled. Bake at 350° for 40 minutes or until golden brown. Brush warm loaf with melted butter. **Yield: 8-10 servings**

Blue Ribbon Rye Bread

3	cups rye flour
⅓	cup brown sugar
1	tablespoon salt
1	tablespoon grated orange peel
1	teaspoon caraway seed
½	teaspoon baking soda
2	packages active dry yeast
1	cup buttermilk
¼	cup molasses
¼	cup shortening
1	cup warm water
3-3½	cups all-purpose flour

Combine rye flour, brown sugar, salt, orange peel, caraway seed, soda, and yeast. In saucepan, heat buttermilk, molasses, and shortening until warm. Add warm water and buttermilk to dry ingredients. Beat with mixer 3 minutes. By hand, stir in enough flour to make a stiff dough. Knead for 5 minutes. Cover; let rise for 1½-2 hours or until doubled. Punch down; shape into 2 loaves; place dough in 2 greased 9" x 5" x 3" loaf pans. Cover; let rise again until doubled. Bake at 350° for 45-55 minutes. **Yield: 2 large loaves**

Desserts

Contents

Almond Tea Cake

From the Mainstay Inn, Cape May, New Jersey

Cake:

4	eggs
2	cups granulated sugar
2	cups all-purpose flour
2	cups butter or margarine, melted

Combine eggs, sugar, flour, and melted butter. Pour into lightly greased 15" x 10" x 1" pan. (Yes, this is a runny batter.) Bake at 350° for 15 minutes. Remove and pour on topping (recipe below). Return cake to oven; broil until top is bubbly and brown, about 15 minutes. Cool and cut into small squares to serve. **Yield: 24 squares**

Topping:

1	cup butter or margarine
1	cup granulated sugar
1	cup sliced almonds
2	tablespoons flour
2	tablespoons milk
2	tablespoons almond extract

In medium saucepan, combine butter, sugar, almonds, flour, and milk and cook over medium heat, stirring constantly until thickened, about 10 minutes. Add almond extract.

Apple Snack Cake

¾	cup vegetable oil
2	eggs
2	cups granulated sugar
2½	cups all-purpose flour
1	teaspoon baking soda
1	teaspoon baking powder
1	teaspoon salt
1	teaspoon cinnamon
3	cups chopped, peeled apples
1	cup chopped nuts
1	cup butterscotch chips, divided

Combine oil, eggs, and sugar in large bowl; beat well. Combine flour, soda, baking powder, salt, and cinnamon; add to egg mixture. Stir in apples, nuts, and half the butterscotch chips. Spoon batter into a greased-and-floured 13" x 9" x 2" pan. Sprinkle remaining chips over batter. Bake at 350° for 55-60 minutes. **Yield: 15 servings**

Old Fashioned Applesauce Cake

This is an original from Cooking Capers.

1	cup unsweetened applesauce
1	teaspoon baking soda
1	cup light brown sugar
½	cup shortening
2	cups all-purpose flour
1	teaspoon ground cloves
1	teaspoon cinnamon
1	teaspoon nutmeg
1	teaspoon salt
1	cup golden raisins
½	cup chopped pecans
1	teaspoon vanilla

In mixing bowl, combine applesauce and soda; let stand 5 minutes. Add sugar and shortening; beat well. Combine flour, cloves, cinnamon, nutmeg, salt, raisins and nuts; add this to applesauce mixture. Stir in vanilla. Spoon batter into a greased and floured 10" tube pan and bake at 350° for 50 minutes. Serve hot with hard sauce (recipe on page 223). **Yield: 16 servings**

Hard Sauce:

½	cup butter
1	pound confectioner's sugar
2	teaspoons cream
4	tablespoons brandy

With mixer, cream butter until fluffy. Gradually beat in sugar until very smooth. Add cream and brandy slowly; continue beating for 10 minutes.

Fresh Apple Cake

2	cups granulated sugar
3	eggs
1¼	cups vegetable oil
1½	teaspoons vanilla
1	teaspoon baking soda
1½	teaspoons combined cinnamon and nutmeg
3	cups all-purpose flour, divided
3½	cups chopped apples
½	cup raisins
1	cup chopped nuts

Mix sugar and eggs. Add oil and vanilla; beat 1 minute. Sift together soda, cinnamon, nutmeg, and flour; add all but ¼ cup to sugar-oil-egg mixture. Dredge apples, raisins and nuts in reserved flour mixture; then fold in apples, raisins and nuts. Spoon into greased-and-floured 10" tube pan; bake at 325° for 90 minutes. Top with glaze (recipe below) or cream cheese frosting (see page 226). **Yield: 16 servings**

Glaze:

¼	cup margarine or butter
½	cup granulated sugar
¼	teaspoon baking soda
¼	cup buttermilk
¾	teaspoon vanilla

Combine margarine, sugar, baking soda, buttermilk, and vanilla in saucepan; bring to a boil. Punch holes in top of cooled cake; pour glaze over cake.

If raisins are heated in the oven before being added to cakes or muffins, they will be more evenly distributed.

Green Apple Cake

1	cup butter or margarine
2	cups granulated sugar
5	eggs
1	teaspoon cinnamon
1	teaspoon nutmeg
1	teaspoon cloves
3	cups all-purpose flour, divided
1	heaping teaspoon baking soda
½	cup cold water
2	cups finely chopped Granny Smith apples

Cream butter and sugar. Add eggs one at a time, beating after each addition. In a separate bowl, combine cinnamon, nutmeg, cloves, and ½ cup flour; add to egg mixture. Dissolve soda in cold water. Stir in soda water, chopped apples, and remaining flour. Spoon batter into greased-and-floured 13" x 9" x 2" rectangular pan. Bake at 325°-350° for 35-40 minutes. Remove cake from oven; spread with Toasted Coconut Topping (recipe below). Return to 375° oven and bake for 10-12 minutes to brown top. **Yield: 12-16 servings**

Toasted Coconut Topping:

1	cup shredded coconut
1	cup light brown sugar
½	cup butter or margarine
4	tablespoons milk
Dash salt	

Combine coconut, sugar, butter, milk, and salt in saucepan. Cook, stirring until sugar melts.

Tips for Successful Cakes

Unless the recipe specifies otherwise, cool cake in the pan for 5-10 minutes before turning out onto a wire rack.

To any yellow or white cake mix, add 1 teaspoon each of vanilla extract and lemon extract for an improved flavor.

To keep chocolate cakes brown on the outside, grease pans and dust with cocoa instead of flour.

Banana Cake

This cake travels well.

1	cup granulated sugar
½	cup shortening
1	egg
3	large bananas, sliced
2	cups cake flour
1	teaspoon baking soda
6-8	dates, chopped

Cream sugar and shortening until fluffy. Add egg and beat well. Add bananas gradually; beat well. Sift flour, then re-measure; add soda. Sift again. Add to batter, beating until flour is absorbed. Add dates. Spoon into greased-and-floured 9" tube pan. Bake at 350° for 40-45 minutes. **Yield: 10 servings**

Banana Nut Cake

2¼	cups sifted cake flour
2	teaspoons baking powder
½	teaspoon baking soda
¾	teaspoon salt
½	cup shortening
1	cup granulated sugar
2	eggs
1	cup chopped black walnuts
1	teaspoon vanilla
1	cup mashed ripe bananas
2	tablespoons milk

Sift together flour, baking powder, baking soda, and salt; set aside. In large bowl, cream shortening and sugar until light and fluffy. Add eggs, one at a time, beating well after each addition. Fold in nuts and vanilla. Add flour mixture to batter alternately with bananas and milk which have been mixed together. Spoon batter into a greased-and-floured 10" tube pan. Bake at 350° for 55 minutes. Cool in pan 10 minutes before cooling on rack. **Yield: 16 servings**

Carrot Cake

1⅓	cups vegetable oil
2	cups granulated sugar
2	cups sifted all-purpose flour
2	teaspoons baking powder
2	teaspoons cinnamon
1	teaspoon baking soda
1	teaspoon salt
4	eggs
3-4	cups grated carrots
1	cup chopped pecans (optional)

Combine oil and sugar; mix well. Sift together flour, baking powder, cinnamon, baking soda, and salt. Mix half the sifted dry ingredients into the sugar mixture. Then add eggs, one at a time, alternately with the remaining dry ingredients, mixing well after each addition. Stir in carrots and nuts; mix well. Spoon batter into a greased-and-floured 10" tube pan. Bake at 325° for 70 minutes. Frost with Cream Cheese Frosting (recipe below). **Yield: 16 servings**

Cream Cheese Frosting:

1	(8-ounce) package cream cheese, at room temperature
½	cup butter or margarine, at room temperature
4	cups confectioner's sugar
1½	teaspoons vanilla
1-8	drops milk if necessary

Beat cream cheese and butter together until light. Gradually add confectioner's sugar and vanilla; beat until smooth. If necessary, add a few drops of milk to thin to spreadable consistency. Frost cake and refrigerate.

❧ *For a simple maple sugar frosting, use 1 cup each maple and granulated sugar, 1 teaspoon butter, and 1 tablespoon cream. Boil 5 minutes; stir until slightly thickened.*

❧ *For a very white cake, add ⅛ teaspoon cream of tartar per layer to cake batter.*

❧ *One cup cake flour equals 1 cup all-purpose flour minus 2 tablespoons.*

Ann's Cake

1   (14.5-ounce) package angel food cake mix
Few drops almond extract
1   (14 to 16-ounce) carton frozen whipped topping, thawed
1   (4.5-ounce) box instant vanilla pudding mix
1   (20-ounce) can crushed pineapple, drained

Prepare angel food cake according to package directions; flavor with almond extract. Bake as directed; cool. Combine whipped topping with pudding mix and pineapple. With serrated knife, slice angel food cake horizontally into 3 layers. Combine pudding mix and pineapple; fold in whipped topping. Frost layers and top with pudding mixture; refrigerate. Make one day ahead for best results. **Variation:** Use yellow cake mix instead of angel food. **Yield: 8-10 servings**

Key Lime Cake

1   (18¼-ounce) package lemon cake mix
1   (3-ounce) package instant lemon pudding
1   cup water
⅓   cup vegetable oil
4   eggs, slightly beaten
1   tablespoon key lime juice
Grated zest of 2 limes

Combine cake mix, pudding mix, water, oil, eggs, lime juice, and lime zest. Beat at medium speed of mixer for 2 minutes. Pour into a greased-and-floured 10" tube pan; bake at 325° for 1 hour. Immediately after removing cake from oven, pierce top with ice pick or fork. Pour glaze (recipe below) over hot cake. Cool cake in pan before inverting onto serving plate. **Yield: 16 servings**

Glaze:

1½   cups confectioner's sugar
⅓   cup key lime juice

Combine sugar and lime juice; pour over cake as directed above.

Pig Pickin' Cake

1	(18¼-ounce) package yellow cake mix
½	cup vegetable oil
1	(11-ounce) can mandarin oranges, undrained
4	eggs

Combine cake mix, oil, and oranges; beat in 1 egg at a time. Beat in electric mixer at medium speed for 4 minutes. Spoon into 2 greased-and-floured 9" round cake pans. Bake at 350° for 20-25 minutes. Cool; slice each layer into 2 thin layers. Spread frosting (recipe below) on each layer, and on top and sides of cake. Refrigerate. **Yield: 12-15 servings**

Icing:

1	(20-ounce) can crushed pineapple
1	(4.5 ounce) package instant vanilla pudding
1	(14-16 ounce) carton frozen whipped topping, thawed

Mix pineapple and juice with pudding mix. Fold in whipped topping.

Piña Colada Cake

Nice for Easter, decorated with jelly beans

1	(18.25-ounce) package white or yellow cake mix
1	(10-ounce) can frozen Piña Colada mix, thawed
1	(16-ounce) carton frozen whipped topping, thawed
2	(6-ounce) packages frozen grated coconut, thawed

Bake cake according to package directions in greased-and-floured 13" x 9" x 2" pan. Remove from oven; immediately punch holes in cake. Spoon Piña Colada mix over entire cake. Let cool completely. Frost with whipped topping; sprinkle with coconut and top with jelly beans, if desired. **Yield: 12-15 servings**

Pound Cake

1½	cups butter or margarine
3	cups granulated sugar
6	eggs, separated
1	cup sour cream
¼	teaspoon baking soda
3	cups all-purpose flour
¾	teaspoon mace
Dash salt	
2	teaspoons vanilla

Cream butter and sugar. Add egg yolks one at a time, beating well after each addition. In separate bowl, combine sour cream and soda. In large bowl, sift flour, mace, and salt 3 times. Add dry ingredients to butter-and-sugar mixture, alternately with sour cream mixture, beginning and ending with flour. Fold in vanilla and stiffly beaten egg whites. Pour into greased-and-floured 10" tube pan. Bake at 300° for 1 hour and 45 minutes. **Yield: 16 servings**

Lois Tankersley's Chocolate Pound Cake

3	cups all-purpose flour
½	cup cocoa
½	teaspoon baking powder
½	teaspoon salt
1	cup butter or margarine
½	cup shortening
3	cups granulated sugar
5	eggs
2	teaspoons vanilla
1	cup milk

Combine flour, cocoa, baking powder, and salt; sift 3 times. Set aside. Cream together butter, shortening, and sugar until light and fluffy. Add eggs, one at a time, beating well after each addition. Add vanilla. Then add dry ingredients, alternately with milk, beginning and ending with flour. Pour into a greased and floured 10" tube pan. Bake at 325° for 1½ hours. Cool for 20 minutes in pan. Remove from pan and continue cooling on rack. **Yield: 16 servings**

Brown Sugar Pound Cake

1	cup butter or margarine
½	cup shortening
5	eggs
3¼	cups light brown sugar
3½	cups all-purpose flour
½	teaspoon baking powder
¼	teaspoon salt
1	cup milk, whole or evaporated

Let butter, shortening, and eggs come to room temperature. Cream butter, shortening, and brown sugar. Add eggs, one at a time, beating well after each addition. Sift together flour, baking powder, and salt. Add dry ingredients alternately with milk to creamed mixture. Spoon batter into a greased-and-floured 10" tube pan. Bake at 325° for 75-90 minutes. Note: If desired, spread with Butter Pecan Frosting (see below). **Yield: 16 servings**

Butter Pecan Frosting:

½	cup butter or margarine
1	cup chopped pecans
4	cups confectioner's sugar
Milk, as needed	

In heavy pan, melt butter; add pecans; stir until pecans are browned. Let mixture cool; beat in confectioner's sugar. Beat in enough milk to achieve spreading consistency.

Tips for Successful Cakes

Heavy cakes are sometimes caused by too slow an oven, or by the use of too much sugar or shortening.

Add a pinch of baking powder to powdered sugar icings. Icing will not get hard or crack and will stay moist.

To help prevent cake layers from sticking to the pans, place pans on a wet towel as soon as they come out of the oven.

Sweet Potato Pound Cake

1	cup butter or margarine
2	cups granulated sugar
2½	cups cooked, mashed sweet potatoes
5	eggs
3	cups all-purpose flour
¼	teaspoon salt
2	teaspoons baking powder
1	teaspoon baking soda
½	teaspoon ground nutmeg
1	teaspoon cinnamon
1	teaspoon vanilla extract
½	cup chopped nuts
½	cup flaked coconut

Cream together butter and sugar. Add potatoes; beat until mixture is light and fluffy. Add eggs, 1 at a time, beating well after each addition; set aside. Combine flour, salt, baking powder, soda, nutmeg, and cinnamon; add to creamed mixture. Add vanilla, nuts, and coconut. Spoon batter into greased-and-floured 10" tube pan and bake at 350° for 75 minutes. Pierce top with fork; pour glaze over hot cake. **Yield: 16 servings**

Glaze:

1	orange
1	lemon
4	cups confectioner's sugar

Grate rinds of orange and lemon. Squeeze all juice. Combine rind, juice, and confectioner's sugar in saucepan; heat, stirring until mixture is translucent.

The Queen's Cake

This is the only cake the Queen makes. Please honor her request that the recipe not be given away, but sold only for Church and charitable purposes as in the manner received.

1	cup boiling water
1	cup chopped dates
1	teaspoon baking soda
1	cup granulated sugar
¼	cup butter or margarine, softened
1	egg, beaten
1	teaspoon vanilla
1⅓	cups all-purpose flour, sifted
½	teaspoon salt
1	teaspoon baking powder
⅓	cup chopped nuts

Pour water over dates and soda; set aside to cool. Cream together sugar, butter, egg, and vanilla. Sift together flour, salt, and baking powder; add to creamed mixture. Fold in nuts. Spoon batter into a lightly greased-and-floured 9" x 9" x 2" pan. Bake at 350° for 30 minutes. Spread the following topping over warm cake; broil until lightly browned. **Yield: 10-12 servings**

Queen's Frosting:

½	cup brown sugar
½	cup heavy cream
3	tablespoons butter or margarine
¾	cup flaked coconut
½	cup chopped nuts

Combine brown sugar, cream, and butter in small saucepan; bring to a boil; cook 3 minutes. Remove from heat; stir in coconut and nuts.

Nana's Cream Sponge Cake

2   cups granulated sugar, divided
2   cups sifted all-purpose flour
10   eggs, separated
3   tablespoons lemon juice
Confectioner's sugar

Sift sugar 2 times; then measure. Sift flour 3-4 times; then measure. Separate eggs; beat whites until stiff, but not dry. Gradually add 10 table-spoons sugar; set aside. Add lemon juice to egg yolks; beat until very thick. Add remaining sugar. Combine egg yolk and egg white mixtures. Gradually fold in sifted flour. Spoon batter into 3-4 ungreased 9" round layer pans. Bake at 350° for 20-30 minutes. Cool layers on wire racks; then spread Nana's Cream Filling (recipe below) between layers. Sprinkle top with confectioner's sugar. Refrigerate. **Yield: 16 servings**

Nana's Cream Filling:

2   cups milk
2   eggs, beaten
4   tablespoons granulated sugar
3   rounded tablespoons all-purpose flour
6   tablespoons butter or margarine, melted
1   teaspoon vanilla

Heat milk in double boiler. Combine eggs, sugar, and flour; gradually add ½ cup hot milk. Add sugar mixture to milk in double boiler; cook and stir until very thick. Mixture may be lumpy, but keep stirring and lumps will disappear. Remove from heat; add butter and vanilla. Spread between cooled cake layers. *Double recipe for extra filling.*

French Fudge Cake

½   cup butter or margarine
4   (1-ounce) squares unsweetened chocolate
2   cups granulated sugar
4   eggs, divided
1   cup all-purpose flour
Pinch salt
1   teaspoon vanilla
1   cup walnut halves
Additional walnut halves for decoration

Melt butter and chocolate; cool slightly. Add sugar and 2 eggs; beat well. Blend in flour and salt. Add remaining eggs, vanilla, and walnuts. Mix well. Spoon batter into 1 greased-and-floured 9" cake pan. Bake at 350° for 30 minutes. Center will be soft. Cool in pan on wire rack. Garnish with walnut halves, if desired. **Yield: 8 servings**

Prize Fudge Cake

¼   cup shortening
2   cups granulated sugar, divided
2   egg yolks
4   (1-ounce) squares unsweetened chocolate, melted
1⅞   cups sifted all-purpose flour
2   teaspoons baking powder
1   teaspoon salt
1½   cups milk
1   teaspoon vanilla
2   egg whites

Cream together shortening, 1½ cups sugar, egg yolks, and chocolate. Sift together flour, baking powder, and salt. Add dry ingredients to creamed mixture; stir in milk and vanilla. Mix thoroughly. In separate bowl, whip egg whites until frothy; add remaining ½ cup sugar, 1 tablespoon at a time. Fold into batter. Spoon batter into 2 greased-and-floured 9" cake pans or 1 greased-and-floured 13" x 9" x 2" pan. Bake at 350° for 35-40 minutes. **Yield: 12 servings**

French Tart

Pastry:

1	cup all-purpose flour
2	tablespoons granulated sugar
3	tablespoons butter or margarine, cut into pieces
2-3	tablespoons ice water

Apple filling:

⅔	cup granulated sugar, divided
¼	teaspoon ground nutmeg or apple pie spice
5	cups baking apples, peeled, cored, and sliced
1	tablespoon lemon juice
2	tablespoons butter or margarine

PASTRY: Combine flour and sugar. With pastry blender or two knives, cut in cold margarine until mixture resembles coarse crumbs. Sprinkle in water, 1 tablespoon at a time, mixing lightly with fork after each addition until pastry just holds together. Form dough into ball, cover; refrigerate. On lightly floured surface, roll dough into 11" circle; set aside.

FILLING: In large bowl combine ⅓ cup sugar and nutmeg or apple pie spice. Add apples and lemon juice; set aside. Put remaining ⅓ cup sugar in skillet. Cook over medium heat, stirring occasionally until sugar melts and turns golden brown. Drain apple mixture; add with butter to skillet. Cook, stirring occasionally until apples are tender. Pour into 10" pie pan. Place pastry on top of apples and cut slits in pastry. Bake at 425° for 20-25 minutes. Let stand 10 minutes and invert into serving platter. *Great served warm with vanilla ice cream or frozen yogurt.* **Yield: 6-8 servings**

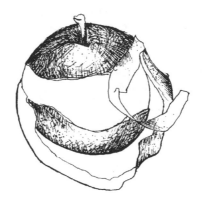

Blackberry Crumb Pie

Filling:

1	cup granulated sugar
⅓	cup all-purpose flour
⅛	teaspoon salt
2	eggs, beaten
½	cup sour cream
3	cups blackberries
1	9" deep-dish pastry shell, unbaked

Topping:

½	cup granulated sugar
½	cup all-purpose flour
½	cup butter or margarine

FILLING: Combine sugar, flour, salt, eggs, and sour cream; gently fold in blackberries. Spoon into pastry shell.

TOPPING: Combine sugar, flour, and butter; crumble over top of pie. Bake at 350° for 50 minutes. **Yield: 6-8 servings**

Deep Dish Cranberry Pie

This was originally published in P. S.

2	cups fresh cranberries
1½	cups granulated sugar, divided
½	cup chopped nuts
2	eggs
1	cup all-purpose flour
½	cup butter or margarine, melted

Gently combine the cranberries, ½ cup sugar, and nuts; spoon into a lightly greased 10" pie plate. Beat eggs with remaining sugar; add flour and butter. Pour batter over berries. Bake at 325° for 1 hour. Serve hot with vanilla ice cream. **Yield: 8 servings**

Cherry Pie

1-2   tablespoons all-purpose flour
1   (16-ounce) can unsweetened red cherries, liquid reserved
1-2   drops red food coloring
¾   cup granulated sugar
1   tablespoon butter or margarine
Pinch of salt
1   teaspoon lemon juice
½   teaspoon vanilla
1   teaspoon brandy
Almond extract
Nutmeg
Pastry for 9" double-crust pie

Combine flour and reserved juice in saucepan; cook and stir over medium heat until thickened. Add red food coloring if necessary to achieve bright red color. Remove sauce from heat; add sugar, butter, salt, lemon juice, vanilla, brandy, almond extract, and nutmeg. Cover saucepan to prevent skim from forming on sauce. Arrange cherries in bottom of pastry-lined pie plate. Pour sauce over fruit. Add top pastry and seal. Bake at 450° for 10 minutes and then at 350° for 30 minutes. **Yield: 6 servings**

Variation: Use 2½ cups fresh pitted red cherries for canned. Arrange cherries in bottom of pastry-lined pie pans. Mix sugar, flour, and salt and sprinkle evenly over cherries. Add lemon juice, vanilla, brandy, almond extract, and nutmeg. Dot with butter. A few drops of water may be added if needed. Add top pastry. Bake at 450° for 10 minutes and then at 350° for 30 minutes.

Tips for Successful Pies

To prevent soggy-bottomed crusts in custard-type pies, brush the unbaked pie crust with a lightly beaten egg white, then bake at 425° for 5-10 minutes before adding filling.

Turn leftover trimmings of pie dough into flaky snacks; Sprinkle the pastry scraps with a little sugar and cinnamon and bake at 375° for 10-12 minutes or until golden.

For a handsome top crust, brush pastry with milk before baking.

Fruit Pie

Lovely, light, and tasty!

1	(20-ounce) can crushed pineapple
1	(21-ounce) can cherry pie filling
1	cup granulated sugar
1	tablespoon all-purpose flour
1	(6-ounce) package orange-flavored gelatin
1	cup chopped pecans
5	bananas, diced
3	9" deep-dish pastry shells, baked

Whipped cream

Mix pineapple, cherry pie filling, sugar and flour in sauce pan. Cook over medium heat until thickened. Cool slightly; add gelatin, pecans, and bananas. Mix well and pour into pastry shells. Refrigerate. At serving time top with whipped cream. **Yield: 18 servings**

Lemon Pie or Tarts

Easy, and oh, so good!

1	cup granulated sugar
2	heaping tablespoons all-purpose flour
1	cup hot water
2	tablespoons butter or margarine
1	tablespoon grated lemon rind
3	tablespoons lemon juice
2	egg yolks, beaten
8	3" tart shells, unbaked *or*
1	9" pastry shell, unbaked

Meringue:

2	egg whites, stiffly beaten
4	tablespoons granulated sugar
1	teaspoon vanilla extract

Mix sugar and flour in top of double boiler. Add hot water, butter, lemon rind, and juice. Cook and stir over simmering water until thickened. Remove from heat; stir in egg yolks. Spoon filling into pastry shell(s). Beat egg whites until foamy; beat in sugar, 1 tablespoon at a time; continue beating until stiff and glossy. Beat in vanilla. Cover tarts or pie with meringue. Brown slightly in 300° oven. **Yield: 8 servings**

Luscious Lemon Pie

1	cup granulated sugar
3	tablespoons cornstarch
4	tablespoons butter or margarine
1	tablespoon grated lemon rind
¼	cup lemon juice
3	egg yolks, unbeaten
1	cup milk
1	cup sour cream
1	9" baked pastry shell
1	cup heavy cream
½	cup chopped walnuts

In a heavy saucepan, combine sugar and cornstarch. Add butter, lemon rind, lemon juice, egg yolks, and milk; cook over medium heat, stirring constantly, until thickened. Cool custard quickly by placing saucepan in a bowl of iced water and stirring occasionally. Then fold in sour cream; spoon filling into pastry shell. Refrigerate at least 2 hours. Prior to serving, beat cream until stiff peaks form; spread over filling. Sprinkle with walnuts. **Yield: 6-8 servings**

Mecklenburg County Lemon Chess Pie

½	cup butter or margarine
1¾	cups granulated sugar
2	tablespoons all-purpose flour
4	eggs, well beaten
6	tablespoons lemon juice
1	tablespoon grated lemon rind
1	unbaked 9" pastry shell

Cream butter, sugar, and flour. Add eggs, lemon juice, and lemon rind. Stir well. Pour into pastry. Bake at 350° for 30-40 minutes. (If using deep-dish pastry shell, bake 40-45 minutes.) **Yield: 8 servings**

Mandarin Orange Pie

1	(11-ounce) can mandarin oranges, drained
1	9" baked graham cracker crumb crust
2-3	firm bananas, sliced
1	(3.4-ounce) package instant banana pudding mix
¾	cup milk
1	cup heavy cream
½	teaspoon vanilla
½	cup flaked coconut

Place oranges on bottom of crust; top with bananas. In small bowl, combine pudding mix, milk, cream, and vanilla. Whip for 2 minutes; do not overbeat. Pour over fruit; sprinkle top with coconut. Refrigerate at least 1 hour before serving. **Yield: 6-8 servings**

Light Pumpkin Pie

½	cup granulated sugar
1½	teaspoons pumpkin pie spice
½	teaspoon salt
½	cup skim milk
2	egg whites
1	whole egg
1	(29-ounce) can pumpkin
1	9" unbaked pastry shell

Combine sugar, spice, salt, milk, egg whites, egg, and pumpkin. Beat at low speed of mixer until smooth. Pour into pastry shell. Bake at 425° for 50 minutes or a knife inserted in center comes out clean.
Yield: 6-8 servings

Tips for Successful Meringue

Separate eggs very carefully while cold. For greatest volume, let whites stand at room temperature 30 minutes before beating.

To make sure meringues don't turn out dry, bake them on a fairly dry, not humid, day.

Cool baked meringue gradually, away from drafts.

Custard Pie

1	(14-ounce) can sweetened condensed milk
1½	cups hot tap water
½	teaspoon salt
½	teaspoon vanilla
3	eggs
1	9" unbaked pastry shell
Nutmeg	

Combine milk, water, salt, and vanilla. Add eggs; beat well. Pour into pastry and sprinkle with nutmeg. Bake at 425° for 10 minutes; reduce heat to 300°. Bake an additional 20-25 minutes or until a knife inserted near pie's center tests clean. Cool to room temperature before refrigerating. **Yield: 8 servings**

Kalman Pie

This is an original from Cooking Capers.

3	egg whites, at room temperature
1	cup granulated sugar
1	cup chopped pecans
20	round buttery crackers, crushed
1	teaspoon baking powder
1	teaspoon vanilla

Using clean bowl and beaters, whip egg whites until stiff. Fold in sugar, pecans, cracker crumbs, baking powder, and vanilla. Spread mixture in lightly greased 9" pie plate. Bake at 350° for 30 minutes. Immediately refrigerate for at least 3-4 hours before cutting into wedges and serving with whipped cream. **Yield: 6-8 servings**

Easy Cream Cheese Pie

1	(8-ounce) package cream cheese
1	(14-ounce) can sweetened condensed milk
⅓	cup lemon juice
1	teaspoon vanilla
1	9" baked pastry shell or graham cracker crumb crust
1	(21-ounce) can commercial fruit pie filling

Combine cream cheese, condensed milk, lemon juice, and vanilla. Pour into pastry shell; refrigerate for 2-3 hours. Top with your favorite fruit pie filling and slice. **Yield: 6 servings**

Peanut Butter Pie

Served at Armbruster's Restaurant, Blackstone, Virginia

1	(8-ounce) package cream cheese
½	cup granulated sugar
½	cup creamy peanut butter
1	teaspoon vanilla extract
1	cup heavy cream
1	9" graham cracker crust
1-2	tablespoons chopped salted peanuts *or*
3	tablespoons melted semi-sweet chocolate

Combine cream cheese and sugar; beat until smooth. Add peanut butter and vanilla; set aside. Beat cream until soft peaks form; fold into cream cheese mixture. Spoon into prepared crust. Garnish with peanuts or drizzle with chocolate. **Yield: 6-8 servings**

Peanut Butter Meringue Pie

¾	cup confectioner's sugar
⅓	cup crunchy peanut butter
1	9" baked pastry shell
⅔	cup granulated sugar
¼	cup cornstarch
1	tablespoon all-purpose flour
½	teaspoon salt
3	egg yolks
3	cups milk
1½	teaspoons vanilla
2	tablespoons butter or margarine, melted

Mix together confectioner's sugar and peanut butter; crumble over pie shell. In a 3-quart saucepan, stir together sugar, cornstarch, flour, salt, egg yolks, and milk. Cook and stir, and bring to a boil. Then lower heat and cook until slightly thickened. Stir in vanilla and melted butter. Pour into baked pastry shell. Top with meringue. Bake at 350° for 6-8 minutes or until meringue peaks are golden. **Yield: 6-8 servings**

Meringue:

3	egg whites
½	cup granulated sugar

Whisk egg whites until foamy. Beat in sugar, 1 tablespoon at a time; continue to beat until stiff and glossy. Spread over pie filling.

Caramel Pie

This surprise recipe comes from the chef at the
Hardware Company Restaurant, Abingdon, Virginia.

2	(14-ounce) cans sweetened condensed milk
1	9" graham cracker-crumb crust
1	cup heavy cream
½	cup confectioner's sugar
1	teaspoon vanilla
½	cup chopped black walnuts

Set unopened cans of condensed milk in saucepan of water, enough to cover; heat to boiling. Cover pan; slow boil for 2 hours, checking frequently to maintain water level. Remove cans; cool under running water. Open cans; pour cooled contents into crust. Refrigerate until set. Beat heavy cream to soft peaks; add sugar and vanilla. Spread over pie; sprinkle with chopped walnuts. **Yield: 8 servings**

Fudge Pie

1	cup granulated sugar
½	cup butter or margarine
2	egg yolks
2	ounces unsweetened chocolate
⅓	cup all-purpose flour
⅛	teaspoon salt
1	teaspoon vanilla
2	egg whites
Vanilla ice cream	

Cream sugar and butter; add egg yolks, melted chocolate, flour, salt, and vanilla. Beat egg whites until soft peaks form. Fold egg whites into chocolate mixture. Pour into greased 9" pie plate; bake at 325° for 20-30 minutes. May be made day before; reheat and serve topped with vanilla ice cream. *This recipe freezes well. Always thaw before reheating.*
Yield: 6-8 servings

Chocolate Meringue Pie

2	ounces unsweetened chocolate
½	cup butter or margarine
4	egg yolks
1	cup granulated sugar
1	teaspoon vanilla
1	(12-ounce) can evaporated milk
1	9" unbaked pastry shell
4	egg whites
1	tablespoon ice water
6	tablespoons granulated sugar

Melt chocolate and butter together over low heat and set aside to cool. Meanwhile, beat egg yolks and sugar together until light and fluffy. Add the chocolate mixture and vanilla; stir well. Add milk. Pour into pastry shell. Bake at 400° for 10 minutes. Reduce heat to 350° and bake an additional 35-40 minutes. Remove from oven; the middle of the pie will be shaky. About 10 minutes before baking time is up, make meringue: Beating the egg whites and ice water. Immediately add sugar, 1 tablespoon at a time. Beat until whites are stiff. Spread on warm pie and continue baking at 350° until meringue is browned. **Yield: 8 servings**

Pecan Pie

2	eggs
¼	cup granulated sugar
½	cup corn syrup
4	tablespoons butter or margarine, melted
½	cup chopped pecans
½	cup milk
½	teaspoon vanilla
½	teaspoon salt
1	8" unbaked pastry shell

Beat eggs until light. Add sugar. Stir in corn syrup, butter, pecans, milk, vanilla, and salt; mix thoroughly. Pour into pastry shell. Bake at 400° for 10 minutes; reduce heat to 350° and bake for 50 minutes more. **Yield: 6 servings**

TO MAKE A RICH BLACK CAKE

(Mount Vernon)

Take 20 eggs; divide the whites from the yolks, and beat the whites to a froth. Then work 2 pounds of butter to a cream, put the whites of eggs to it, a spoonful at a time, until well mixed. Then put 2 pounds of sugar, finely powdered, in it in the same manner. Then add the yolks of eggs, well beaten, 2½ pounds of flour, and 5 pounds of fruit. Add to this ¼ ounce of mace, a nutmeg, ½ pint of wine, and some French brandy. Five and one-quarter hours will bake it.

MRS. WASHINGTON,
Mount Vernon.

FRITTERS

(Arlington)

Make up 1 quart of flour with 1 egg well beaten; a large spoonful of yeast, and as much milk as will make it a little softer than muffin dough. Mix it early in the evening. In the morning, when well risen, work in 2 tablespoonfuls of melted butter. Make into balls the size of a walnut and fry a light brown in boiling lard. Serve with wine and sugar or molasses.

Christt Church

ALEXANDRIA, VIRGINIA

CIRCA 1766 - 1773

THE TOWN OF Alexandria was first called Hunting Creek Warehouse. In 1762, the town was enlarged to include the land of the Alexander family (hence, the name Alexandria) and was also included in the Fairfax Parish, established 1764. Christ Church was one of two parish churches built in 1766. Construction materials consisted of a mortar mixed two-thirds lime and one-third sand (opposite of modern mortar), which accounts for the durability of the walls. The roof was covered with ¾" cypress or juniper shingles. When the church was completed in 1773, ten pews were immediately sold, with George Washington paying the highest price. His pew has remained in the Washington family for generations. Robert E. Lee worshipped here in 1861, just before travelling to Richmond to accept command of the Army of Northern Virginia.

Apple Crisp

This recipe is a wonderful breakfast dish, too.

3	cups sliced or chopped cooking apples
1	tablespoons all-purpose flour
¼	cup granulated sugar
1	teaspoon salt
1	tablespoon water

Place apples in 1½-quart casserole. Combine flour, sugar, salt and water; pour over apples.

Topping:

½	cup oatmeal
¼	teaspoon salt
6	tablespoons butter or margarine, melted

Mix oatmeal, salt, and butter; sprinkle over apples. Bake at 375° for 35 minutes. **Variation:** Substitute ¼ cup peanut butter plus 2 tablespoons butter for butter listed above. **Yield: 4-6 servings**

Apple Dumplings

1	(5-ounce) can buttermilk biscuits
2½	medium-sized cooking apples, peeled, cored, and quartered
¾	cup granulated sugar
¾	cup water
¼	cup butter or margarine
½	teaspoon vanilla
¼	teaspoon ground cinnamon

Roll each biscuit into a 5½" circle on a lightly floured surface. Cut each circle in half. Place 1 apple quarter on each piece of dough. Moisten edges of dough with water; bring ends to center, pinching to seal. Place dumplings in an 8" x 8" x 2" baking dish. Repeat procedure with remaining dough and apples. Combine sugar, water, margarine, vanilla, and cinnamon in a saucepan; cook over medium heat until mixture boils. Pour syrup over dumplings. Bake at 350° for 30 minutes until dumplings are golden brown. Baste with syrup. **Yield: 6-8 servings**

Blueberries and Peaches with Mint Sauce

4 fresh peaches, peeled, pitted and sliced
1 cup blueberries, rinsed and drained
3 tablespoons fresh lemon juice
¼ cup loosely packed fresh mint leaves, chopped
4 teaspoons granulated sugar

Mix together sliced peaches and blueberries; set aside. In food processor or blender, combine lemon juice, mint, and sugar. Process until blended. Pour over fruit, toss gently, and refrigerate. **Yield: 4 servings**

Lucy's Blueberry Bump

½ cup butter or margarine
1 cup granulated sugar
¾ cup all-purpose flour
2 teaspoons baking powder
⅛ teaspoon salt
¾ cup milk
2 cups fresh blueberries, rinsed and picked over

Preheat oven to 325°. Put butter in 9" x 9" x 2" glass baking dish; set in oven to melt. Meanwhile, whisk together sugar, flour, baking powder, salt, and milk. Remove dish from oven; pour in batter. Do not stir. Scatter fruit over top. Bake for 1 hour, or until pudding pulls away from sides of dish. **Yield: 8 servings**

Cherry Ritz

3 egg whites
¾ cup granulated sugar
½ teaspoon vanilla
½ cup chopped pecans
1 cup crushed round, buttery crackers (not too fine)
1 (8-ounce) carton frozen whipped topping, thawed
1 (16-ounce) can cherry pie filling

Beat egg whites until stiff. Beat in sugar and vanilla. Fold in pecans and cracker crumbs. Spread mixture in 13" x 9" x 2" pan. Bake at 350° for 25 minutes. Remove from oven and cool completely. Spread whipped topping over baked meringue. Then carefully spread cherry pie filling over the whipped topping. **Yield: 12-15 servings**

Bebe's Lemon Chiffon Cups

Nice, light, "company" dessert

4	eggs, separated
¾	cup granulated sugar, divided
1	grated lemon rind
1½	tablespoons lemon juice
4	tablespoons lemon gelatin dessert mix
1	cup hot water
1	cup heavy cream
4	egg whites, beaten
2	tablespoons butter or margarine, melted
4-6	vanilla wafers, crumbled
Granulated sugar	

In saucepan over medium heat, combine egg yolks, ½ cup sugar, grated lemon, and lemon juice; cook until thickened. Remove from heat. Dissolve lemon gelatin mix in hot water; add to custard. Refrigerate. Beat egg whites until stiff. Beat cream until stiff. When lemon mixture cools, fold in the stiffly beaten egg whites and whipped cream. Spoon mixture into small dessert cups or parfait glasses; refrigerate. Combine butter, vanilla wafers, and remaining sugar; sprinkle on tops.
Yield: 10 (3-ounce) servings

Godiva Cream Strawberries

To Die For!

1	pint strawberries, capped and halved
6	ounces Godiva liqueur
1	(12-ounce) carton frozen whipped topping
4	sprigs chocolate-flavored mint

Divide strawberries into 4 balloon-shaped wine glasses. Pour 1½ ounces of liqueur over berries. Top with whipped cream, garnish each glass with mint and one beautiful strawberry. **Yield: 4 servings**

Piña al Homo con Natillas

Baked Pineapple with Custard Sauce

1	large, fresh pineapple
¼	cup granulated sugar
3	tablespoons all-purpose flour
3	tablespoons light rum
¼	cup butter or margarine

Lay pineapple on its side; cut a thick slice on 1 side that does not include green top. Carefully scoop out flesh and cut into bite-sized chunks. In a bowl, combine pineapple chunks, sugar, flour, and rum; spoon mixture back into pineapple boat. Dot with butter. Cover pineapple (including leaves) with aluminum foil. Bake at 350° for 20 minutes. Serve warm with cold Natillas Sauce (recipe below). **Yield: 8-12 servings**

Natillas Sauce:

2	cups half-and-half
¼	cup granulated sugar
¼	teaspoon salt
1	teaspoon cornstarch
1	egg
2	egg yolks
1	teaspoon vanilla

Scald half-and-half; cool slightly. Combine sugar, salt, and cornstarch; whisk in whole egg and egg yolks. Add half-and-half. Cook in top of double boiler over simmering water until sauce thickens slightly. Add vanilla. Refrigerate. **Yield: 2½ cups**

English Trifle

A true English recipe - the best ever!

2	dozen ladyfingers
1	(8-12 ounce) jar strawberry jam

Dry Madeira or Sherry

2	cups broken fresh bakery macaroons
¾	cup toasted, slivered almonds
4	cups thick boiled custard (see recipe below)
2	cups heavy cream

Maraschino cherries for garnish

Split ladyfingers; spread each with strawberry jam. Drizzle Madeira or Sherry over macaroons. (All of these steps may be done a day ahead and refrigerated.) Layer ladyfingers, almonds, and wine-soaked macaroons in large serving bowl; repeat until all is used. Cover and refrigerate until serving time. Prepare custard ahead and refrigerate. Pour custard over trifle. Whip cream; spread over custard; garnish with cherries.
Yield: 10-12 servings

Boiled custard:

1	quart milk
5-6	whole eggs, lightly beaten
½	cup granulated sugar
¼	teaspoon salt
2	tablespoons vanilla

Combine milk, eggs, sugar, salt, and vanilla in large saucepan; cook slowly, stirring, until custard thickens and coats a silver spoon. Refrigerate.

Tips for Successful Desserts

A gelatin dessert will not congeal if frozen pineapple is added. Bring the pineapple to a boil and cook it a minute or two, then it will work perfectly.

To flame a dessert or other dish without using brandy, sprinkle drops of fresh lemon extract over the dish and flame.

If custard curdles during cooking due to high heat, pour immediately into a cold bowl and beat hard with a whisk.

Macaroon Soufflé

8	eggs, separated
1½	cups granulated sugar
½	teaspoon salt
2	cups milk
3	tablespoons unflavored gelatin
3	tablespoons water
4	cups broken fresh bakery macaroons
2	tablespoons vanilla
2	cups heavy cream

Separate egg yolks and whites. Beat yolks. Combine sugar, salt, and milk in double boiler; add egg yolks. Dissolve gelatin in water; add to custard. Cook and stir over simmering water until thickened. Remove from heat; cool completely. Fold in macaroons and vanilla. Beat egg whites until stiff; fold into custard mixture. (Note: be sure egg yolk mixture is cold, but not jellied, before adding egg whites, as they tend to fall if custard is warm at all.) Pour into lightly oiled 10" ring mold; refrigerate overnight. Unmold soufflé by placing in very hot water for a few seconds and then inverting mold on serving plate. Meanwhile, whip cream until soft peaks form; frost soufflé ring. **Yield 6-8 servings**

Ginger Mousse

1	quart heavy cream
⅓	cup granulated sugar
2	teaspoons chopped ginger root
1⅓	cups shredded coconut
1	cup chopped walnuts
9	tablespoons Drambuie liqueur
2	tablespoons Scotch whisky
1	(16-ounce) package ginger snap cookies

Beat cream until stiff; add sugar as mixture thickens. Fold in the following ingredients, one at a time, in this order: ginger, coconut, walnuts, Drambuie, and Scotch. Spoon a layer of the cream mixture into the bottom of a large glass or ceramic bowl. Cover the cream with a layer of cookies. Repeat layering process until all ingredients are used; end with cream mixture. This may be prepared one day in advance; refrigerate until serving time. **Yield: 10 servings**

Chocolate Mousse

1   tablespoon unflavored gelatin
⅓   cup cold water
½   cup boiling water
3   ounces unsweetened chocolate
4   eggs, beaten separately
1   cup sugar
1   teaspoon vanilla

Whipped cream:

1   cup heavy cream
3   tablespoons confectioner's sugar
1   teaspoon vanilla
Grated semi-sweet or milk chocolate

Dissolve gelatin in cold water, then add boiling water. Melt chocolate. Combine sugar and beaten egg yolks. Add chocolate; slowly stir in gelatin mixture. Fold in stiffly beaten egg whites and vanilla. Pour into a serving bowl. Refrigerate. Just before serving, whip cream until stiff peaks form; add sugar and vanilla. Top mousse with whipped cream; garnish with grated chocolate. *Be sure to blend thoroughly after each ingredient is added in making this mousse. That's the secret.* **Yield: 6-8 servings**

Chocolate Almond Custards

Here's a refreshing dessert that's light and soooo good!

2   cups milk
½   cup semi-sweet chocolate chips
½   cup granulated sugar
3   eggs, slightly beaten
¼   teaspoon almond extract

Combine milk and chocolate in a saucepan. Cook and stir over low heat until chocolate melts. Combine sugar, eggs, and extract; gradually add chocolate mixture, beating with mixer on low speed until smooth. Put six 6-ounce glass baking cups in a 13" x 9" x 2" pan. Pour chocolate mixture into cups. Pour boiling water into pan to a depth of 1". Bake at 325° for 40-45 minutes or until custards test done. Serve warm or chilled.
Yield: 6 servings

Frozen Chocolate Mousse

Simply elegant. Can be made a week in advance.

Crust:

8	ounces chocolate wafer cookies
6	tablespoons butter or margarine

Adjust oven rack a ⅓ up from oven bottom. Separate bottom from side of 9" springform pan. Butter sides only; replace bottom; and set pan aside. Crush cookies in food processor. Melt butter; mix with crumbs. Pour ⅔ of the mixture into pan. Tilt and press thin layer of crumbs against the sides. Pat remaining crumbs on bottom. Bake at 375° for 7-8 minutes. Remove from oven and cool.

Mousse:

1	teaspoon instant coffee
½	cup boiling water
1¼	cups granulated sugar, divided
8	ounces semi-sweet chocolate
3	eggs, separated
2	cups heavy cream
Pinch salt	
⅛	teaspoon cream of tartar

In medium saucepan, dissolve coffee in water. Add ½ cup sugar; stir over moderate heat until dissolved. Add chocolate; stir until melted. Remove from heat. Whisk in egg yolks one at a time; cool.

In a large bowl, whip the cream until soft peaks form; set aside. In small bowl, beat egg whites with salt until foamy. Gradually add cream of tartar and remaining ¾ cup of sugar. Beat until firm, but not stiff and dry. Fold in chocolate mixture. Fold whipped cream into chocolate mixture. Spoon into crumb crust.

Freeze. After a few hours, cover top with plastic wrap. To serve, run thin knife around insides of pan; remove sides. Slide spatula under bottom crust; slide onto serving plate. **Yield: 12 servings**

Raisin Bread Pudding

2½	cups skim milk
6	(1-ounce) slices raisin bread, cubed
2	eggs, lightly beaten
2	tablespoons honey
1	teaspoon vanilla
¼	teaspoon salt
¼	teaspoon cinnamon
⅛	teaspoon nutmeg

Pour milk into a large saucepan; heat until warm. Remove from heat; add bread, eggs, honey, vanilla, salt, cinnamon, and nutmeg; mix well. Spoon mixture evenly into 6 (4-ounce) ramekins coated with nonstick vegetable cooking spray. Place ramekins in 13" x 9" x 2" pan and add hot water to a depth of 1". Bake at 350° for 20 minutes; shield with aluminum foil; bake an additional 15 minutes or until knife inserted in center comes out clean. Remove ramekins from water and serve warm or chilled.
Yield: 6 servings

New York-Style Cheesecake

Divine!

1	pound cream cheese
1	pound ricotta cheese
1½	cups granulated sugar
3	tablespoons all-purpose flour
3	tablespoons cornstarch
4	eggs, beaten
½	cup butter or margarine, melted
2	tablespoons lemon juice
1	teaspoon vanilla
2	cups sour cream

Beat cream cheese and ricotta together until light and fluffy. Combine sugar, flour, and cornstarch; stir into cheese mixture. Add eggs and butter. Then add lemon juice and vanilla. Fold in sour cream, mixing well. Pour into a greased-and-floured 9" springform pan. Bake at 325° for 70 minutes. Do not open oven door. Turn off oven; leave cake in oven for at least 3 hours, preferably overnight. Refrigerate.
Yield: 15 servings

Pumpkin Cheesecake

A new Thanksgiving tradition!

Crust:

1½	cups graham cracker crumbs
¼	cup granulated sugar
⅓	cup butter or margarine, melted

Filling:

3	(8-ounce) packages regular or light cream cheese
1	cup granulated sugar
¼	cup light brown sugar
1	(16-ounce) can pumpkin
2	eggs
1	(5-ounce) can evaporated milk, undiluted
2	tablespoons cornstarch
1¼	teaspoons cinnamon
½	teaspoon nutmeg

Topping:

2	cups regular or light sour cream
⅓	cup granulated sugar
1	tablespoon vanilla

CRUST: Combine graham cracker crumbs, sugar, and butter. Press onto bottom and up 1" on side of 9" spring form pan. Bake at 350° for 6-8 minutes. Remove from oven; cool.

FILLING: Beat cream cheese and sugars until fluffy. Beat in pumpkin, eggs, and milk. Add cornstarch, cinnamon, and nutmeg. Pour into crust; bake at 350° for 55-60 minutes or until edge is set.

TOPPING: Combine sour cream, sugar, and vanilla. Spread over warm cheesecake. Return to 350° oven; bake 5 minutes. Cool on wire rack. Chill several hours or overnight before serving. **Yield: 12 servings**

Vanilla Ice Cream

This family recipe was designed for the old-fashioned, hand-cranked machine.

3   quarts half-and-half, divided
2½-3 cups granulated sugar
Dash salt
1   vanilla bean
6   eggs

In large heavy saucepan, scald 1 quart half-and-half with sugar, salt, and vanilla bean. In a separate bowl, beat eggs; add 1 quart half-and-half. Remove softened vanilla bean from heated milk and sugar mixture, split and scrape out pulp and seeds into pan, saving the bean. Pour hot mixture into egg mixture; beat. Return to pan with split vanilla bean. Add last quart of half-and-half. Cook over low heat, stirring constantly until thick and creamy. Do not boil! Cool, remove vanilla bean; refrigerate. Next day, pour custard into ice cream freezer. Following manufacturer's directions, crank until frozen. **Yield: 1 gallon**

Pavlova

4   egg whites
¾   cup granulated sugar
1   cup heavy cream
½   cup confectioner's sugar
½   teaspoon vanilla
1   (1.45-ounce) milk chocolate bar, grated

Beat whites of eggs stiff; gradually add granulated sugar. Line cookie sheet with brown paper. Spread meringue in 9" circle on brown paper. Bake at 275° for 45 minutes. Turn off oven and open door slightly to cool. Remove and invert on platter. Beat cream to soft peaks; add confectioner's sugar and vanilla. Cover baked meringue with whipped cream and sprinkle with grated chocolate. Refrigerate at least 4 hours before serving. **Yield: 8 servings**

Applesauce Cookies

½	cup vegetable oil
1	cup granulated sugar
1	egg
1¾	cups thick applesauce
2½	cups sifted all-purpose flour
1	teaspoon baking powder
½	teaspoon baking soda
½	teaspoon salt
¾	teaspoon cinnamon
¼	teaspoon cloves
½	cup raisins

Blend together the oil, sugar and egg. Add applesauce and mix well. Mix flour, baking powder, soda, salt, cinnamon, cloves and raisins; stir into sugar mixture. Drop on ungreased cookie sheets. Bake at 375° for 10-12 minutes. These cookies spread, so space accordingly.

Ellie's Cookies

My grandfather's cousin, Ellie, used to make these for us when we visited them years ago in Georgia.

1	cup butter, margarine, or shortening
2	cups brown sugar
2	eggs
3½	cups all-purpose flour
½	teaspoon baking soda
2	teaspoons cinnamon
½	teaspoon salt
1	cup chopped pecans

Cream butter or shortening, brown sugar, and eggs. Sift flour, baking soda, salt, and cinnamon together. Combine butter mixture with dry ingredients. Add nuts to make a stiff dough. Roll dough into logs and refrigerate overnight. Slice into ¼" slices; place on ungreased cookie sheets. Bake at 350° for 8-10 minutes. This cookie burns easily, so watch carefully. **Yield: 3-4 dozen**

Cinnamon Sledge Cookies

Old New England Recipe

1   cup butter (no substitutions)
1   cup granulated sugar
1   teaspoon cinnamon
½   teaspoon salt
1   egg, separated
2   cups sifted all-purpose flour
½   cup (or more) chopped nuts

Beat the butter until fluffy. Mix the sugar, cinnamon and salt together; beat into butter. Add egg yolk. Add the flour, ½ cup at a time, mixing well after each addition. Spoon into ungreased 15" x 10" x 1" jelly roll pan. Use fingers to pat dough evenly over pan. Lightly beat egg white; brush on surface of dough. Sprinkle chopped nuts on top and lightly press into dough. Bake at 325° about 30 minutes - watch closely. While warm, cut into squares; leave in pan to cool. Store in airtight container. **Yield: 4 dozen**

Pound Cake Cookies

1   cup butter or margarine
1   cup granulated sugar
2   eggs
2   cups all-purpose flour
2   teaspoons vanilla
Pecan halves or candied cherries (optional)

Cream butter and sugar. Add eggs. Gradually add flour and vanilla. Drop mixture in small amounts from the tip of a teaspoon onto ungreased cookie sheets. If desired, press pecan half or cherry on each cookie. Bake at 325° for 12-15 minutes. **Yield: 5 dozen**

White Chocolate Chip Cookies

2½	cups all-purpose flour
⅔	cup cocoa
1	teaspoon baking soda
¼	teaspoon salt
1	cup butter or margarine, softened
¾	cup granulated sugar
⅔	cup brown sugar
1	teaspoon vanilla
2	eggs
1	(12-ounce) package white chocolate chips

Combine flour, cocoa, baking soda, and salt in small bowl. Beat butter, sugars, and vanilla in large bowl until creamy. Blend in eggs. Gradually add flour mixture. Stir in chips. Drop by well-rounded teaspoonfuls onto ungreased cookie sheets. Bake at 350° for 9-11 minutes. Let stand for 2 minutes; remove to wire racks to cool completely. **Yield: 5 dozen**

Chocolate Biscotti

6	ounces shelled hazelnuts
4	ounces unsweetened chocolate
½	cup butter or margarine
½	teaspoon vanilla
3	eggs, separated
1¼	cups granulated sugar, divided
3¼	cups sifted all-purpose flour
½	teaspoon baking powder
1	egg white, lightly beaten

Toast nuts in 375° oven for 5-8 minutes. Remove from oven. While still warm, wrap nuts in clean dish towel; let steam for 1-2 minutes. Rub nuts together vigorously to remove as much of the skin as possible. Leave half the nuts whole; finely chop ¼, and coarsely chop the rest. Melt chocolate with butter; stir in vanilla; set aside to cool. Beat the egg yolks with half the sugar until pale and thick. Fold in cooled chocolate mixture.

In a separate bowl, beat the egg whites until frothy; gradually add remaining sugar; beat until stiff and glossy. Fold meringue into yolk mixture. Re-sift flour with baking powder; gradually fold into egg-sugar mixture. Add nuts. With lightly floured hands, shape the dough into a cylinder 1½" wide and 10" long. Place on greased cookie sheet. Brush with egg white. Bake at 350° for 45 minutes or until dough is set. Remove from sheet; cut diagonally into ½" slices. Toast the biscotti on cookie sheets for 5-8 minutes on each side or until slightly dry. *Stored in an airtight container, the cookies will keep for 2 weeks.* **Yield: 3 dozen**

Holiday Fruit Drops

1	(18¼-ounce) package orange cake mix
½	cup shortening
⅓	cup butter or margarine, softened
2	eggs
2	tablespoons milk
1	cup chopped pecans
½	cup chopped candied green cherries, halved
½	cup chopped candied red cherries, halved
½	cup chopped dates
1	cup confectioner's sugar
2	teaspoons lemon juice
2	teaspoons orange juice

Combine cake mix, shortening, butter, eggs, and milk in large bowl; beat until well blended. Stir in pecans, cherries, and dates. Drop by rounded teaspoonfuls 2" apart onto ungreased cookie sheets. Bake at 375° for 8-9 minutes. Cool 2 minutes on cookie sheets; remove to wire racks. Cool completely before glazing. In a small bowl, combine confectioner's sugar and juices to make a thin glaze. Drizzle over cookies. Allow glaze to set before storing. **Yield: 5 dozen**

Honey Bunches

3	cups quick-cooking oats
2	cups flaked coconut
1	cup all-purpose flour
1½	cups brown sugar
1	cup butter or margarine
½	cup honey

In a large bowl, combine oats, coconut, and flour. In a heavy saucepan, combine sugar, butter, and honey; bring to a boil. Pour over dry ingredients; mix well. Drop dough by teaspoonfuls into greased 1¾" muffin tins. Bake at 350° for 12-15 minutes or until browned. Cool completely in pans before removing. **Yield: 4 dozen**

Lemon Crinkles

½   cup shortening
1   cup firmly packed brown sugar
1   egg
1   tablespoon grated lemon rind
1½   cups all purpose flour
½   teaspoon baking soda
½   teaspoon cream of tartar
¼   teaspoon ground ginger
Pinch of salt
2   tablespoons granulated sugar

Cream shortening and brown sugar until fluffy. Add egg and grated lemon rind; beat well. Combine flour, soda, cream of tartar, ginger and salt. Stir dry ingredients into creamed mixture. Roll dough into 1" balls; then roll each in granulated sugar. Place 2" apart on ungreased cookie sheet. Bake at 350° for 10-12 minutes. **Yield: 3½ dozen**

Loreta's Date Sticks

A loving grandmother's gift

6   tablespoons all-purpose flour, sifted
⅛   teaspoon salt
½   teaspoon cinnamon
1   teaspoon baking powder
2   eggs
¾   cup brown sugar
2   teaspoons grated orange rind
1   cup chopped walnuts or pecans
1   cup chopped pitted dates
½   teaspoon vanilla
Confectioner's sugar

Sift flour once, measure, and re-sift with salt, cinnamon, and baking powder. Beat eggs; add brown sugar. Stir in sifted ingredients. Add orange rind, nuts, dates, and vanilla. Blend well. Spoon mixture into a greased, waxed paper-lined 8" square pan. (Both the pan and the waxed paper should be greased with shortening.) Bake at 325° for 30-35 minutes. Sprinkle with confectioner's sugar. Cool. Cut into strips of desired size. **Yield: 1 dozen**

Scottish Shortbread

1	cup butter or margarine
½	cup granulated sugar
2½	cups all-purpose flour

Cream butter and sugar until light and fluffy. Gradually add flour. Refrigerate dough for 30 minutes. Divide into 3 equal parts. With floured hands, pat into 3 rectangles ½" thick on ungreased cookie sheets. With a sharp knife, score each rectangle into 12 squares. Prick each square with fork. Bake at 300° for 30-35 minutes or until cream-colored, but not brown. **Yield: 3 dozen**

Cornmeal Shortbread Cookies

1	cup butter or margarine
½	cup brown sugar
1	cup confectioner's sugar
1	cup cornmeal
1¼	cups all-purpose flour
½	teaspoon salt
1	cup chopped, toasted almonds

Cream butter and sugars in a large bowl until light and fluffy. Add cornmeal, flour, and salt; mix until well blended. Add almonds. Roll dough into four 1½"-2" diameter cylinders about 6" long. Refrigerate until firm. Line cookie sheets with parchment or waxed paper. When dough is firm, cut into ¼" slices with a sharp knife. Place cookies on sheets and bake at 325° for 10-12 minutes, or until golden brown. *These pack and ship well.* **Yield: 4 dozen**

Tips for Successful Cookies

To soften hard butter quickly, fill a bowl with very hot water for 3 minutes. Drain and dry bowl and invert it over the sticks of butter.

Always use a shiny cookie sheet. Dark or stained cookie sheets absorb heat and may over-brown cookie bottoms.

Store soft cookies in an airtight container and place a slice of bread in the container to keep them soft. Store crisp cookies in containers with loose fitting tops.

Melting Moments

1	cup all-purpose flour, sifted
½	cup cornstarch
½	cup confectioner's sugar
¼	cup cocoa (optional)
¼	teaspoon salt (optional)
¾	cup butter or margarine
1	teaspoon vanilla

Combine, flour, cornstarch, sugar, cocoa, and salt; set aside. In large bowl, cream butter until light and fluffy. Beat in vanilla and reserved dry ingredients. Cover and refrigerate 1 hour. Shape dough into 1" balls. Place balls 1½" apart on ungreased cookie sheets; flatten slightly with fork tines. Bake at 375° for 10-12 minutes or until edges are lightly browned. **Yield: 3 dozen**

Mexican Tea Cakes

This is an original from Cooking Capers.

1	cup butter or margarine, softened
1	cup confectioner's sugar
2	cups all-purpose flour
½	teaspoon salt
1	tablespoon vanilla
1	cup chopped pecans
	Additional confectioner's sugar

In large bowl of mixer, combine butter or margarine, sugar, flour, salt and vanilla and beat until blended. Stir in nuts by hand. Shape into balls using a rounded teaspoon for each. Place on ungreased cookie sheets. Bake at 325° for 15-18 minutes. Do not brown. Roll warm cookies in additional sugar. **Yield: 4-5 dozen**

Molasses Sugar Cookies

This is an original from Country Capers.

¾	cup real butter
1	cup granulated sugar
¼	cup sorghum molasses
1	egg
2	cups all-purpose flour
2	teaspoons baking soda
½	teaspoon salt
½	teaspoon ground cloves
½	teaspoon ginger
1	teaspoon cinnamon

Melt butter in large saucepan over low heat. Cool slightly. Stir in sugar, molasses, and egg and beat well. Sift together flour, soda, salt, cloves, ginger, and cinnamon. Combine with butter mixture until well blended. Refrigerate dough at least 1 hour. Form into marble-sized balls and roll in granulated sugar. Place on greased cookie sheets and flatten each ball slightly with fingertip. Bake at 375° for about 8 minutes. **Yield: 6 dozen**

Nana's Ice Box Cookies

This is an original from Cooking Capers.

1	cup butter or margarine
1½	cups granulated sugar
2	eggs
3	cups all-purpose flour
1	teaspoon baking soda
½	teaspoon salt
2	teaspoons nutmeg *or*
1	tablespoon grated orange or lemon rind *and*
2	teaspoons Sherry

Cream butter and sugar together until light. Add eggs. Mix together flour, soda, salt, and nutmeg or rind and sherry; add to egg mixture. Divide dough into two parts. Place on waxed paper and shape into rolls 1½" in diameter. Wrap and refrigerate 3-4 hours. Cut into ⅛" slices with a sharp knife. Place on ungreased cookie sheets. Bake at 375° for 8-10 minutes. **Yield: 8-9 dozen**

Texas Pecan Pie Bars

1	(18¼-ounce) package butter-recipe yellow cake mix, divided
4	eggs, divided
½	cup butter or margarine, melted
1½	cups dark corn syrup
½	cup dark brown sugar
1	teaspoon vanilla
1	cup chopped pecans

Measure ⅔ cup cake mix; set aside. Combine remaining mix with 1 egg and butter. Spread in greased and floured 13" x 9" x 2" pan. Bake at 350° for 15-20 minutes. Meanwhile, beat remaining eggs; combine with reserved cake mix, corn syrup, brown sugar, and vanilla. Pour over baked crust. Sprinkle with pecans. Bake at 350° for 30-35 minutes. Cool in pan on rack. Run sharp knife around edge when cooling. When cool, cut into squares. **Yield: 3 dozen**

Chocolate Revel Bars

1	cup semi-sweet chocolate chips
1	cup + 3 tablespoons butter or margarine, divided
1	(14-ounce) can sweetened condensed milk
2	teaspoons vanilla
¾	cup coarsely chopped pecans
2	cups light brown sugar
2	eggs
2½	cups all-purpose flour
1	teaspoon baking powder
¾	teaspoon salt
¾	cup quick-cooking oats

Melt chocolate chips, 3 tablespoons butter, and milk together in microwave. Stir until smooth. Add vanilla and nuts; cool slightly. Cream 1 cup butter and brown sugar; add eggs. Sift together flour, baking powder, and salt. Add oats to creamed mixture. Spread three-quarters of the dough in greased 15" x 10" x 1" jelly roll pan. Carefully spread fudge mixture evenly over dough, leaving ½" border all around. Dot remaining dough over the top. Bake at 350° for 20-25 minutes. Cool; cut into bars. **Yield: 4 dozen**

THE Best Brownies

Supposedly, this is Katharine Hepburn's recipe—it's divine!

½   cup butter or margarine
2   ounces unsweetened chocolate
1   cup granulated sugar
½   teaspoon salt
2   eggs, lightly beaten
1   cup all-purpose flour
1   cup chopped walnuts
1   teaspoon vanilla

Melt butter and chocolate together. While hot, add sugar and salt. Cool slightly. Alternately add eggs and flour. Stir in nuts and vanilla. Pour into lightly greased 8" x 8" x 2" square pan. Bake at 325° for 40-45 minutes. Cool before cutting into bars. **Yield: 1 dozen**

Caramel Brownies

1   cup butter or margarine
1   cup chopped pecans
4   cups dark brown sugar
2   cups unsifted all-purpose flour
1   teaspoon baking powder
4   eggs, separated
Confectioner's sugar

Melt butter with nuts and sugar in an iron skillet; pour into large bowl. Add flour, baking powder, and egg yolks. Mix thoroughly. Beat egg whites until stiff peaks form; fold into batter. Pour into a greased 9" x 9" x 2" square pan or 13" x 9" x 2" pan, depending on desired thickness. Bake at 300° for 45 minutes. Cut into squares. Sprinkle with confectioner's sugar if desired. **Yield: 1-2 dozen**

Church Windows

1   (12-ounce) package semi-sweet chocolate chips
½   cup margarine or butter
1   (10½-ounce) package colored miniature marshmallows
½   cup chopped nuts (optional)
Confectioner's sugar

Melt chocolate chips and margarine in top of double boiler. When completely melted, remove from heat; beat until cool. Add marshmallows in folding motion. Stir in nuts. Sprinkle confectioner's sugar on sheets of waxed paper; spoon candy mixture on sugar and form into 3-3" logs. Refrigerate until firm. Slice and serve. **Yield: 4 dozen**

M&M Party Mix

Fun for Easter with pastel M&M's

3   cups doughnut-shaped oat cereal
3   cups bite-sized crisp rice cereal squares
3   cups bite-sized crisp corn cereal squares
3   cups small, round pretzels
1   cup salted peanuts
1   cup M&M's candies
1   pound white chocolate coating wafers

In a large bowl, combine cereals, pretzels, peanuts, and M&M's. Melt white chocolate; pour over cereal mixture. Stir and mix well. Refrigerate, stirring every 10 minutes until chocolate has solidified. Store in airtight container; this doesn't have to be refrigerated after chocolate sets. **Yield: 11 cups**

Party Mints

This originally appeared in P. S.

2   cups granulated sugar
2   tablespoons white corn syrup
Pinch salt
¾   cup cold water
¼   teaspoon cream of tartar
Peppermint extract

Combine sugar, syrup, salt, and water in large, heavy saucepan. Cook and stir over medium-high heat. When mixture boils, add cream of tartar. Let boil to soft-ball stage (235°). Place saucepan in a large non breakable bowl of iced water; beat with electric mixer until creamy. Beat in 3-4 drops of peppermint extract. Return pan to low heat and let candy melt. Drop mixture by teaspoonfuls onto waxed paper. **Yield: 1 pound**

German Chocolate Fudge

1   (12-ounce) package semi-sweet chocolate chips
3   (4-ounce) bars sweet chocolate
1   (7-ounce) jar marshmallow creme
4½   cups granulated sugar
2   tablespoons butter or margarine
1   (13-ounce) can evaporated milk, undiluted
¼   teaspoon salt
2   cups chopped nuts

Combine chocolate chips, sweet chocolate, and marshmallow creme in a large bowl; set aside. Combine sugar, butter, milk, and salt in a heavy skillet. Bring mixture to a boil; boil for 6 minutes, stirring constantly. Pour hot syrup over chocolate mixture. Stir with a wooden spoon until smooth. Add nuts and mix well. Spread in a buttered 15" x 10" x 1" jelly roll pan. Cool; when firm, cut into squares. **Yield: 2 pounds**

Creamy Marshmallow Fudge

Hubby always makes this for Christmas gifts. It's very creamy.

1	(6¼-ounce) package miniature marshmallows
1½	cups granulated sugar
⅔	cup evaporated milk
¼	cup butter or margarine
¼	teaspoon salt
1	(12-ounce) package semi-sweet chocolate morsels
½	cup chopped nuts (optional)
1	teaspoon vanilla

In medium saucepan, combine marshmallows, sugar, evaporated milk, butter, and salt. Bring to a full boil over moderate heat. Stir constantly until all marshmallows are melted. Boil 5 minutes more over moderate heat, stirring constantly. Remove from heat. Add chocolate chips. Stir until chocolate melts and mixture is smooth. Stir in nuts and vanilla. Pour into 8" x 8" x 2" foil-lined pan. Refrigerate until firm, at least 2 hours. **Yield: 1¾ pounds**

Peanut Butter Fudge

1	cup granulated sugar
1	cup firmly packed brown sugar
½	cup half-and-half
2	tablespoons light corn syrup
¼	cup butter or margarine
½	cup crunchy peanut butter
½	cup marshmallow cream
2	teaspoons vanilla

Combine sugars, half-and-half, and corn syrup in Dutch oven. Cook over low heat, stirring gently, until sugar dissolves. Cover; cook over medium heat 2-3 minutes to wash down sugar crystals from sides of pan. Uncover; cook to soft ball stage (235°), stirring occasionally. Remove from heat. Add butter, peanut butter, marshmallow cream, and vanilla. Stir until smooth. Spread mixture in buttered 8" x 8" x 2" pan. Cool and cut into squares. **Yield: 1¾ pounds**

Bourbon Butter Creams

1	pound confectioner's sugar
¼	cup butter or margarine, softened
3	ounces Bourbon whisky
½-1	cup chopped pecans or walnuts
6-8	squares unsweetened chocolate

Mix sugar and butter together. Add Bourbon gradually. Fold in nuts and chill. Shape into balls. Refrigerate 3 hours. Heat baking chocolate in double boiler over hot water until completely melted. Pick up each ball with a toothpick; dip ball in chocolate, then place on rack until cold. Refrigerate. **Yield: 1½ pounds**

Buckeyes

Our family makes these every Christmas!

1	cup butter or margarine, softened
2	cups peanut butter
5¾	cups sifted confectioner's sugar
1	teaspoon vanilla extract
1	(12-ounce) package chocolate chips
¼	cake paraffin wax

Mix butter and peanut butter in a medium bowl until well blended. Add confectioner's sugar and vanilla. Roll into 1" balls. Place on baking sheet; refrigerate. Melt chocolate chips and paraffin wax in double boiler set over hot water. Use toothpicks to dip peanut butter balls into chocolate. Cover the bottom and sides with chocolate, leaving the "eyes" on top uncovered. Place on wax paper-covered baking sheet; refrigerate. **Yield: 2+ pounds**

Tips for Successful Candy Making

Fudge placed in an airtight container for 24 hours will be softer and more velvety.

Humidity will cause pralines to become sugary.

For creamier and smoother fudge, add 1 teaspoon cornstarch to each cup of sugar specified in recipe.

Chocolate Roll

1	cup firmly packed brown sugar
¼	cup white corn syrup
¼	cup evaporated milk, undiluted
1	teaspoon vanilla extract
1	cup semi-sweet chocolate chips
1½	cups coarsely chopped nuts

In a medium saucepan, mix together the sugar, syrup, and evaporated milk. Boil for 2 minutes, stirring constantly. Remove from heat. Add vanilla and chocolate chips. Beat until smooth. Stir in nuts. Shape on waxed paper or plastic wrap in two 12" rolls. Roll up and chill. Cut into ½" slices. **Yield: 4 dozen**

Toffee Bars

¼	pound saltine crackers
1	cup butter (no substitute)
1	cup granulated sugar or brown sugar
1	(12-ounce) package semi-sweet chocolate chips
1	(3-ounce) package slivered almonds (optional)

Line a 15" x 10" x 2" pan with aluminum foil. Lay out enough crackers to cover pan, breaking if necessary. Melt butter with sugar; boil 3 minutes, stirring constantly. Pour hot mixture over the saltines. Bake in 350° oven for 10-12 minutes. Sprinkle chocolate chips over bubbling mixture. Spread with knife to cover. Sprinkle almonds over entire surface. Refrigerate 45 minutes or until hard. Then break into unevenly shaped pieces (not cracker-shaped). Store in sealed container in refrigerator. **Yield: 1 pound**

Butterscotch Sauce

Elegant on vanilla ice cream.

1   (1-pound) box light brown sugar
1⅔   cups light corn syrup
¾   cup butter or margarine
1   (12-ounce) can evaporated milk
Pinch cream of tartar
Dash vanilla

Combine brown sugar, syrup, and butter in double boiler or heavy saucepan; bring to a boil over medium heat, stirring constantly, to hard ball stage (256°). Remove from heat. Add evaporated milk, cream of tartar, and vanilla; beat well. **Yield: 4 cups**

White's Chocolate Sauce

4   ounces unsweetened chocolate
1   (5-ounce) can evaporated milk
1   cup granulated sugar
1   cup whole milk
1   teaspoon vanilla

Melt chocolate in top of double boiler. Gradually stir in evaporated milk, sugar, and milk. Cook and stir until thickened. Add vanilla. Refrigerate. *Best made the day before serving, this sauce is wonderful served over ice cream or angel food cake.* **Yield: 2 cups**

Custard Sauce

3   eggs
2   tablespoons granulated sugar
1   teaspoon cornstarch
2⅓   cups whole milk
2   teaspoons vanilla

Blend together eggs, sugar, and cornstarch. Heat milk until just below boiling point. Whisk into egg mixture. Return to saucepan. Cook, stirring constantly, over medium-low heat until thickened. Cool saucepan quickly in a basin of ice cubes. Serve warm or cold. **Yield: 3 cups**

Dessert Topping for Ice Cream

1   cup granulated sugar
2   teaspoons cornstarch
1   (6-ounce) can frozen orange juice, undiluted and thawed
1   cup water
1   cup drained crushed pineapple
⅓   cup chopped maraschino cherries
1   cup flaked coconut

Combine sugar, cornstarch, orange juice, and water in saucepan. Cook over moderate heat, stirring constantly, until slightly thickened. Stir in pineapple, cherries, and coconut; cook for an additional 2 minutes. Cool before serving. *Keeps well for about 2 weeks in the refrigerator.*
Yield: 2 cups

Praline Sauce for Ice Cream

1   cup firmly packed brown sugar
½   cup half-and-half
½   cup butter or margarine
½   cup chopped pecans
1   teaspoon vanilla

Combine brown sugar, half-and-half, and butter in a small saucepan. Bring to a boil over medium heat, stirring constantly. Remove from heat. Stir in pecans and vanilla. Serve warm over ice cream. *Keeps well in refrigerator for several weeks.* **Yield: 2 cups**

Lemon Curd

*This is traditionally used as a bread spread,
as a dessert sauce, or to fill pastries.
Fresh lemon juice is the secret to intense flavor.*

2	cups granulated sugar
1	cup butter or margarine
¼	cup grated lemon rind
⅔	cup fresh lemon juice
4	large eggs, slightly beaten

Combine sugar, butter, lemon rind, and lemon juice in top of double boiler. Bring water to boil, reduce to low; cook until butter melts. Gradually stir about one fourth of hot mixture into eggs: add to remaining hot mixture, stirring constantly. Cook over medium-low heat, stirring constantly until mixture thickens and coats a spoon (about 15 minutes). Remove from heat; cool. Cover and refrigerate up to 2 weeks. *Serve chilled as a topping for pound cake or gingerbread.* **Yield: 3¼ cups**

Vanilla Extract

12	ounces dark rum
2-3	vanilla beans, split lengthwise

Pour rum into an airtight container; add beans and cover tightly. Let steep for 2-3 weeks. Strain through cheesecloth into a bottle. *Substitute 2 teaspoons of homemade vanilla for 1 teaspoon commercial.* **Yield: 1½ cups**

Contributors

THE CHOIR COOKBOOK COMMITTEE of *O Taste & Sing* wishes to express their deep appreciation to the following parishioners and friends of St. Stephen's Church who so generously contributed many of their favorite time-tested recipes. Names followed by an asterisk denote contributors to two earlier cookbooks, *Cooking Capers* (1960) and *P.S.* (1964) published by the Women of St. Stephen's and whose recipes are featured in this book. Due to cost factors and similarity of recipes, we were unable to publish all recipes received. We hope that our friends will understand this compromise and share in our enthusiasm for the finished product of *O Taste & Sing*.

Bobbie Arnall	Anne Denny	Tho. Hollandsworth	Carter Pollard
Cari Arnall	Sara Frances Derieux	Jacqueline Hoofnagle*	Dorris Prevette
Lauren Aswell	Mary Lou Doherty	Margaret Horsley	Danny Prevette
Eloise Atkinson	Susan Dull	Margaret Hotchkiss	Lindsay Prevette
Lucille Baber	Leslie Douthat	Bette Huntting	Ruth Prevette
Frances Bales	Laurie Dudley	Ann Hyer	Jan Price
Ellen Barry	Linda Dusenbury	Molly Hyer	Martha Purcell
Joyce Bell	Debbie DuVal	Libba Irby	Ravenel Rhoads
Ray Bell	Frank DuVal	Betty Ann Johns	Anne Rhodemyre
Rudy Berger	Phyllis DuVal	Ludmilla Jollie	Becky Roche
Elizabeth Blackburn	Harry Easterly	Betty Joynes	Mary Kay Rose
Margaret Blackburn	Jane Edwards	Anne Kay	Mimi Rose
Ann Blair	Lisa Edwards-Burrs	Edie Kjellstrom	Jane Rowe
Eugenia Borum	Jean Roche Elliott	Polly Kloeti	Jane Ruth
Jean Bounds*	Janie Eppes	Jeannie Knight	Ray Ruth
Carolyn Bowman	Marion Farmer	Anne Larus	Mary Ann Sartin
Carol Bradley	Betty Ann Fleenor	Virginia Lawson	Anne Satterfield
Betty Brill	Barbara Fleming	Harry Lee	Betsy Saunders
Cass Brill	Bill Fleming	Tina Lewis	Harriet Schnell
Kate Brill	Adelaide Flippen	Anne Lumpkin	Jean Shields
Maud Brown	Susan Foy	Emma Lou Martin	Mary Frances Siersema
Suzanne Brown	Justin Frackelton	Joanna Martin	Caroline Smithers
Wendy Bugg	Le Frazier	Ann Mason	Mary Snyder
Marnie Bushnell	Peg Freeman	Daryl Mathers	Ruth Stopps
Gwynn Campbell	Nancy Gachet	Gloria Matthews	Mary Strother
Peggy Cardwell	Martha Garner	May Fair House	Terry Taylor
Jane Chappell	Katherine Gill	Adelia Mayer	Jana Thomas
Kay Clary	Nancy Gillespie	Carolyn McCue	Helen Tripp
Liz Cone	Kathryn Goodman	Georgia McDaniel	Mary-Joe Vaughan
Beese Craigie	Amy Goolsby	Marge McGlynn	Bob Vaughan
Beth Crews	Betty Graham	Alexa McGrath	Eileen Walker
Anne Cronly	Liza Graham	Anne McGraw	Jane Ware
Ruth Cunningham	Gayle Gray	Virginia Mills	Marianne Watkinson
Eileen Curry	Pan Greene*	Evelyn Mooney	Marsden Williams
Margaret Curtis	Helen Gregory*	Martha Moore	Camilla Williamson
Toni Dabel	Karen Hamlett	Nancy Morris	Kitty Wiltshire*
Donna Dabney	Kathleen Hamlett	Elizabeth Morton*	Elizabeth Winfree*
Jo Daniel	Anne Hardage	Lynn Newman	Carol Womack
Lucy K. Daniel	Ruth Harp*	Jean Oakey	Thyra Wood*
Judy Daughtry	Susan Hayden	John Oakey	Janet Woolwine
Nancy David	Emily Peyton Higgins	Emma G. Oppenhimer	Elise Wright
Dorothy Deane*	Catharine Hill*	Laila Pearsall*	Page Wright
Jane deButts	Bob Hodder	Dorothy Pelouze*	Elsie Yates
Cynthia Delafield	Nancy Hodder	Edwina Phillips	Gretchen Young

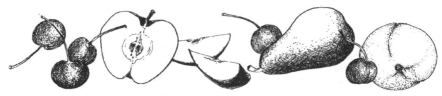

St. Stephen's Choir Cookbook
St. Stephen's Episcopal Church
P. O. Box 8500
Richmond, VA 23226

Please send _____copies of *O Taste & Sing*   @ $17.95 each _____

        Postage and handling   @   2.75 each _____

        Virginia residents add sales tax   @   .81 each_____

                                     Total _____

Name _____

Address _____

City _____ State _____ Zip _____

Please make checks payable to *O Taste & Sing*.

- -

St. Stephen's Choir Cookbook
St. Stephen's Episcopal Church
P. O. Box 8500
Richmond, VA 23226

Please send _____copies of *O Taste & Sing*   @ $17.95 each _____

        Postage and handling   @   2.75 each _____

        Virginia residents add sales tax   @   .81 each_____

                                     Total _____

Name _____

Address _____

City _____ State _____ Zip _____

Please make checks payable to *O Taste & Sing*.

- -

St. Stephen's Choir Cookbook
St. Stephen's Episcopal Church
P. O. Box 8500
Richmond, VA 23226

Please send _____copies of *O Taste & Sing*   @ $17.95 each _____

        Postage and handling   @   2.75 each _____

        Virginia residents add sales tax   @   .81 each_____

                                     Total _____

Name _____

Address _____

City _____ State _____ Zip_____

Please make checks payable to *O Taste & Sing*.